Treasures

A Reading/Language Arts Program

Macmillan/McGraw-Hill

Contributors

Time Magazine

 RFB&D
learning through listening

Students with print disabilities may be eligible to obtain an accessible, audio version of the pupil edition of this textbook. Please call Recording for the Blind & Dyslexic at 1-800-221-4792 for complete information.

A

The **McGraw·Hill** Companies

Macmillan/McGraw-Hill

Published by Macmillan/McGraw-Hill, of McGraw-Hill Education, a division of The McGraw-Hill Companies, Inc., Two Penn Plaza, New York, New York 10121.

Printed in the United States of America

1 2 3 4 5 6 7 8 9 006/055 13 12 11 10 09

Treasures

A Reading/Language Arts Program

Program Authors

Dr. Diane August
Senior Research Scientist, Center for
 Applied Linguistics
Washington, D.C.

Dr. Donald R. Bear
University of Nevada, Reno
Reno, Nevada

Dr. Janice A. Dole
University of Utah
Salt Lake City, Utah

Dr. Jana Echevarria
California State University, Long Beach
Long Beach, California

Dr. Douglas Fisher
San Diego State University
San Diego, California

Dr. David J. Francis
University of Houston
Houston, Texas

Dr. Vicki L. Gibson
Educational Consultant, Gibson Hasbrouck
 and Associates, Massachusetts

Dr. Jan E. Hasbrouck
Educational Consultant – J.H. Consulting
Los Angeles, California

Dr. Scott G. Paris
Center for Research and Practice,
National Institute of Education
Singapore

Dr. Timothy Shanahan
University of Illinois at Chicago
Chicago, Illinois

Dr. Josefina V. Tinajero
University of Texas at El Paso
El Paso, Texas

Macmillan/McGraw-Hill

Program Authors

Dr. Diane August

Center for Applied Linguistics, Washington, D.C.

- Principal Investigator, Developing Literacy in Second-Language Learners: Report of the National Literacy Panel on Language-Minority Children and Youth
- Member of the New Standards Literacy Project, Grades 4–5

Dr. Donald R. Bear

University of Nevada, Reno

- Author of *Words Their Way* and *Words Their Way with English Learners*
- Director, E.L. Cord Foundation Center for Learning and Literacy

Dr. Janice A. Dole

University of Utah

- Investigator, IES Study on Reading Interventions
- National Academy of Sciences, Committee Member: Teacher Preparation Programs, 2005–2007

Dr. Jana Echevarria

California State University, Long Beach

- Author of *Making Content Comprehensible for English Learners: The SIOP Model*
- Principal Researcher, Center for Research on the Educational Achievement and Teaching of English Language Learners

Dr. Douglas Fisher

San Diego State University

- Co-Director, Center for the Advancement of Reading, California State University
- Author of *Language Arts Workshop: Purposeful Reading and Writing Instruction* and *Reading for Information in Elementary School*

Dr. David J. Francis

University of Houston

- Director of the Center for Research on Educational Achievement and Teaching of English Language Learners (CREATE)
- Director, Texas Institute for Measurement, Evaluation, and Statistics

Dr. Vicki Gibson

Educational Consultant Gibson Hasbrouck and Associates, Massachusetts

- Author of *Differentiated Instruction: Grouping for Success*

Dr. Jan E. Hasbrouck

Educational Consultant JH Consulting, Los Angeles

- Developed Oral Reading Fluency Norms for Grades 1–8
- Author of *The Reading Coach: A How-to Manual for Success*

Dr. Scott G. Paris

Center for Research and Practice, National Institute of Education, Singapore

- Principal Investigator, CIERA, 1997–2004

Dr. Timothy Shanahan

University of Illinois at Chicago

- Member, National Reading Panel
- President, International Reading Association, 2006
- Chair, National Literacy Panel and National Early Literacy Panel

Dr. Josefina V. Tinajero

University of Texas at El Paso

- Past President, NABE and TABE
- Co-Editor of *Teaching All the Children: Strategies for Developing Literacy in an Urban Setting* and *Literacy Assessment of Second Language Learners*

Consulting and Contributing Authors

Dr. Adria F. Klein
Professor Emeritus,
California State University,
San Bernardino

- President, California Reading Association, 1995
- Co-Author of *Interactive Writing* and *Interactive Editing*

Dolores B. Malcolm
St. Louis Public Schools
St. Louis, MO

- Past President, International Reading Association
- Member, IRA Urban Diversity Initiatives Commission
- Member, RIF Advisory Board

Dr. Doris Walker-Dalhouse
Minnesota State University,
Moorhead

- Author of articles on multicultural literature and reading instruction in urban schools
- Co-Chair of the Ethnicity, Race, and Multilingualism Committee, NRC

Dinah Zike
Educational Consultant

- Dinah-Might Activities, Inc. San Antonio, TX

Program Consultants

Kathy R. Bumgardner
Language Arts Instructional
Specialist
Gaston County Schools, NC

Elizabeth Jimenez
CEO, GEMAS Consulting
Pomona, CA

Dr. Sharon F. O'Neal
Associate Professor
College of Education
Texas State University
San Marcos, TX

Program Reviewers

Mable Alfred
Reading/Language Arts Administrator
Chicago Public Schools, IL

Suzie Bean
Teacher, Kindergarten
Mary W. French Academy
Decatur, IL

Linda Burch
Teacher, Kindergarten
Public School 184
Brooklyn, NY

Robert J. Dandorph
Principal
John F. Kennedy Elementary School
North Bergen, NJ

Suzanne Delacruz
Principal, Washington Elementary
Evanston, IL

Carol Dockery
Teacher, Grade 3
Mulberry Elementary
Milford, OH

Karryl Ellis
Teacher, Grade 1
Durfee School, Decatur, IL

Christina Fong
Teacher, Grade 3
William Moore Elementary School
Las Vegas, NV

Lenore Furman
Teacher, Kindergarten
Abington Avenue School
Newark, NJ

Sister Miriam Kaeser
Assistant Superintendent
Archdiocese of Cincinnati
Cincinnati, OH

LaVonne Lee
Principal, Rozet Elementary School
Gillette, WY

SuEllen Mackey
Teacher, Grade 5
Washington Elementary School
Decatur, IL

Jan Mayes
Curriculum Coordinator
Kent School District
Kent, WA

Bonnie Nelson
Teacher, Grade 1
Solano School, Phoenix, AZ

Cyndi Nichols
Teacher, Grade K/1
North Ridge Elementary School
Commack, NY

Sharron Norman
Curriculum Director
Lansing School District
Lansing, MI

Renee Ottinger
Literacy Leader, Grades K–5
Coronado Hills Elementary School
Denver, CO

Michael Pragman
Principal, Woodland Elementary School
Lee's Summit, MO

Carol Rose
Teacher, Grade 2
Churchill Elementary School
Muskegon, MI

Laura R. Schmidt-Watson
Director of Academic Services
Parma City School District, OH

Dianne L. Skoy
Literacy Coordinator, Grades K–5
Minneapolis Public Schools
Minneapolis, MN

Charles Staszewski
ESL Teacher, Grades 3–5
John H. William School, No. 5
Rochester, NY

Patricia Synan
New York City Department
of Education

Stephanie Yearian
Teacher, Grade 2
W. J. Zahnow Elementary
Waterloo, IL

Unit 8   The Big Question

What do plants need to grow?

Enduring Understanding and Essential Questions

In this unit, children will read and write about how plants grow. As they progress through the unit, they will also develop and apply key comprehension skills that good readers use as they read.

Big Idea	Enduring Understanding	Essential Questions
Theme: Plants	Plants require a lot of care in order to grow.	What do plants need to grow?

Comprehension	Enduring Understanding	Essential Questions
Identify Sequence of Events Week 1	Good readers use the words and pictures to understand the sequence of events.	What is the sequence of events in the selection?
Retell Week 2	Good readers can retell important facts by understanding how a book is organized.	How does the author group important facts?
Draw Conclusions Week 3	Good readers use clues from the story to draw conclusions about what they read.	What clues from the story help you draw conclusions about the characters in the story?

Theme: Plants

Planning the Unit

Literature Selections

Teaching the Unit

Wrapping Up the Unit

Additional Resources

Unit Assessment

Theme: Plants

Unit Theme Opener, page xvi

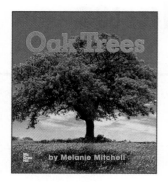

Big Book

Big Book

ORAL LANGUAGE	WEEK 1	WEEK 2
• Oral Vocabulary	**Theme**	**Theme**
	How Trees Grow	Seeds and Plants
• Phonemic Awareness	✔ **Phonemic Awareness**	✔ **Phonemic Awareness**
	Phoneme Isolation	Phoneme Isolation
	Phoneme Blending	Phoneme Blending
	Phoneme Segmentation	Phoneme Deletion
WORD STUDY		
• Phonics	✔ **Phonics**	✔ **Phonics**
	Introduce /k/k	Introduce /u/u
	(Initial) /k/k	(Initial and Medial)
	(Final) /k/ck	
• High-Frequency Words	✔ **High-Frequency Words**	✔ **High-Frequency Words**
	little , said	*here , was*
READING		
• Listening Comprehension	✔ **Comprehension**	✔ **Comprehension**
	Strategy: Recognize Text Structure	**Strategy:** Recognize Text Structure
	Skill: Identify Sequence of Events	**Skill:** Retell
• Fluency	**Fluency**	**Fluency**
	Build Fluency: Word Automaticity	Build Fluency: Word Automaticity
	Echo-Read, Read for Fluency	Echo-Read, Choral-Read, Read for Fluency
• Leveled Readers	**Approaching** *The Little Tree*	**Approaching** *Seeds*
	On Level *Seeds Make Trees*	**On Level** *From Seed to Plant*
	Beyond *How a Tree Grows*	**Beyond** *Seeds, Seeds, Seeds!*
	ELL *We Like Trees*	**ELL** *Seeds*
LANGUAGE ARTS		
• Grammar	**Grammar**	**Grammar**
	Describing Words	Describing Words
• Writing	**Writing**	**Writing**
	Directions	Similes

Read-Aloud Trade Book

WEEK 3

Theme
What's in My Garden?

Phonemic Awareness
Phoneme Deletion
Phoneme Segmentation
Phoneme Blending

Phonics
Review Initial /k/k, /u/u; Medial /u/u; Final /k/ck; -ot, -op, -ick Word Families

High-Frequency Words
little , said , here , was

Comprehension
Strategy: Recognize Story Structure
Skill: Draw Conclusions

Fluency
Build Fluency: Word Automaticity
Echo-Read, Choral-Read, Read for Fluency
Approaching *It Was Here!*
On Level *I Like This Flower*
Beyond *Kim's Garden*
ELL *I Will Sit Here*

Grammar and Writing
Describing Words, Poem

Half-Day Kindergarten

Use the chart below to help plan your half-day kindergarten schedule. Choose Small Group and Workstation Activities as your time allows during the day.

ORAL LANGUAGE

- **Phonemic Awareness**
- **Build Background**
- **Oral Vocabulary**

WORD STUDY

- **Phonics:** /k/k, /k/ck, /u/u
- **High-Frequency Words:** *little, said, here, was*

READING

- **Share the Big Books:** *Oak Trees; Seed Secrets*
- **Read-Aloud Trade Book:** *Sunflower House*
- **Read-Aloud Anthology**
- **Big Book of Explorations**
- **Fluency Practice**

LANGUAGE ARTS

- **Shared Writing**
- **Interactive Writing**
- **Independent Writing**

INDEPENDENT PRACTICE

- **Activity Book Pages**
- **Practice Book Pages**
- **Handwriting Practice**

Theme: Plants

Literature

Big Book

Big Book

Read-Aloud Trade Book

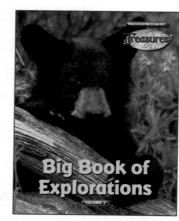

Big Book of Explorations (2)

Decodable Readers

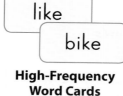
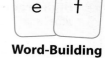

Approaching Level

On Level

Beyond Level

ELL

Leveled Readers

Read-Aloud Anthology
Includes Plays for Readers Theater

Oral Vocabulary Cards
(30 sets)

Retelling Cards

Teaching Support

Teacher's Edition

Teacher's Resource Book

Home-School Connection

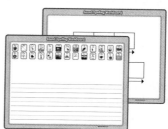

High-Frequency Word Cards

Word-Building Cards

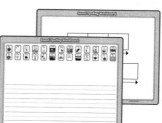

Sound-Spelling WorkBoards

Puppet

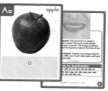

Sound-Spelling Cards

Photo Cards

Student Practice

Teaching Chart

Activity Book

Practice Book

Handwriting
- Ball and Stick
- Slant

Literacy Workstation Flip Charts

Class Management Tools

How-to Guide

Rotation Chart

Weekly Contracts

Differentiated Resources

English Language Learners

ELL Resource and Practice Books

Visual Vocabulary Resources

Response to Intervention

Tier 2

- Phonemic Awareness
- Phonics
- Vocabulary
- Comprehension
- Fluency

Tier 3

Assessment

Assess Unit Skills
- Phonemic Awareness
- Phonics
- High-Frequency Words
- Listening Comprehension

Unit Assessment

Digital Solutions

Go to **ConnectED** http://connected.mcgraw-hill.com
Online Center

☑ Prepare/Plan

ONLINE www.macmillanmh.com

Teacher's Edition Online

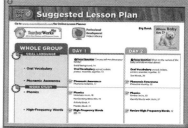

TeacherWorks™ Plus
All-In-One Planner and Resource Center

Available on CD-ROM
• Interactive Teacher's Edition
• Printable Weekly Resources

Implementation Modules

 • Support on how to implement the reading program

Balanced Literacy Planner

Balanced Literacy Lesson Plan
▸ Oral Language Development
▸ Word Work
▾ Focus Lesson
  ▸ Shared Reading
  ▸ Read Aloud
▾ Guided Reading
  ▸ Literacy Centers
▸ Writing Workshop

• Create customized weekly balanced literacy planners

ELL Strategies

 • Teaching strategies for English Language Learners

Reading Video Library

 • Video clips of instructional routines

Leadership Handbook

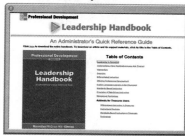

 • Professional development for school principals

☑ Teach/Learn

ONLINE www.macmillanmh.com

Animated Activities

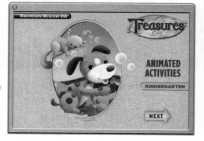

• Animated comprehension activities

Classroom Presentation Toolkit

• Weekly transparencies, graphic organizers, and guided instruction and practice

Additional Professional Development

• **Instructional Routine Handbook**
• **Writing Professional Development Guide**
• **Managing Small Groups**
• **Leadership Handbook:**
  An Administrator's Quick Reference Guide

Also available
Reading Yes!
Video Workshops on CD-ROM

LOG ON ▶ VIEW IT · READ IT · LEARN IT · FIND OUT

☑ **Assess**

Leveled Reader Database

- Search and print Leveled Reader titles

Weekly Activities

- Oral Language
- Research Roadmap
- Research and Inquiry
- Vocabulary and Spelling
- Author and Illustrator

ONLINE www.macmillanmh.com

Progress Monitoring

Unit 1 Reteaching and Intervention Opportunities

- Prescriptions for Reteaching
- Student Profile System

Online and CD-ROM materials are **Interactive White Board Ready!**

IWB

Available on CD

- **Listening Library**
- **Sound Pronunciation**

- **New Adventures with Buggles and Beezy**

Theme: **Plants**

Diagnostic Assessment

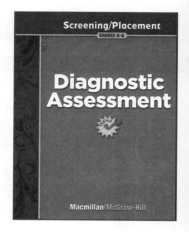

Screening, Diagnosis, and Placement

Use your state or district screener to identify children at risk. In addition, see tests in the **Diagnostic Assessment** book for information on determining the proficiency of children according to specific skills. Use the results to place children in the program.

- Diagnostics should be given at the beginning of the school year after you have had time to observe children and they become familiar with classroom routines. Use the diagnostics to determine children in need of intervention or to identify specific prerequisite skill deficiencies that you need to teach during Small Group differentiated instruction time.

Progress Monitoring Assessment

Meeting Grade-Level Expectations

Use these tests at the end of each unit (every 3 weeks). Multiple questions and next-steps information are provided.

Ongoing Informal Assessments

- Daily Quick Check Observations

Formal Assessments

- **Unit Assessment**

Benchmark Assessment

Give once a year to determine whether children have mastered the grade-level content standards and to document long-term academic growth.

Test Alignment

GRADE K UNIT 8 ASSESSED SKILLS	TerraNova/ CAT 6	SESAT	TPRI	DIBELS*
COMPREHENSION STRATEGIES AND SKILLS				
• Strategies: Recognize text/story structure	◆	◆	◆	◆
• Skills: Sequence of events, Retell, Draw conclusions	◆	◆	◆	◆
VOCABULARY/HIGH-FREQUENCY WORDS				
• Position words				
• *little, said, here, was*	◆	◆	◆	◆
PHONEMIC AWARENESS				
• Phoneme isolation, Phoneme segmentation, Phoneme deletion, Phoneme blending	◆	◆	◆	◆
PHONICS				
• *Uu, Kk, Ll*	◆	◆	◆	◆
TEXT FEATURES				
• Photographs				
GRAMMAR				
• Describing words (adjectives)				

*Data from DIBELS serve as indicators of overall reading comprehension performance, not specific skills.

KEY

TerraNova/CAT 6	TerraNova, The Second Edition
SESAT	Stanford Early School Achievement Test
TPRI	Texas Primary Reading Inventory
DIBELS*	Dynamics Indicators of Basic Early Literacy Skills

Theme Project: How Does Your Garden Grow?

Introduce the Theme

Sing the theme song. Then guide children to generate questions related to the theme and topic of class-wide interest. For example: *What do plants need to grow? How do plants help people?*

Seeds

*A lot of trees start from
seeds so small,*

*You gotta look close or
you can't see them at all.*

*It's hard to believe
trees grow so tall*

From seeds that start so small.

Song on Listening Library Audio CD

Research and Inquiry
Self-Selected Theme Project

 Step 1 **Planning a Project**

What do I want to learn about plants?

- Use the **Big Books** and **Photo Cards** to show pictures of plants.
- Have children ask themselves: *What do I want to learn about plants and how they grow?*
- Help children decide what people or sources can help answer their research questions.

 Step 2 **Doing the Project**

- Guide children to use informational books, encyclopedias, and videos to answer their questions about plants.

 Step 3 **Document and Evaluate Research**

How can I share what I have learned?

You might suggest:

- making diagrams of plants or trees
- using gardening catalogs to cut out plant pictures to create a classroom garden mural
- making a book showing and labeling how seeds grow.

Help children decide what materials they will need for their presentation. See the Unit Closer on pages 2070–2071.

Research Strategy

As you decide which resources to use for your project, here are a few questions to ask: *Does this resource have information that will answer my questions? Do I understand what the information means?* Answering these questions can help you choose the best resources for your project.

Unit 8
Plants

The
Big
Question

What do plants
need to grow?

50A

Teaching Chart 50A

Introduce Theme Project

PLANTS

Let's look at this photo. It is a young girl watering a plant. It also shows another girl, possibly her sister, helping her. Point to each girl, the watering can, and the garden as you describe the picture. *Why is the girl watering the plants? Is she being responsible?*

- Ask: *What do plants need to grow besides water?*

- Ask: *Have you ever taken care of a plant?*

- Throughout this unit we will be learning about how trees grow, seeds and plants, and what you can find in a garden.

Connect to Content

Listening and Speaking

Explain to children that when they listen, they should listen with full attention. They should sit quietly and look at the speaker while he or she is talking. Point out that when children want to share information and ideas in a discussion, they should speak clearly so everyone can hear them. They should respond clearly in complete and coherent sentences.

Unit 8 Opener

Connect to Content

Make a Terrarium

Ask: *How can we grow plants if we do not have a garden?*

- Have children work in small groups to talk about ways we can grow plants.

- Help children create simple terrariums using two plastic bottles or cups, pebbles, potting soil, and small plants. Have them water the plants and close up the terrarium.

- Tell children to observe their plants daily and draw pictures to record data.

- At the end of the observation period, write down children's summaries of the results.

Minilesson

Following Directions

Explain In a science experiment, it is important to **follow directions**. The directions will tell us how to set up the experiment so that we get the results we want. Sometimes, directions use pictures to make it easier for us to understand what we are supposed to do. They also use **sequence words** to tell us the order in which to do things.

Discuss Ask: *Why is it important to do the steps of an experiment in order?* (to be safe, to not waste materials, to be successful)

Apply Supply children with pictorial directions showing the steps to create a terrarium. Before children begin their experiments, carefully review the directions and any sequence words used.

Connect to Content

Seed Mosaics

Ask: *What kinds of seeds have you seen? Tell about them.*

- Provide children with small containers of various types of dried seeds, such as pumpkin seeds, kidney beans, lima beans, etc.
- Ask them to compare the seeds and make observations about their size, color, and shape.
- Have children glue their seeds onto poster board to create interesting designs.
- Then display the seed designs on a mural. Ask children to identify as many different seeds as they can.

Listening and Speaking

Guide children to

- participate in a conversation on a specific topic with you;
- describe people, places, things, and locations;
- be polite, take turns, and speak one at a time.

Character Building: Caring

Use the Make a Terrarium activity to discuss how people care for plants. Explain that taking care of a garden is hard work. Remind children that caring also means we do not pick flowers from someone's garden without permission.

Minilesson

Plan and Develop a Draft

Explain Once they finish their experiments, scientists use words and pictures to record their results. This way, they can share what they have learned with other people. Scientists first write a **draft** of what they want to say. A draft is a first try at writing a paper. In a draft, you should make sure to record your details in an order that makes sense.

Discuss Ask: *What kinds of words might you use to list details in a draft?* (sequence words, such as *first*, *next*, and *last*)

Apply Have children write a draft about the results of their experiment using words and pictures. Remind children to use details in their writing.

LOG ON ▶ **FIND OUT**

Research For technology research and presentation strategies, see the Computer Literacy lesson on pages 2068–2069. For additional research and inquiry, go to **www.macmillanmh.com**.

Week 1 ★ At a Glance

Priority Skills and Concepts

 ### Comprehension
- **Genre:** Folktale, Expository
- **Strategy:** Recognize Text Structure
- **Skill:** Identify Sequence of Events
 - **Skill:** Identify Main Ideas and Details

 ### High-Frequency Words
- *little*, *said*

Oral Vocabulary
- Build Robust Vocabulary: *charming*, *conceited*, *equal*, *grow*, *plant*

Fluency
- Echo-Read
- Word Automaticity

 ### Phonemic Awareness
- Phoneme Isolation
- Phoneme Blending
- Phoneme Segmentation

 ### Phonics
- *Kk, ck*

Grammar
- Describing Words (Adjectives)

Writing
- Steps in a Process

Key    Tested in Program    Review Skill

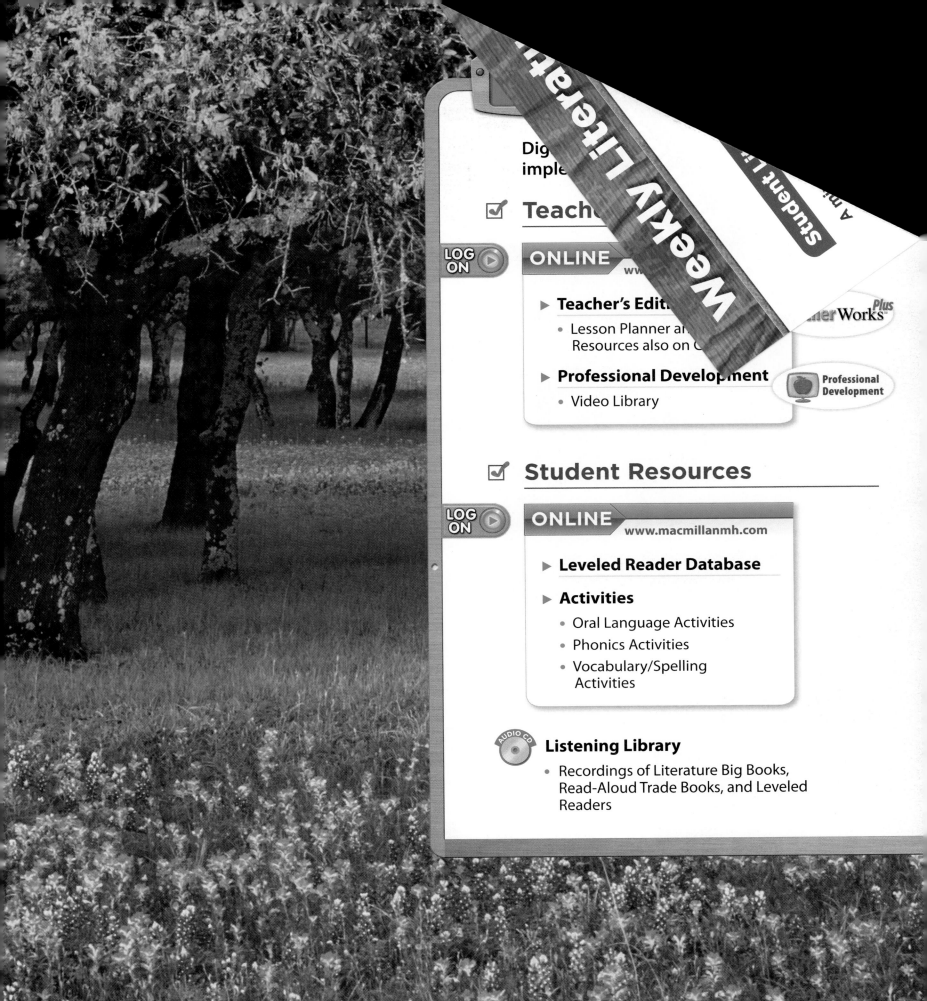

Dig
imple

Weekly Literature

Student Li

☑ **Teacher**

LOG
ON ▶

ONLINE

ww

Plus
...ner Works™

▶ **Teacher's Editi**
• Lesson Planner a
  Resources also on C

▶ **Professional Development**
• Video Library

Professional
Development

☑ **Student Resources**

LOG
ON ▶

ONLINE
www.macmillanmh.com

▶ **Leveled Reader Database**

▶ **Activities**
• Oral Language Activities
• Phonics Activities
• Vocabulary/Spelling
  Activities

AUDIO CD

Listening Library
• Recordings of Literature Big Books,
  Read-Aloud Trade Books, and Leveled
  Readers

Theme: How Trees Grow

Literature

ix of fiction and nonfiction

Big Book

Genre Expository

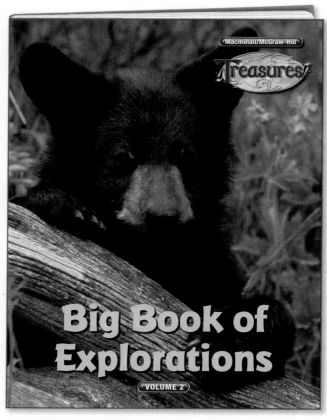

Big Book of Explorations

Genre Poetry

Support Literature

**Interactive
Read-Aloud Anthology**

Genre Folktale

Oral Vocabulary Cards
- Listening Comprehension
- Build Robust Vocabulary

Decodable Reader

Resources for Differentiated Instruction

Leveled Readers: Science

GR Levels A–G

Genre   Fiction

- Same Theme
- Same Vocabulary/Phonics
- Same Comprehension Skills

Approaching Level

On Level

Beyond Level

ELL

Leveled Reader Database
Go to www.macmillanmh.com.

Practice

Activity Book

Practice Book

ELL Practice Book

Response to Intervention

Tier 2

Tier 3

- Phonemic Awareness
- Phonics
- Vocabulary
- Comprehension
- Fluency

Unit Assessment

Assess Unit Skills

- Phonemic Awareness
- Phonics
- High-Frequency Words
- Listening Comprehension

HOME-SCHOOL CONNECTION

- Family letters in English and Spanish
- Take-home stories and activities

Go to **www.macmillanmh.com** for Online Lesson Planner

TeacherWorks *Plus*
All-In-One Planner and Resource Center

Professional Development
Video Library

Big Book

Oak Trees
by Melanie Mitchell

WHOLE GROUP

ORAL LANGUAGE

	DAY 1	**DAY 2**
• **Oral Vocabulary**	**❓ Focus Question** Trees grow in many places. What do you know about trees? Build Background, 1826 **Oral Vocabulary** *charming, conceited, equal, grow, plant*, 1826	**❓ Focus Question** Can you name something that starts out very little and then grows tall? **Oral Vocabulary** *charming, conceited, equal, grow, plant*, 1834 Position Words, 1841
• **Phonemic Awareness**	**Phonemic Awareness** Phoneme Isolation, 1829	**Phonemic Awareness** Phoneme Blending, 1842

WORD STUDY

• **Phonics**	**Phonics** Introduce /k/*k*, 1830 Handwriting: Write *Kk*, 1831 Activity Book, 4 Practice Book, 161	**Phonics** Review /l/*l*, /k/*k*, /b/*b*, 1842 Blend with /k/*k*, 1843
• **High-Frequency Words**	**High-Frequency Words** *little*, *said*, 1828	**Review High-Frequency Words**, 1844

READING

• **Listening Comprehension** • **Apply Phonics and High-Frequency Words** • **Fluency**	**Share the Big Book** *Oak Trees* **Strategy:** Recognize Text Structure, 1827 **Skill:** Identify Sequence of Events, 1827 Big Book	**Reread the Big Book** *Oak Trees* **Strategy:** Recognize Text Structure, 1836 **Skill:** Identify Sequence of Events, 1836 Big Book Retell, 1840 **Decodable Reader:** *Sad Hen*, 1844 Activity Book, 5 Practice Book, 162 **Fluency** Echo-Read, 1840

LANGUAGE ARTS

• **Writing** • **Grammar**	**Shared Writing** Steps in a Process, 1833 **Grammar** Describing Words (Adjectives), 1832	**Interactive Writing** Steps in a Process, 1845

ASSESSMENT

• **Informal/Formal**	**Quick Check** Phonemic Awareness, 1829	**Quick Check** Comprehension, 1840

SMALL GROUP Lesson Plan ▷ **Differentiated Instruction 1820–1821**

Priority Skills

Half-Day Kindergarten

Teach Core Skills
Focus on tested skill lessons, other lessons, and small group options as your time allows.

Phonemic Awareness/Phonics	High-Frequency Words	Oral Vocabulary	Comprehension
/k/k, /k/ck	*little, said*	Position Words	**Strategy:** Recognize Text Structure **Skill:** Identify Sequence of Events

DAY 3

? Focus Question What would you say if a tree said, "What do you like best about me?"

Oral Vocabulary *charming, conceited, equal, grow, plant,* 1846

Oral Vocabulary Cards: "The Conceited Apple Branch"

✔ **Phonemic Awareness**
Phoneme Isolation, 1851

✔ **Phonics**
Introduce /k/*ck*, 1852
Blend with /k/*ck*, 1853
Read Words, 1853

✔ **High-Frequency Words**
little , said , 1850
Activity Book: "A Little Acorn," 7–8
Practice Book, 163–164
Read for Fluency, 1850

Read the Big Book of Explorations:
"Acorn," 25

Literary Element: Rhyme and Rhythm, 1848

Big Book of Explorations

Independent Writing
Prewrite and Draft Steps in a Process, 1855
Grammar
Describing Words (Adjectives), 1854

Quick Check High-Frequency Words, 1850

DAY 4

? Focus Question How do little pine trees and big pine trees look alike?

Oral Vocabulary *charming, conceited, equal, grow, plant,* 1856

Position Words, 1859

✔ **Phonemic Awareness**
Phoneme Blending, 1860

✔ **Phonics**
Word Sort, 1860
Blend with /k/*ck*, 1861
Activity Book, 9–10
Practice Book, 165

✔ **Review High-Frequency Words**, 1862

Interactive Read Aloud
Listening Comprehension, 1858

Read Aloud: "The Sticky-Sticky Pine"

Decodable Reader: *Sad Hen,* 1862

Read Aloud

Fluency Reread for Fluency, 1862

Independent Writing
Revise and Edit Steps in a Process, 1863

Quick Check Phonics, 1861

DAY 5
Review and Assess

? Focus Question What have we said about trees this week?

Oral Vocabulary *charming, conceited, equal, grow, plant,* 1864

Position Words, 1866

✔ **Phonemic Awareness**
Phoneme Segmentation, 1867

✔ **Phonics**
Read Words, 1868
Dictation, 1868
Activity Book, 12

✔ **High-Frequency Words**
little , said , this , do , and , what , 1866

Read Across Texts
Strategy: Recognize Text Structure, 1865
✔ **Skill:** Identify Sequence of Events, 1865
Activity Book, 11

Fluency Word Automaticity, 1866

Independent Writing
Publish and Present Steps in a Process, 1869

✔ **Weekly Assessment, 1896–1897**

Differentiated Instruction

What do I do in small groups?

Teacher-Led Small Groups

Independent Activities

Focus on Skills

IF... children need additional instruction, practice, or extension based on your Quick Check observations for the following priority skills

 Phonemic Awareness
Phoneme Isolation, Blending, Segmentation

 Phonics
Kk, ck

 High-Frequency Words
little, *said*

 Comprehension
Strategy: Recognize Text Structure
Skill: Identify Sequence of Events

THEN...

Approaching	Preteach and
ELL	Reteach Skills
On Level	Practice
Beyond	Enrich and Accelerate Learning

 ## Suggested Small Group Lesson Plan

	DAY 1	**DAY 2**
Approaching Level **Tier 2** • **Preteach/Reteach** **Tier 2 Instruction**	• Oral Language, 1870 • High-Frequency Words, 1870 **ELL** High-Frequency Words Review, 1870 • Phonemic Awareness, 1871 • Phonics, 1871 **ELL** Sound-Spellings Review, 1871	• Oral Language, 1876 • High-Frequency Words, 1876 **ELL** • Phonemic Awareness, 1877 • Phonics, 1877
On Level • **Practice**	• High-Frequency Words, 1872 • Phonemic Awareness/Phonics, 1872 **ELL**	• Phonics, 1878
Beyond Level • **Extend/Accelerate** **Gifted and Talented**	• High-Frequency Words/Vocabulary, 1873 **ELL** Expand Oral Vocabulary, 1873 • Phonics, 1873	• Phonics, 1878
ELL • **Build English Language Proficiency** • See **ELL** in other levels.	• Oral Language Warm-Up, 1874 • Academic Language, 1874 • Vocabulary, 1875	• Access to Core Content, 1879

Focus on Leveled Readers

Levels A–G

A

Approaching

C

On Level

G

Beyond

B

ELL

Additional Leveled Readers

 Leveled Reader Database

www.macmillanmh.com

Search by

- Comprehension Skill
- Content Area
- Genre
- Text Feature
- Guided Reading Level
- Reading Recovery Level
- Lexile Score
- Benchmark Level

Subscription also available

Manipulatives

Sound-Spelling WorkBoards

Sound-Spelling Cards

Photo Cards

High-Frequency Word Cards

Visual Vocabulary Resources

DAY 3

- High-Frequency Words, 1880 **ELL**
- Phonemic Awareness, 1880
- Phonics, 1881
- Decodable Reader, 1881

- Decodable Reader, 1882

- Decodable Reader, 1882

- Access to Core Content, 1883
- Grammar, 1883

DAY 4

- Phonemic Awareness, 1884
- Phonics, 1884 **ELL**
- Leveled Reader Lesson 1, 1885

- Leveled Reader Lesson 1, 1886 **ELL**

- Leveled Reader Lesson 1, 1887
- Evaluate, 1887

- Leveled Reader, 1888

DAY 5

- Phonemic Awareness, 1890
- Phonics, 1890 **ELL**
- Leveled Reader Lesson 2, 1891
- High-Frequency Words, 1891

- Leveled Reader Lesson 2, 1892

- Leveled Reader Lesson 2, 1893
- Expand Vocabulary, 1893 **ELL**

- Fluency, 1894
- High-Frequency Words, 1895
- Writing, 1895

Managing the Class

What do I do with the rest of my class?

- Activity Book
- Practice Book
- ELL Practice Book
- Leveled Reader Activities
- Literacy Workstations
- Online Activities
- Buggles and Beezy

Classroom Management Tools

Weekly Contract

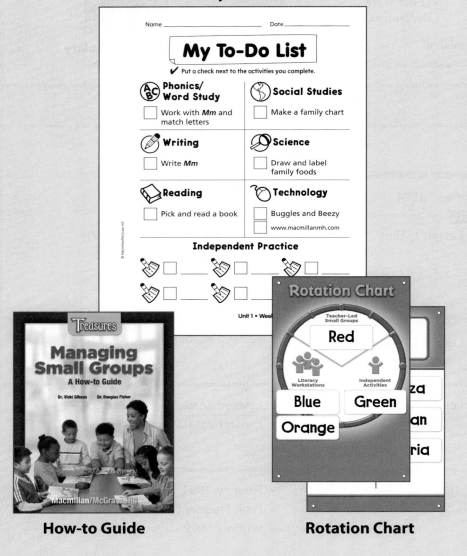

Name _____ Date _____

My To-Do List

✓ Put a check next to the activities you complete.

(ABC) Phonics/ Word Study
☐ Work with *Mm* and match letters

🌐 Social Studies
☐ Make a family chart

✏️ Writing
☐ Write *Mm*

🎷 Science
☐ Draw and label family foods

📖 Reading
☐ Pick and read a book

⚙ Technology
☐ Buggles and Beezy www.macmillanmh.com

Independent Practice

Unit 1 • Week

Rotation Chart

Teacher-Led Small Groups

Red

Literacy Workstations | Independent Activities

Blue | Green

Orange

How-to Guide

Treasures
Managing Small Groups
A How-to Guide
Dr. Vicki Gibson Dr. Douglas Fisher
Macmillan/McGraw-Hill

Rotation Chart

Digital Learning

Phonics Activities

- Match Letters
- Match Letters to Sounds
- Blend Words

Meet the Author/Illustrator

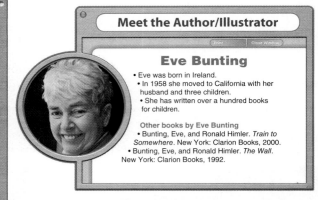

Eve Bunting
- Eve was born in Ireland.
- In 1958 she moved to California with her husband and three children.
- She has written over a hundred books for children.

Other books by Eve Bunting
- Bunting, Eve, and Ronald Himler. *Train to Somewhere*. New York: Clarion Books, 2000.
- Bunting, Eve, and Ronald Himler. *The Wall*. New York: Clarion Books, 1992.

- Read Other Books by the Author or Illustrator

Practice

Activity Book

Practice Book

ELL Practice Book

Independent Activities

ONLINE INSTRUCTION www.macmillanmh.com

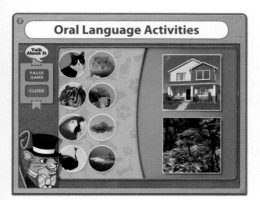

Oral Language Activities

- Focus on Unit Vocabulary and Concepts
- English Language Learner Support

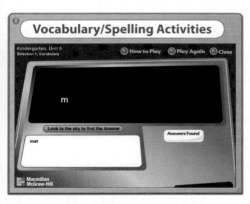

Vocabulary/Spelling Activities

- Differentiated Lists and Activities

Leveled Reader Database

- Leveled Reader Database
- Search titles by level, skill, content area, and more

Available on CD

LISTENING LIBRARY
Recordings of selections

- Literature Big Books
- Read-Aloud Trade Books
- Leveled Readers
- ELL Readers

NEW ADVENTURES WITH BUGGLES AND BEEZY
Phonemic awareness and phonics activities

Leveled Reader Activities

Approaching

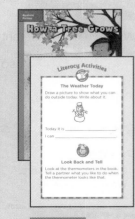

On Level

Beyond

ELL

See inside cover of all Leveled Readers.

Literacy Workstations

See lessons on pages 1824–1825.

Managing the Class

What do I do with the rest of my class?

Reading

Objectives

- Select a nonfiction book to read independently
- Read a book; add a page to tell what happens next

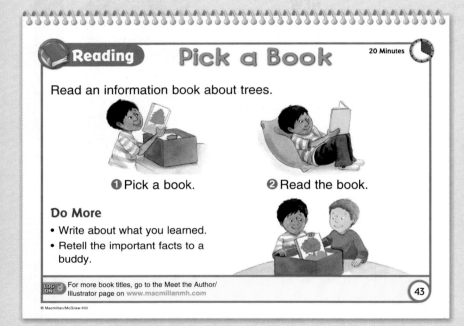

Reading — Pick a Book
20 Minutes

Read an information book about trees.

❶ Pick a book.　　❷ Read the book.

Do More
- Write about what you learned.
- Retell the important facts to a buddy.

For more book titles, go to the Meet the Author/Illustrator page on www.macmillanmh.com

43

© Macmillan/McGraw-Hill

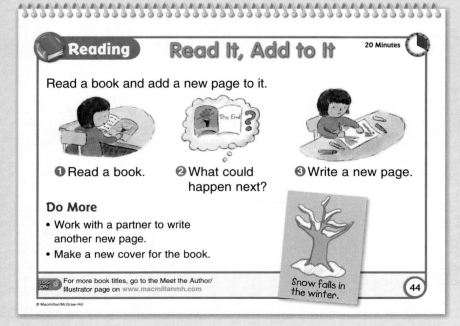

Reading — Read It, Add to It
20 Minutes

Read a book and add a new page to it.

❶ Read a book.　　❷ What could happen next?　　❸ Write a new page.

Do More
- Work with a partner to write another new page.
- Make a new cover for the book.

The End?

Snow falls in the winter.

For more book titles, go to the Meet the Author/Illustrator page on www.macmillanmh.com

44

© Macmillan/McGraw-Hill

Phonics/Word Study

Objectives

- Make a list of words that end in *-ick*
- Write high-frequency words in different colors

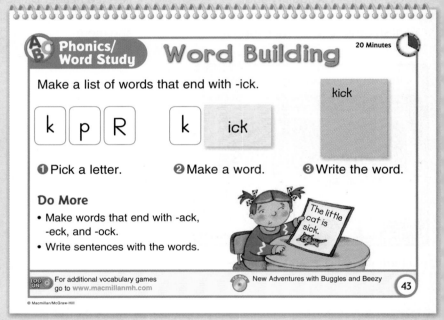

Phonics/Word Study — Word Building
20 Minutes

Make a list of words that end with -ick.

k　p　R　　k　ick　　kick

❶ Pick a letter.　　❷ Make a word.　　❸ Write the word.

Do More
- Make words that end with -ack, -eck, and -ock.
- Write sentences with the words.

The little cat is sick.

For additional vocabulary games go to www.macmillanmh.com　New Adventures with Buggles and Beezy

43

© Macmillan/McGraw-Hill

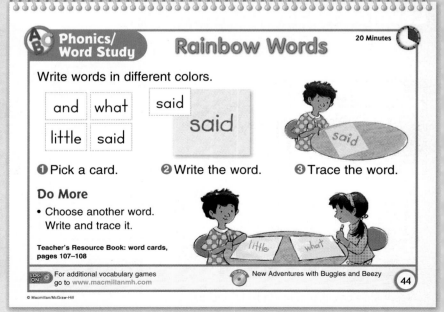

Phonics/Word Study — Rainbow Words
20 Minutes

Write words in different colors.

and　what　said　little　said　　said

❶ Pick a card.　　❷ Write the word.　　❸ Trace the word.

Do More
- Choose another word. Write and trace it.

Teacher's Resource Book: word cards, pages 107–108

For additional vocabulary games go to www.macmillanmh.com　New Adventures with Buggles and Beezy

44

© Macmillan/McGraw-Hill

Literacy Workstations

Reading · **Phonics/ Word Study** · **Writing** · **Science/ Social Studies**

Literacy Workstation Flip Charts

Writing

Objectives

- Write one or more facts about trees
- Write sentences using the word *little*

Content Literacy

Objectives

- Compare and contrast different leaves
- Make posters that tell how trees are useful

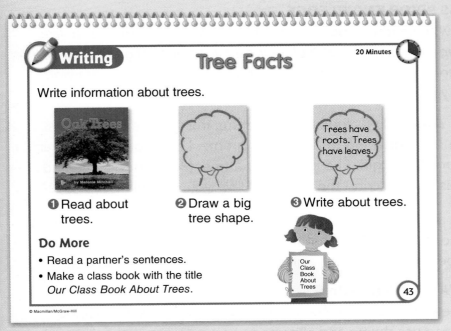

Writing — **Tree Facts** — 20 Minutes

Write information about trees.

❶ Read about trees. ❷ Draw a big tree shape. ❸ Write about trees.

Trees have roots. Trees have leaves.

Do More
- Read a partner's sentences.
- Make a class book with the title *Our Class Book About Trees*.

43

© Macmillan/McGraw-Hill

Science — **Let's Look at Leaves** — 20 Minutes

See how leaves are the same and different.

❶ Look at different leaves. ❷ Talk about size, shape, and color.

Do More
- Make leaf rubbings.
- How are the leaf rubbings alike and different?

oak

Internet Research and Inquiry Activity
www.macmillanmh.com

44

© Macmillan/McGraw-Hill

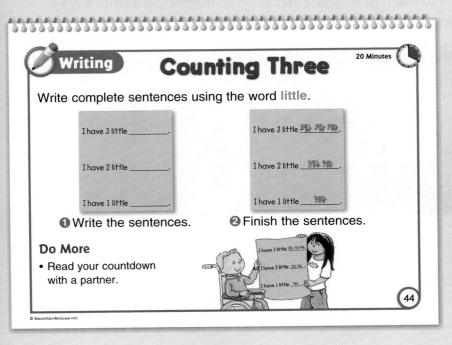

Writing — **Counting Three** — 20 Minutes

Write complete sentences using the word little.

I have 3 little _____.
I have 2 little _____.
I have 1 little _____.

❶ Write the sentences. ❷ Finish the sentences.

Do More
- Read your countdown with a partner.

44

© Macmillan/McGraw-Hill

Social Studies — **Save the Trees Posters** — 20 Minutes

Make posters about how trees are useful.

Take care of trees.
Trees give us food.

❶ Think about trees. ❷ Draw a picture. ❸ Write about trees.

Do More
- Read and talk about each other's posters.

Take care of trees.
Animals live in trees.

Internet Research and Inquiry Activity
www.macmillanmh.com

43

WHOLE GROUP

Oral Language
- Build Background

✔ **Comprehension**
- Read *Oak Trees*
- Strategy: Recognize Text Structure
- Skill: Identify Sequence of Events

✔ **High-Frequency Words**
- Introduce *little, said*

✔ **Phonemic Awareness**
- Phoneme Isolation

✔ **Phonics**
- Introduce /k/*k*
- Handwriting: Write *Kk*

Grammar
- Describing Words (Adjectives)

Writing
- Shared Writing: Steps in a Process

SMALL GROUP

- Differentiated Instruction, pages 1870–1895

Oral Vocabulary

Week 1

charming   conceited   equal
grow   plant

Review

clear   cozy   experience
hibernate   retreat

Use the **Define/Example/Ask** routine in the **Instructional Routine Handbook** to review last week's words.

Oral Language

Build Background: *How Trees Grow*

INTRODUCE THE THEME
Tell children that this week they will be talking and reading about how trees **grow**. *A tree is a type of* **plant** *that grows from a seed.*

Write the following message on the board: *Trees grow in many places. What do you know about trees?* Track the print as you read aloud the message. *Printed materials provide us with information. The first sentence tells us that trees grow in many places. The information printed here can also be found in some books.*

ACCESS PRIOR KNOWLEDGE
- Talk with children about plants that grow. *To grow means "to live, change, and get bigger." A plant is a living thing that grows and cannot move from place to place. What plants do you see growing near your home?*

Think Aloud Let's look at this picture. It is a huge tree. It must have been growing for a very long time. Let's look at the other picture. It is a girl. She is planting a tree. **(Point to the tree and girl as you describe the picture.)** Have you ever planted a tree?

- Look at the photographs of the girl and the sequoia tree. Then sing the song. Talk about what the plants in the photographs looked like before and after they grew by speaking audibly and clearly.

INNOVATE ON THE SONG
Write new lyrics about other things that grow from seeds. Guide children to use rhyme and alliteration to model the author's way of writing.

A lot of trees
start from seeds so small,
You gotta look close
or you can't see them at all.

Oral Language   Plants Week 1   50

Teaching Chart 50

Share the Big Book

Listening Comprehension

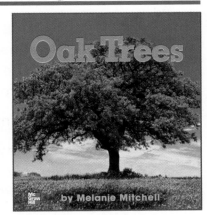

Big Book

PREVIEW Display the cover. *I see a big tree. It looks like an oak tree. Now let's read about how an oak tree **grows**.*

Read aloud the title and the author/photographer. *Is this tree young or old? When was it **planted**? Why?*

GENRE: INFORMATIONAL TEXT/ EXPOSITORY Tell children that this book is **expository**. Discuss that the purpose of reading expository text is to learn facts and information.

STRATEGY Recognize Text Structure

EXPLAIN/MODEL Remind children that understanding how a book is organized can help them to understand it.

Think Aloud This is a huge tree. I know trees start from seeds. This tree must have been growing a long time. I wonder if the book will be organized by how a tree grows.

SKILL Identify Sequence of Events

EXPLAIN/MODEL Tell children that some books tell the order in which things happen. Page through the book.

Think Aloud The photographs show a large tree and then how an acorn sprouts and grows into a tree. I think the book will tell about the steps in which an acorn grows into an oak tree.

Read the Big Book

SET PURPOSE Tell children to think about how the book is organized and how trees grow. Use the **Define/Example/Ask** routine to teach the story words on the inside back cover.

Respond to Literature

MAKE CONNECTIONS Discuss the book. Have children respond to information in *Oak Trees* by relating to their own experience with growing plants or with putting a story in a logical sequence.

Objectives

- Discuss the theme
- Use oral vocabulary words *grow* and *plant*
- Listen and respond to a story
- Recognize text structure/ identify sequence of events

Materials

- Teaching Chart 50
- Big Book: *Oak Trees*

ELL

Use the Interactive Question-Response Guide for *Oak Trees*, **ELL Resource Book** pages 208–211, to guide children through a reading of the book. As you read *Oak Trees*, make meaning clear by pointing to the pictures, demonstrating word meanings, paraphrasing text, and asking children questions.

Digital Learning

Song and Story on **Listening Library Audio CD**

Objectives

- Read the high-frequency words *little, said*
- Review the high-frequency words *this, do, and, what*
- Identify the words *little* and *said* in speech and text

Materials

- High-Frequency Word Cards: *little, said, this, do, and, what*
- Teaching Chart 51

Reinforce Vocabulary
Review the high-frequency words *little, said, this, and, do, what*. Display the High-Frequency Word Cards *little, said, this, and, do, what*. Point to various children and classroom objects and ask questions, such as: *Does Juanita have a little sister? Who said Juanita has a little sister? Whose seat is this? What are Carla and Kiku doing?* Guide children to answer in complete sentences using the high-frequency words.

High-Frequency Words

 little, said

little · said

INTRODUCE Display the **High-Frequency Word Card** for **little**. Use the **Read/Spell/Write** routine to teach the word. Repeat the routine with the word **said**.

- **Read** Point to and say the word *little*. *The kitten is* little.

- **Spell** *The word* little *is spelled* l-i-t-t-l-e. *What's the first sound in* little? *That's right. The first sound in* little *is /l/. That's why the first letter is* l. *Repeat with the remaining letters. Let's read and spell* little.

- **Write** *Now let's write the word* little *on our papers. Let's spell aloud the word as we write it:* little, l-i-t-t-l-e.

SPIRAL REVIEW **REVIEW *this, do, and, what*** Display each card and have children read the word.

this

READ THE RHYME AND CHIME
Tell children to point to *little* and *said* each time they see them. Repeat the rhyme together for fluency. Then add *little* and *said* to the class Word Wall.

what

Kid and Kitten
Goat Kid gave a kick.
Little Chick said, "Cheep!"
Duck kept paddling in the pond.
And Kitten fell asleep.

High-Frequency Words: *little, said*
Phonics: /k/k, /k/ck

Plants Week I | 51

Teaching Chart 51

TIME TO MOVE!

Play a game. One child whispers an action, such as, *Jump,* to another child. The class asks: *What did [first child's name] say?* The second child says: *[First child's name] said, "Jump."* The class does the action. Then another child begins.

Phonemic Awareness

 Phoneme Isolation

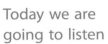

Model

Display the Photo Card for *kite*.

Repeat with the Photo Card for *kitten*.

Today we are going to listen for a new sound. Listen for the sound at the beginning of *kite*: /k/. *Kite* has /k/ at the beginning. Say the sound with me: /k/. What is the sound? We'll clap our hands when we hear /k/ at the beginning of a word!

Say the "Kid and Kitten" Rhyme and Chime again. Have children clap every time they hear /k/.

Goat Kid gave a kick.
Little Chick said, "Cheep!"
Duck kept paddling in the pond.
And Kitten fell asleep.

 SPIRAL REVIEW

Review /b/ and /l/

Display the Photo Card for *book*.

Repeat for *lamp*.

This is a book. The beginning sound in *book* is /b/. (Emphasize the beginning sound.) What is the sound?

Guided Practice/Practice

Display and name each Photo Card. Children identify the initial sound. Guide practice with the first card, using the same routine. Continue orally with the words *koala, be, keep, kin, leaf, bath, kitten, buy, leap, bubbly.*

Say the name of the picture with me. Tell me the sound you hear at the beginning of the word.

Quick Check

Can children identify the initial /k/ sound?

During **Small Group Instruction**

If No → **Approaching Level** For additional practice isolating sounds, page 1871.

If Yes → **On Level** Children blend words with /k/, page 1872.

Beyond Level Children read words with /k/, page 1873.

Objectives

- Identify initial /k/
- Review initial /b/ and /l/

Materials

- Photo Cards: *banana, book, bus, key, kite, kitten, koala, lamp, leg, lock,*

ELL

Pronunciation Display and have children name Photo Cards from this and prior lessons to reinforce phonemic awareness and word meanings. Point to a card and ask: *What do you see?* (a key) *What is the sound at the beginning of the word key?* (/k/) Repeat using Photo Cards with words that begin with the /b/ and /l/ sounds.

Objectives

- Match the letter *k* to the /k/ sound
- Handwriting: Write *Kk*

Materials

- Sound-Spelling Card: *Koala*
- Teaching Chart 51
- Word-Building Cards
- Handwriting
- Handwriting Teacher's Edition
- Activity Book, p. 4
- Practice Book, p. 161

ELL

Variations in Languages
Speakers of Hmong may have difficulty perceiving and pronouncing /k/. Use the Approaching Level Phonics lessons for additional pronunciation and decoding practice.

 Sound Pronunciation

See **Sound-Pronunciation CD** for a model of the /k/ sound. Play this for children needing additional models.

Phonics

✔ Introduce /k/k

Model

Display the *Koala* **Sound-Spelling Card**.

This is the *Koala* card. The sound is /k/. The /k/ sound is spelled with the letter *k*. Say it with me: /k/. This is the sound at the beginning of the word *koala*. Listen: /k/ . . . *oala, koala*.
What is the name of this letter? What sound does this letter stand for?

Read the "Kid and Kitten" Rhyme and Chime. Reread the title. Point out that the words *Kid* and *Kitten* begin with /k/*k*. Tell children that the words begin with the letter *K*. Model placing a self-stick note below the letter *K* in *Kid* and *Kitten*.

Kid and Kitten
Goat Kid gave a kick.
Little Chick said, "Cheep!"
Duck kept paddling in the pond.
And Kitten fell asleep.

High-Frequency Words: *little, said*
Phonics: /k/*k*, /k/*ck*

Plants Week I 51

Teaching Chart 51

Guided Practice/Practice

Read the rest of the rhyme. Stop after each line. Children place self-stick notes below words that begin with the letter *k*. Guide practice with *Kid* in line 1.

Let's place a sticky note below the words in the line that begin with *k*. The words *Kid* and *kick* begin with the letter *k*.

Corrective Feedback

If children need help with /k/, review the word *kid*. Emphasize the /k/ sound as you demonstrate the proper mouth position. *This is the /k/ sound in the beginning of* kid: /kiiid/, kid. Repeat with *kick, key,* and *kit.*

Build Fluency: Sound-Spellings

 Display the following **Word-Building Cards:** *a, b, c, d, e, h, i, k, l, m, n, o, r, s, p, t.* Have children chorally say each sound. Repeat and vary the pace.

Handwriting: Write *Kk*

MODEL Say the handwriting cues below as you write the capital and lowercase forms of *Kk* on the board. Then trace the letters on the board and in the air as you say /k/. Identify the uppercase and lowercase forms of the letter.

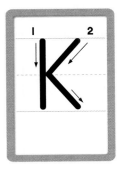

Straight down. Go back to the top. Slant in, slant out.

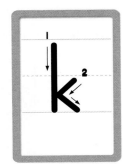

Straight down. Slant in, slant out.

PRACTICE Ask children to hold up their writing hand.

- To provide extra support, have children trace with their index finger the letters you wrote on the board. Have children identify the uppercase and lowercase forms of the letter.

- Have children write *K* and *k* in the air as they say /k/ multiple times.

- Distribute handwriting practice pages. Observe children's pencil grip and paper position, and correct as necessary. Have children say /k/ every time they write *k*.

For Tier 2 instruction, see page 1871.

Daily Handwriting
Check that children form letters starting at the top and moving to the bottom. See **Handwriting Teacher's Edition** for ball-and-stick and slant models.

Activity Book, page 4
Practice Book, page 161

Objective

- Recognize describing words (adjectives)

Materials

- Big Book: *Oak Trees*
- Photo Cards: *soup, yolk, mop*

ELL

Basic and Academic Vocabulary Display the Photo Cards from the lesson and pair English Language Learners with fluent speakers. Have partners make up sentences using *mop* and a describing word. Write their sentences, read them chorally, and ask: *What describing word tells about* mop?

Grammar

Describing Words (Adjectives)

MODEL Use the **Big Book** *Oak Trees* to discuss describing words. Tell children that describing words tell more about something. Display page 10 of *Oak Trees* and read aloud the sentence "It **grows** into a small tree." Tell children that *small* is a describing word that tells more about the tree.

- Use *small* to start a list. Add other describing words that tell about the trees on pages 11 and 14 (*young, leafy, big, tall, old*). Point out that these words tell more about trees, too.

PRACTICE Display **Photo Cards** of *soup, yolk,* and *mop.*

- Help children identify each picture. Model using describing words by making up sentences about the pictures, such as:

> *We are eating* hot *soup.*
>
> *The mop was* wet.

- After each sentence, ask children to name the describing word. Then have them make up their own complete sentences about the pictures. Have children say the describing word after each sentence. Dictate a sentence for each child to illustrate. Have partners share their sentences and point out the describing words. Use words that describe color, size, and location.

Writing

Shared Writing: Steps in a Process

BRAINSTORM

Remind children that in *Oak Trees* they learned the steps to how an acorn **grows** into an oak tree that later makes acorns, which then grow into new trees. *How did the acorn grow into a tree? What happened first? Today will write about how something is done or made.* Tell children that this kind of writing is named **Procedural Writing**.

WRITE

- Make a list showing the process of how an oak tree grows. Read the heading together as you track the print.

- Tell children they will make a list of how oak trees grow. They will use the words *first, next,* and *last* to write the steps in order.

- Model by reading pages 6–7 of *Oak Trees. The first step is that an acorn falls or is **planted** in the ground, so I will write:* 1. First, an acorn is planted.

- Continue by reading pages 8–17. After you read each spread, have children tell you what to write.

- Read the completed list together with children. Save the list to refer to in other writing activities this week.

How Oak Trees Grow

1. First, an acorn is planted.
2. Next, the acorn grows roots.
3. Next, the acorn grows a stem.
4. Next, the acorn grows into a small tree.
5. Next, the tree grows bigger.
6. Next, the tree makes flowers.
7. Next, acorns grow from the flowers.
8. Next, the acorns fall to the ground.
9. Last, the acorns grow into new oak trees.

Write About It

Tell children to draw a picture of a tree with fruit growing on it. Ask them to label their drawing.

Objective

- Write a numbered list

Materials

- Big Book: *Oak Trees*

5-Day Writing

Procedural Text: Steps in a Process	
DAY 1	Shared: Steps in a Process
DAY 2	Interactive: Steps in a Process
DAY 3	Independent: Prewrite and Draft Steps in a Process
DAY 4	Independent: Revise and Edit Steps in a Process
DAY 5	Independent: Publish and Present

ELL

Prewriting Planning
Provide the **Big Book** *Oak Trees* for children to look through. Have them look at the words and pictures in the glossary. Then help children name the different parts of each tree shown before beginning work on their notebook drawing.

Transitions That Teach

While children are packing up, have them name things that **grow**. Ask: *Do trees grow? What else can grow?*

Oral Language
- Build Robust Vocabulary

✓ **Comprehension**
- Reread *Oak Trees*
- Strategy: Recognize Text Structure
- Skill: Identify Sequence of Events
- Fluency: Echo-Read

Vocabulary
- Position Words
- Story Words: *acorns, roots, stem*

✓ **Phonemic Awareness**
- Phoneme Blending

✓ **Phonics**
- Review /k/k, /b/b, /l/l
- Blend with /k/k
- Decodable Reader: *Sad Hen*

Writing
- Interactive Writing: Steps in a Process

- Differentiated Instruction, pages 1870–1895

Oral Vocabulary

Week 1

charming   conceited   equal
grow   plant

Review

clear   cozy   experience
hibernate   retreat
Use the **Define/Example/Ask** routine in the **Instructional Routines Handbook** to review last week's words.

Oral Language

Talk About It ## Build Robust Vocabulary

INTRODUCE WORDS

Tell children that today they are going to talk about the **Big Book** *Oak Trees*. Read aloud pages 2–11. *See how big the oak tree is in this photograph? Oak trees can grow to be very big. Oak trees first start out as seeds called acorns. Then the seeds grow into small plants.*

Vocabulary Routine

Use the routine below to discuss the meaning of each word.

Define: A **plant** is a living thing that usually grows in the ground. Say the word with me.
Example: Trees and flowers are plants.
Ask: What do you need to do to take care of a plant?

Define: **Grow** means "to live, change, and become bigger." Say the word with me.
Example: Many trees grow in the forest.
Ask: Which of the things I name can grow: a duck, a book, grass, a vine, a child, a plane, a bed?

CREATE A CHART

Create a three-column chart as shown, or use **Teaching Chart G4**, to sequence the events in the life cycle of a tree, using pictures. Read the headings together as you track the print. *I know that an acorn is the first stage in the life of an oak tree. I put* acorn *under* First *and drew a picture. Next the acorn grows into a small tree. Where should I write that?* Guide children to speak audibly and clearly, using complete sentences to communicate.

Listen for Rhyme

IDENTIFY RHYME

Remind children that words rhyme when they have the same ending sounds. *The word* red *rhymes with* bed. Tell children *red* and *bed* end with the sounds /ed/. *What word rhymes with* bed? Sing the song and have children say the words that rhyme.

SING ABOUT TREES

Let's sing a fun song about trees. Play the fingerplay "Little Red Apple," using the **Listening Library Audio CD**. Then teach children the words and actions, and recite the fingerplay several times together.

Little Red Apple

A little red apple hung high in a tree.

Point up high.

I looked at it.

Look up.

And it looked down at me.

Look down.

"Come down, please," I called.

Put hands to mouth as if calling.

And what do you suppose?

Shrug shoulders.

The little red apple fell right on my nose!

Put hands on nose.

Objectives

- Discuss the theme
- Discuss the life cycle of an oak tree
- Use oral vocabulary words *plant* and *grow*
- Complete a chart

Materials

- Big Book: *Oak Trees*
- Graphic Organizer; Teaching Chart G4
- Listening Library Audio CD

Digital Learning

Fingerplay on Listening Library Audio CD

ELL   ENGLISH LANGUAGE LEARNERS

Beginning	**Intermediate**	**Advanced**
Confirm Understanding Ask children to point to the chart as they complete sentences. For example: *First, an oak tree is an _____. Next, the acorn grows _____. Last, it becomes a _____.*	**Enhance Understanding** Help children elaborate on the events on the chart. Ask: *Does a small tree grow before or after the roots are formed? What happens after the oak tree makes flowers?*	**Retell Sequence** Have children use *first, next,* and *last* in complete sentences to tell about the life of an oak tree.

Objectives

- Recognize text structure/ways authors group information
- Identify sequence of events
- Retell important facts and events in a book

Materials

- Big Book: *Oak Trees*
- Activity Book, p. 5
- Practice Book, p. 162

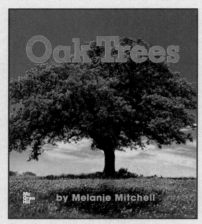

Big Book

Digital Learning

Story on **Listening Library Audio CD**

ELL

Use gestures and other strategies to help make the text comprehensible.

p. 3

grow very big: Call attention to the picture on page 3. Point to the roof of the house and say *big*. Slide your finger up from the roof to the top of the tree. Say: *It's very big.* Have a few children take turns repeating the action and words in complete sentences.

Reread the Big Book

Listening Comprehension

CONCEPTS ABOUT PRINT Display the cover and read the title aloud with children as you track the print. Have them tell what they remember about the book, using complete, coherent sentences.

STRATEGY **Recognize Text Structure**

Explain to children that paying attention to how a book is organized can help them to understand it. *Do you remember how the book was organized? It showed the stages in which an oak tree **grows**.*

SKILL **Identify Sequence of Events**

Tell children that yesterday they learned that some books tell about things in order. *Today you are going to read the Big Book again and look for clues to help you know the order in which things happen.* Display and explain "Life Cycle of an Oak Tree" on page 18.

Think Aloud These pictures show how an acorn sprouts and slowly grows into a big tree. I remember that the book is organized to show what happens first, next, and last in the growth of an oak tree.

Read the **Big Book** and use the prompts on the inside covers.

pages 2–3

This is an **oak tree.**

②

Oak trees can grow very big.

③

Develop Comprehension

pages 4–5

SEQUENCE OF EVENTS

Think Aloud These pages tell me that oak trees grow from seeds called acorns. This is at the beginning of the book, so acorns must be the first step of an oak tree growing.

pages 6–7

TEXT STRUCTURE

- *How is the book organized?* (by how an oak tree grows)

SEQUENCE OF EVENTS

- *What do you think happens after an acorn is planted?*

pages 8–9

CONCEPT WORDS: SEQUENCE WORDS

- *I am going to read these pages again. Which two words help us know when things happen?* (*first, next*)

How do oak trees grow?

④

Oak trees grow from seeds called **acorns.**

⑤

Some acorns are planted.

⑥

Others just fall to the ground.

⑦

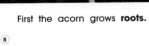

First the acorn grows **roots.**

⑧

Next it grows a **stem.**

⑨

Comprehension

Recognize Text Structure

- (pages 6–7) I see that the book is organized by how an oak tree grows. Each page tells the next step in the process.

Sequence of Events

- (pages 8–9) I see that after an acorn is planted, it grows roots underground. What happens next?
- (pages 12–13) Does an oak tree make flowers or acorns first?
- (page 14) When does an oak tree grow acorns?

Story Word

(page 5) acorns

About the Author: Melanie Mitchell

Melanie Mitchell is the author of many books about animals, food, nature, and people. She also tackled loftier topics in such books as *Stars, Moon,* and *Sun.*

**Big Book
Inside Back Cover**

ELL

pp. 4–5

seeds, acorns: Explain that acorns are the seeds of an oak tree. Talk about other seeds children know such as apple seeds, avocado seeds, and sunflower seeds.

pp. 6–7

planted: Lead children in showing the action of planting a seed in soil. Then together say: *We planted a seed.*

pp. 8–9

roots, stem: Point to the roots on page 8 and the stem on page 9. Then say *roots* or *stem* again and have children point to the correct part on page 9 and repeat the appropriate word.

Recognize Text Structure

Explain Remind children that they must support their answers with text evidence.

Discuss Have children listen to pages 10–15. *Does an oak tree make flowers or acorns first?* (flowers) Recognizing text structure helps us find text evidence. Recognizing that the page about flowers comes before the page about acorns helps me to find information.

ELL

pp. 10–11
small, bigger, taller: Draw three trees on the board going from smallest to largest. Point to the first two trees. *Which tree is big? Which is bigger? Which is biggest?* Repeat with *tall, taller, tallest.*

p. 12
flowers: Help children recognize oak flowers as flowers. Show photos of flowers with which children are familiar. Point to each and say *flower.* Then, point to the oak flowers on page 12. Say: *This is a flower.* Have children name a flower they know: _____ *is a flower.*

pp. 14–15
fall to the ground: Have children pretend to be trees. Give them paper with acorns drawn on it. Say *fall to the ground* and model letting a paper acorn fall. Have them let their paper acorns fall as they repeat your words.

Develop Comprehension

pages 10–11

✓ SEQUENCE OF EVENTS
- *What happens as a tree grows?* (It gets bigger and taller.)

It grows into a small tree. ⑩   The tree grows bigger and taller. ⑪

pages 12–13

✓ TEXT STRUCTURE
- *Does an oak tree make flowers or acorns first?* (flowers) *How can you tell?* (The page about flowers comes first, before the page about acorns.)

Many years later, the tree grows **flowers.** ⑫   Acorns grow from the flowers. ⑬

pages 14–15

SELF-QUESTION
Think Aloud The beginning of the book talked about acorns on the ground. Why are there acorns on the ground again on this page? First, the author told us that trees grow from acorns. Now, the author describes what happens when a tree gets old and makes acorns. Those acorns fall on the ground and can grow into trees. It starts all over. What questions about the book do you have?

Oak trees must be very old to grow acorns. ⑭   The acorns fall to the ground. ⑮

pages 16–17

IDENTIFY MAIN IDEA

- *What is the big idea of this book?* (Possible answer: The book is about how oak trees grow.)

Animals eat some of the acorns.

The rest grow into new oak trees.

16   17

page 18

SEQUENCE OF EVENTS

- *Which picture shows what happened first? What happens next? How does the illustrator use pictures to help us understand the life cycle of an oak tree?*

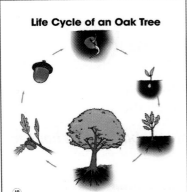

Life Cycle of an Oak Tree

Oak Trees

Oak trees grow all over the world. There are almost 300 kinds of oak trees. Different kinds of oak trees grow in different places.

Oak trees grow very slowly. It takes many years for an oak tree to grow big enough to produce acorns. Oak trees produce acorns in the fall. Some oak trees produce thousands of acorns. Only a few acorns will actually grow into trees and continue the life cycle of an oak tree.

18   19

ELL

pp. 16–17
some, rest: Use several small items to demonstrate keeping some and giving a child the rest. *I have some. You have the rest.*

pages 20–21

AUTHOR'S PURPOSE

- *These pages have more facts about oak trees. Why do you think the author put these pages in the book?* (Possible answer: She wanted to tell other facts about oak trees that did not fit into the rest of the book.)

Oak Tree Facts

 Oak trees can live for hundreds of years. A famous oak tree in Maryland called the Wye Oak lived for over 400 years. It was destroyed by lightning in 2002.

 Some oak trees are 50 years old before they produce acorns.

 An average oak tree sheds about 700,000 leaves each fall.

 Oak trees seem to be struck by lightning more than any other kind of tree.

 Connecticut, Georgia, Illinois, Iowa, Maryland, and New Jersey all have an oak tree as their state tree.

 The bark from the cork oak tree can be peeled away and used to make corkboards, shoe soles, and insulation. The tree regrows its bark in about nine years.

20   21

page 22

PARTS OF A BOOK

Think Aloud This page is called the *glossary*. It lists important words used in the book and tells what each one means. This glossary also has a photograph for each word.

Glossary

 acorns – the seeds of an oak tree

 flowers – the parts of plants that grows seeds

 oak tree – a tree that makes acorns

 roots – the parts of plants that grow down into the soil

 stem – the supporting part of plants that grows above ground

22

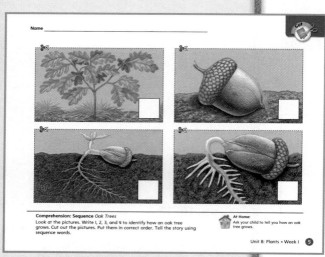

Activity Book, page 5
Practice Book, page 162

Respond to Literature

TALK ABOUT IT Ask children to talk about the words and photographs that they liked and to refer to the book as they answer the questions.

- *What does an oak tree begin as?* (Oak trees begin as acorns.) LOCATE

- *How was the book organized?* (in the order that an oak tree grows) COMBINE

- *How is an oak tree like a person?* (It starts out small and gets taller.) CONNECT

Retell

GUIDED RETELLING

Explain to children that as they listened to *Oak Trees,* they used the words, photographs, and illustrations to understand the book. Now they will retell the story.

- *What did the book tell us happens first?* (Oak trees grow from acorns.)

- *What happens next?* (The acorn seed grows into a little plant.)

- *What happens last?* (The tree gets big enough to make acorns. The acorns fall to the ground, and some make new trees.)

- Discuss the book. *What did you learn about how oak trees are* **planted** *and* **grow**?

- Ask children to act out how an oak tree grows.

- Have children write, share, and discuss friendly notes about their favorite plants and trees.

Fluency: Echo-Read

MODEL Reread page 5, emphasizing the word in boldface. Then reread pages 8–9 the same way and have children echo-read as you track the print.

> **Quick Check**
>
> **Can children identify sequence of events to help understand a book?**
> **Can children retell information in a book in sequence?**

Retelling Rubric

 4   Excellent

Retells the selection without prompting, using detailed information, and referring to text structure and features. Clearly describes the main idea.

 3   Good

Retells the selection with little guidance, using some details, and occasionally referring to text structure and features. Generally describes the main idea.

2   Fair

Retells the selection with some guidance, using limited details. Partially describes the main idea.

 1   Unsatisfactory

Retells the selection only when prompted, using limited details. Does not describe the main idea.

Vocabulary

Position Words

Chant the following jingle:

Let's make a sandwich:

A piece of bread on the bottom,

A slice of cheese in the middle,

And another piece of bread on top!

■ Repeat the second line and tell children which word tells a place or position. Repeat with the other lines.

Make a tower using colored blocks. Describe the tower saying phrases such as: *a red block on* top, *a blue block in the* middle, *and a yellow block on the* bottom.

NAME POSITION WORDS Have children build block towers and describe the position of the blocks to each other.

Story Words: *acorns, roots, stem*

Display page 5 of *Oak Trees*. Point out the picture of *acorns* and the written word. *Have you ever seen acorns? Where were they? An acorn is the seed of an oak tree.*

Display pages 8 and 9. Point out the pictures of the *roots* and *stem*. *Which part is being* **planted** *into the ground? Which part is above the ground?*

TIME TO MOVE!

Put groups of three objects in a pile, one on top of the other.
Give directions such as:
Show me the book on the bottom.
Tap the box of crayons in the middle.
Bring me the pad of paper on the top.

Objectives

- **Use position words**
- **Learn story words** *acorns, roots, stem*

Materials

- **Big Book:** *Oak Trees*
- **building blocks in various colors**

Digital Learning

LOG ON For children who need additional language support and oral vocabulary development, use the activities found at **www.macmillanmh.com**.

ELL

Reinforce Meaning Have two children place their hands on top of each other to form a pile. As they lift their hands, ask children to say the position words with you: *top, middle, bottom.*

Objectives

- Orally blend sounds in words with /k/
- Match the letters *k, b, l* to their sounds
- Blend sounds in words with /k/k

Materials

- Puppet
- Word-Building Cards
- pocket chart

/s/c

Explain Hold up Word-Building Card *c*. *This letter is* c. *We know that* c *can stand for* /k/ *as in* cat. C *can also stand for* /s/.

Hold up the **Photo Card** for *circle*. Write *circle* on the board. *This is the word* circle. *The sound at the beginning of the word* circle *is* /s/. *The* c *stands for* /s/. *What is the word? What sound does* c *stand for in the word* circle?

Model Write *cereal, cut, cent, cot,* and *center* on the board. Read the words aloud. *I am going to place a sticky note under each* c *that stands for* /s/. Point to the word *cereal*. *This word is* cereal. Cereal *begins with* c *and the sound* /s/. *I will place a sticky note beneath* c *in* cereal. Continue with the other words.

Guided Practice/Practice Remove the self-stick notes from the board. Have children work in groups of two or three to determine which words on the board begin with /s/c and which words begin with /k/c, using self-stick notes.

Phonemic Awareness

Phoneme Blending

Model

Use the **Puppet** to model how to blend the word *kit*.

Repeat the routine with *kite*.

Happy is going to say the beginning and ending sounds in a word. Listen to Happy as he says these sounds: /k/ /it/. Happy can blend these sounds together: *kit*. Say the sounds with Happy: /k/ /i/ /t/, /kiiit/, *kit*. What is the word? (*kit*)

Guided Practice/Practice

Say the sounds.

Children blend the sounds to form words. Guide practice with the first word.

Happy is going to say the sounds in a word. Listen to Happy as he says each sound. Then blend the sounds together to make a word.

/k/ /i/ /s/	/k/ /i/ /d/	/k/ /e/ /n/
/k/ /ē/ /p/	/k/ /ē/	/k/ /i/ /k/

Phonics

Review

k	b	l

Model

Display **Word-Building Card** *k*.

Repeat the routine for the letters *b* and *l*.

This is the letter *k*. The letter *k* stands for /k/ at the beginning of *kite*. Say /k/.

Say the word. Write the letter *k*.

Repeat with *bed*.

Listen as I say a word: *kit*. The sound at the beginning of the word *kit* is /k/. The letter *k* stands for /k/ that we hear at the beginning of *kit*. I'll write *k*.

Guided Practice/Practice

Children write *k, b,* and *l*. Guide practice with the first word.

Listen as I say a word. Write the letter that stands for the beginning sound.

king	bus	kiss	lock
lamp	key	keep	bike

Build Fluency: Sound-Spellings

 Display the following **Word-Building Cards**: *a, b, c, d, e, m, n, h, i, k, o, r, s, p, t.* Have children chorally say each sound. Repeat and vary the pace.

✔ Blend with /k/k

Model

Place Word-Building Card *K* in the pocket chart.

This letter is *K*. It stands for the /k/ sound. Say /k/.

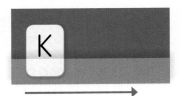

Place Word-Building Card *i* next to *K*. Move your hand from left to right.

This letter is *i*. It stands for the /i/ sound. Listen as I blend the two sounds together: /kiii/. Now you blend the sounds with me. (/kiii/)

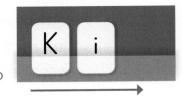

Place Word-Building Card *m* next to *Ki*. Move your hand from left to right.

Repeat with *kit*.

This is the letter *m*. It stands for the /m/ sound. Listen as I blend the three sounds together: /kiiimmm/. Now you blend the sounds with me. (/kiiimmm/, *Kim*)

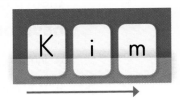

Guided Practice/Practice

Children repeat the blending routine after you. Guide practice with *kid*.

kid	lot	kin	let	lab
bib	Ken	net	not	bid

Objectives

- Read decodable words with /k/k
- Read the words *little, said, a, for, is,* and *the*
- Reread for fluency

Materials

- High-Frequency Word Cards: *little, said, a, for, is, the*
- pocket chart
- Decodable Reader: *Sad Hen*

Decodable Text

For additional decodable passages, see pages 35–36 of the **Teacher's Resource Book**.

Decodable Reader

Read *Sad Hen*

Sad Hen

 REVIEW HIGH-FREQUENCY WORDS Display **High-Frequency Word Cards** for **little, said, a, for, is,** and **the** in the pocket chart. Say each word. Review the words using the **Read/Spell/Write** routine.

MODEL CONCEPTS ABOUT PRINT Demonstrate book handling. *I hold the book so that the cover is on the front and the words are not upside down. I turn the cover. Then I turn each page as I read it.*

PREDICT Ask children to describe the cover. *Do you think the story will be a made-up story or one that could really happen? Why?*

FIRST READ Turn to page 2. Children point to each word, sounding out decodable words and saying the high-frequency words quickly. If children have difficulty, provide corrective feedback and guide them page by page.

DEVELOP COMPREHENSION Ask the following:

- *What is this book about?* (a sad hen with a kind friend)

- *What did Ken Cat give to Kit Hen? Why?* (a red hat; she was sad)

SECOND READ Have partners reread the book together.

Ken Cat met Kit Hen.
Is Kit Hen sick?

2

Kit Hen is not sick.
Kit Hen is a little bit sad.

3

Let's sit on the back deck.

4

Kit Hen sits.
Ken Cat sits.

5

Ken Cat has a red sack.
It is for Kit Hen.

6

"It is a red hat!" said Kit.

7

The hat fits.
Kit Hen is not sad.

8

Decodable Reader

Writing

Interactive Writing: Steps in a Process

REVIEW

■ Display and read aloud the list, the **Procedural Writing**, that children created for the Shared Writing activity.

WRITE

■ *Today we are going to write sentences about how oak trees **grow**. We are going to write the first four steps.*

■ Collaborate with children to write the following sentence frames.

_____, an acorn is _____.

Next, the acorn grows _____.

_____, the acorn grows a _____.

Last, the acorn grows into

_____ _____ _____.

■ Children suggest words to complete each sentence, using the list made on Day 1. Write words in the frames to complete the sentences. Ask children to help by writing the letters that they know.

■ Read the completed sentences aloud with children as you track the print.

■ Tell children that the words *first, next,* and *last* help us tell things in order.

■ To extend the lesson, children can write about the other steps to how an oak tree grows.

Write About It

Tell children to draw a picture of a fruit tree. Have them label their drawing, using one of the high-frequency words *this, do, and,* or *what. This is a cherry tree.*

Objectives

- Write sentences
- Use letter knowledge to write letters in a word

Materials

- Shared Writing lists from Day 1

5-Day Writing

Procedural Text: Steps in a Process	
DAY 1	Shared: Steps in a Process
DAY 2	Interactive: Steps in a Process
DAY 3	Independent: Prewrite and Draft Steps in a Process
DAY 4	Independent: Revise and Edit Steps in a Process
DAY 5	Independent: Publish and Present

ELL

Use New Language
Ask children to dictate a sentence that describes a fruit tree they have seen in books, in the area where they live, or in their country of origin. Have children add any phonetic elements or high-frequency words they know.

Transitions That Teach

While lining up, have children tell about how a **plant** grows up from a seed.

Day 3
At a Glance

WHOLE GROUP

Oral Language
- Build Robust Vocabulary
- Oral Vocabulary Cards: "The Conceited Apple Branch"

✓ **Comprehension**
- Read "Acorn"

✓ **High-Frequency Words**
- Review *little*, *said*

✓ **Phonemic Awareness**
- Phoneme Isolation

✓ **Phonics**
- Introduce /k/*ck*
- Blend with /k/*ck*

Grammar
- Describing Words (Adjectives)

Writing
- Independent Writing: Prewrite and Draft Steps in a Process

SMALL GROUP

- Differentiated Instruction, pages 1870–1895

Additional Vocabulary

To provide 15–20 minutes of additional vocabulary instruction, see Oral Vocabulary Cards 5-Day Plan. The pre- and posttests can be found in the **Teacher's Resource Book**, pages 228–229.

Oral Language

Talk About It **Build Robust Vocabulary**

BUILD BACKGROUND
Introduce the story "The Conceited Apple Branch" using **Oral Vocabulary Card 1** and read the title aloud. *Can you name some plants or flowers? What do they look like?* Ask children to tell what they think is happening in the picture and to predict what will happen in the story.

■ Read the story on the back of the cards. You may wish to check children's understanding using the Identify Story Elements, Ask Questions, and Words with Multiple Meanings prompts. Pause at each oral vocabulary word and read the definition.

Oral Vocabulary Cards

Vocabulary Routine

Use the routine below to discuss the meaning of each word.

Define: Someone who is **conceited** is too proud of himself or herself. Say the word with me.
Example: The conceited baseball player thought he was better than the others on his team.
Ask: Is it nice to be conceited? Why or why not?

Define: **Equal** means "to be the same as something else." Say the word with me.
Example: The two girls are equal in height.
Ask: How could you make two circles that are equal in size?

Define: If something is **charming**, it is very pleasing and delightful. Say the word with me.
Example: The baby's gurgling sounds and laughter were very charming.
Ask: Would you prefer a friend that was conceited or charming? Why?

SPIRAL REVIEW

■ Use the routine on Cards 1 and 2 to review the words **plant** and **grow**.

■ Review last week's words: *clear, cozy, experience, hibernate,* and *retreat*.

Listen for Rhyme

IDENTIFY RHYME

Review rhyme with children by asking them to identify the rhyming word pairs: *chunk/crust, last/past, star/car, plot/plate, truck/duck.*

Tell children that they will sing another song about a type of tree. Play the song and have children join in.

Say the word *frosty* as you clap for each syllable. Then explain that if you omit the /ē/ at the end of *frosty*, you will get the word *frost.* Have children clap to identify how many syllables are in the words *may, today,* and *gathering.*

TREE TALK

Tell children that trees grow from seeds. *Some trees have nuts that are seeds. The seeds fall to the ground, and a new tree may start to grow. Have partners discuss types of trees they know and how they grow.*

Nuts in May

Here we come gathering nuts in May,

Nuts in May, nuts in May.

Here we come gathering nuts today,

All on a frosty morning.

We can have nuts for Nan in May,

Nuts in May, nuts in May.

We can have nuts for Nan today,

All on a frosty morning.

Objectives

- Discuss the theme
- Use oral vocabulary words *grow, plant, charming, conceited,* and *equal*
- Listen and respond to a folktale

Materials

- Oral Vocabulary Cards: "The Conceited Apple Branch"

Digital Learning

Song on **Listening Library Audio CD**

Objectives

- Read and respond to a poem
- Identify rhythm and rhyme
- Use a picture dictionary

Material

- Big Book of Explorations, Vol. 2: "Acorn," p. 25

Vocabulary

acorn a nut that grows on an oak tree

shell the hard outside part of something

Use a Picture Dictionary
Guide children to find each word in a picture dictionary.

Poetry

Genre

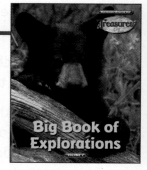

Big Book of Explorations

LITERARY TEXT: POETRY

Tell children that today they will listen to a poem. Explain that poems help us say things in a special way. This poem will be about a playful squirrel.

LITERARY ELEMENT: RHYME AND RHYTHM

Explain/Model Tell children that some poems use words that rhyme. Remind them that rhyming words, such as *bake* and *cake*, have the same sounds at the end. Also explain to children that *rhythm* is another word for *beat*. Say: *Listen for the rhyming words and the rhythm in the poem "Acorn."*

Think Aloud As I read, I will pay attention to the rhyming words I hear. I will also tap my hand softly to the beat, or rhythm, of the poem.

READ "ACORN"

- **Preview and Predict** Display the page as you read the title "Acorn" and point to the illustration. *What is the girl doing? What is the squirrel doing? What will this poem be about?* Explain to children that squirrels eat acorns in autumn. They also gather and save them to eat later.

- **Vocabulary** Introduce and discuss the vocabulary words.

- **Set Purpose** Tell children to listen for the rhythm and words that rhyme in "Acorn." Read the poem aloud as you track the print and softly tap out the rhythm.

page 25

Retell and Respond

- *Which word rhymes with* tree*? What other words rhyme with* tree *and* me*?*

- *Let's clap out the rhythm in "Acorn."*

- *Why did the squirrel want the girl's acorn?*

Connect to Content

Seasonal Activities

- Explain that animals do different things during different seasons of the year. Name the seasons, and remind children that squirrels eat and gather acorns in autumn, or fall.

- Divide a sheet of poster board or chart paper into four squares. In each square, write the name of a season, and have children briefly discuss the weather. Then help children brainstorm activities that they do during each season. Write their ideas in the chart.

- Tell children to draw a picture of themselves doing one of the activities. Help them write a sentence to tell about their drawing.

ELL

Beginning

Use Illustrations Reinforce content words by pointing to an acorn, the shell, the tree, and the squirrel in the illustration. Have children name each one. Point out that the girl in the illustration is talking in the poem.

Intermediate

Act Out Have children work in pairs as you reread "Acorn." Have one child pretend to be the little girl while the other child pretends to be the squirrel. Encourage children to repeat words and sentences from the poem, such as *I took the acorn and ran, ran, ran* and *Give me back my acorn!*

Advanced

Summarize Have children use their own words to summarize "Acorn."

Objectives

- Read the high-frequency words *little, said*
- Review the high-frequency words *I, see, the*

Materials

- High-Frequency Word Cards: *little, said, see, the, I*
- High-Frequency Word Cards; Teacher's Resource Book, pp. 103–110
- pocket chart
- Photo Cards: *dog, doll, feather, key, mouse*
- index card with: period mark
- Activity Book, pp. 7–8
- Practice Book, pp. 163–164

Activity Book, pages 7–8
Practice Book, pages 163–164

High-Frequency Words

 little, said

SPIRAL REVIEW **REVIEW** Display the **High-Frequency Word Cards** for **little, said**. Review the words using the **Read/Spell/Write** routine. Repeat the routine with **I, see**, and **the**.

MODEL *I am going to say a sentence. The dog said to the little squirrel, "Give me back my acorn."* Hold up the appropriate card when you say the words *said* and *little*.

PRACTICE Tell children to hold up their High-Frequency Word Cards when you say the words *little* and *said*. Say the sentences: *The little squirrel ran up the tree. The squirrel said, "This acorn is for me."*

APPLY Build sentences in the pocket chart using High-Frequency Word Cards and **Photo Cards**. Have children point to the high-frequency words.

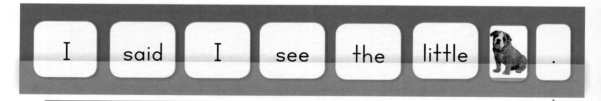

READ FOR FLUENCY Have children use the Take-Home Book to review high-frequency words and practice fluency.

Quick Check

Can children read the words *little* and *said*?

During **Small Group Instruction**

If No → **Approaching Level** Provide additional practice with the words *little* and *said*, pages 1880, 1882.

If Yes → **On Level** Children can read the Take-Home Book.

Beyond Level Children can read the Take-Home Book.

TIME TO MOVE!

Children form two facing lines. Have them point to themselves and chant: *We said, "Did you see the little dog?"* Then have children across from them say: *You said, "Did you see the little dog?"* Continue the chant using a different animal each time.

Phonemic Awareness

Phoneme Isolation

Objective

- Listen for initial and final /k/ in words

Materials

- Photo Cards: *book, key, kite, rake*
- Sound Box
- WorkBoard Sound Boxes; Teacher's Resource Book, p. 136
- markers

Model

Display the **Photo Card** for *kite*. Use the **Sound Box**.

Repeat with *key*.

Listen for the /k/ in the word *kite*. Say the word with me: *kite*. I hear /k/ at the beginning of *kite*. I'll place the marker in the first box because I hear /k/ at the beginning of *kite*.

Repeat for final /k/, using the Photo Cards for *rake* and *book*.

Listen for /k/ in *rake*. Say the word with me: *rake*. I hear /k/ at the end of *rake*. I'll place the marker in the last box because I hear /k/ at the end of *rake*.

Guided Practice/Practice

Distribute a Sound Box and markers to each child. Children identify the position of /k/ in words. Guide practice with the first word.

Listen to each word. You say the word after me and then place a marker in a box to show where you hear /k/.

back	keep	sack	king	tack	kiss
brick	pack	kind	kit	deck	kite

Objectives

- Match *ck* to the /k/ sound
- Blend sounds in words with /k/*ck*

Materials

- pocket chart
- Word-Building Cards
- Word-Building Cards; Teacher's Resource Book, pp. 95–102

ELL

Variations in Languages
Speakers of Hmong may have difficulty pronouncing /k/. Use the Approaching Level Phonics lessons for additional pronunciation and decoding practice.

Phonics

c   k

✓ Introduce /k/*ck*

Model

Display **Word-Building Cards** *c, k*.

The names of these letters are *c* and *k*. When these letters are together, they stand for one sound: /k/. We hear the /k/ sound at the end of *truck*.

Repeat with *lick*.

Listen to the word I say: *lick*. I will hold up the Word-Building Cards *c, k* because I hear the /k/ sound at the end of the word *lick*.

Guided Practice/Practice

Distribute Word-Building Cards. Children identify final /k/*ck*. Guide practice with the first two words.

When these letters are together at the end of a word, they stand for the /k/ sound. Listen as I say each word. Hold up Word-Building Cards *c, k* if you hear the /k/ sound at the end of the word.

pick	can	tack	Rick
ran	fun	track	pack
sock	set	soup	truck

Build Fluency: Sound-Spellings

Display the following Word-Building Cards: *a, b, c, d, e, h, i, k, l, m, n, s, p, t*. Have children chorally say each sound. Repeat and vary the pace.

For Tier 2 instruction, see page 1881.

Blend with /k/ck

Model

Place Word-Building Card _p_ in the pocket chart.

This is the letter _p_. The letter _p_ stands for the /p/ sound.

Place Word-Building Card _i_ next to _p_. Move your hand from left to right.

This letter is _i_. The letter _i_ stands for the /i/ sound. Listen as I blend the two sounds together: /piii/. Now you blend the sounds. (/piii/)

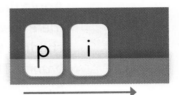

Place Word-Building Cards _c_ and _k_ next to _pi_. Move your hand from left to right.

These letters are _ck_. When these letters are together at the end of a word, they stand for the /k/ sound. Listen as I blend the three sounds together: /piiik/, _pick_. Now you blend the sounds with me. (/piiik/, _pick_)

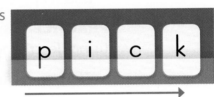

Repeat with _sick_.

Guided Practice/Practice

Children repeat the blending routine using these words. Guide practice with the first two words.

back	peck	kick	sack	tick
tack	neck	rock	lick	lock

Read Words

Apply

Write the words and sentences. Guide practice with the first word.

Rick
rock
pack
Rick said the rock is red.
I see the little rock.
Did Ken pack the map?

Corrective Feedback

Blending: Sound Error Model the sound that children missed, then have them repeat the sound. For example, for the word _pick_, say: _My turn._ Tap under the letters _ck_ in the word _pick_ and say: _Sound? What's the sound?_ Then return to the beginning of the word. Say: _Let's start over._ Blend the word with children.

Objective

- Recognize describing words (adjectives)

Materials

- Oral Vocabulary Cards: "The Conceited Apple Branch"
- Photo Cards: *cloud, ruby, sun*

ELL

Basic and Academic Vocabulary Display the Photo Cards from the lesson and pair English Language Learners with fluent English speakers. Have partners make up sentences that describe the pictured items. Encourage them to use more than one descriptive word. Write children's sentences, read them chorally, and ask: *What descriptive words did you use in your sentence? What other descriptive words can you use?*

Grammar

Describing Words (Adjectives)

MODEL Use the **Oral Vocabulary Cards** for "The Conceited Apple Branch" to discuss describing words. Remind children that describing words tell more about something. Display Card 1 of "The Conceited Apple Branch" and read aloud the first sentence: *Long, long ago there lived a pretty apple branch covered with soft pink blossoms.* Tell children that *pretty* is a describing word that tells about the *apple branch.* Then identify the two words *soft* and *pink* that describe the *blossoms.*

- Use *pretty* to start a list. Add other describing words that tell about apple trees (*leafy, big, tall*). Point out that these words tell more about apple trees.

PRACTICE Display **Photo Cards** for *cloud, ruby,* and *sun.* Model using describing words by making up sentences about the pictures.

- *The cloud is* fluffy.

- *The* shiny *ruby is on her finger.*

After each sentence, ask children to name the describing word. Then have them make up their own complete sentences about the pictures. Have children say the describing word after each sentence. Ask children to use words that describe color, size, and location.

Writing

Independent Writing: Steps in a Process

Display sentences from the Shared and Interactive Writing activities.

BRAINSTORM

WRITING TRAIT: ORGANIZATION Explain that children will write about the steps in the process of something they know how to do. First they need to decide how to organize their sentences.

Think Aloud Good writers plan their writing and make a clear beginning, middle, and end. I want to write about how I write a sentence. I'll be sure to use the words *first, next,* and *last.*

PREWRITE

Write the following numbered steps and read them aloud.

> ## How to Write a Sentence
> 1. First, write a capital letter.
> 2. Next, write the words.
> 3. Last, write a period.

- Read the steps aloud as you track the print.

- Have partners choose a process of something they know how to do and write about such things as putting on a shirt, building a block building, or throwing a ball.

DRAFT

- Have children work with partners to write a heading and then three or more numbered steps in a process. Then have them draw a picture to go with their instructions.

- Collect and save children's work to use tomorrow.

Write About It
Tell children to draw animals that live in trees. Ask them to label the drawing.

Objectives

- Write steps in a process
- Use letter knowledge to write letters in a word
- Use writing trait: organization

Materials

- Interactive Writing from Day 2

5-Day Writing

Procedural Text: Steps in a Process	
DAY 1	Shared: Steps in a Process
DAY 2	Interactive: Steps in a Process
DAY 3	Independent: Prewrite and Draft Steps in a Process
DAY 4	Independent: Revise and Edit Steps in a Process
DAY 5	Independent: Publish and Present

ELL

Prewriting Planning Provide appropriate **Photo Cards** and/or nonfiction books about animals. Guide children to use the books to find other animals that live in trees before they start their drawing.

Transitions That Teach

While children pick up, have them tell about what a **conceited** person is like.

WHOLE GROUP

Oral Language
- Build Robust Vocabulary

✔ **Comprehension**
- Read Aloud: "The Sticky-Sticky Pine"

Vocabulary
- Position Words
- Story Words: *acorns, roots, stem*

✔ **Phonemic Awareness**
- Phoneme Blending

✔ **Phonics**
- Word Sort
- Blend with /k/ck
- Decodable Reader: *Sad Hen*

Writing
- Independent Writing: Revise and Edit Steps in a Process

SMALL GROUP

- Differentiated Instruction, pages 1870–1895

Oral Language

 Talk About It ## Build Robust Vocabulary

PARTS OF A PINE TREE
Discuss how trees are alike and different.

- *What is the same about pine trees and oak trees? What **grows** on the branches of an oak tree? What grows on the branches of a pine tree?*

CREATE A WORD WEB
Draw an outline of a pine tree and pinecones as shown below, or use **Teaching Chart G1**. Write the heading and read it aloud as you track the print.

MODEL *I know that pine trees have trunks and branches. I know that a pine tree also has sap. So I will write the words* trunk, branches, *and* sap *for parts of a pine tree.*

Have children name other parts of a pine tree, or provide additional information as you add parts such as *pine needles, pinecones,* and *roots*. Read the words with children as you track the print.

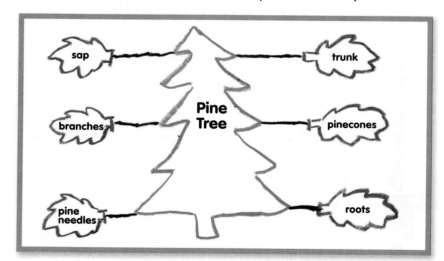

ELL ENGLISH LANGUAGE LEARNERS

Beginning	Intermediate	Advanced
Confirm Understanding Use the word web to point out various parts of the pine tree, such as the branches and pinecones. Have children say the words aloud. Bring in examples from nature if possible.	**Enhance Understanding** Prompt children to select words from the word web to state facts about pine trees, such as: *All pine trees have a trunk and roots. Pine trees have branches and sap. Pine trees have needles. Pinecones grow on pine trees.*	**Compare and Contrast** Prompt children to compare and contrast the pine tree with an oak tree. *What do pine trees and oak trees both have? Oak trees have acorns. What do pine trees have? Oak trees have large leaves. What do pine trees have?*

Listen for Rhyme

IDENTIFY RHYME

Remind children that words rhyme when they have the same ending sounds. *The word* nose *rhymes with* hose. They have the same sounds at the end. When words do not rhyme they do not end with the same sounds. Sing the song with children. Have them identify the rhymes. Then have children distinguish rhyming pairs from non-rhyming pairs: *red/bed; hung/pop; jet/fin; tip/sip; Ned/Ted; fan/flap; yell/bell.*

SONG ABOUT TREES

Tell children that they will sing "Little Red Apple," the song they learned about an apple tree. Play the song and have children join in. Ask children to use complete sentences to name and describe the kinds of trees and how they grow that they have learned.

Little Red Apple

A little red apple hung high in a tree.

Point up high.

I looked at it.

Look up.

And it looked down at me.

Look down.

"Come down, please," I called.

Put hands to mouth as if calling.

And what do you suppose?

Shrug shoulders.

The little red apple fell right on my nose!

Put hands on nose.

Objectives

- Discuss the theme
- Contribute to a word web
- Use oral vocabulary words *charming, conceited, equal, grow,* and *plant*
- Distinguish rhyming pairs from non-rhyming pairs of words

Materials

- Graphic Organizer; Teaching Chart G1

Oral Vocabulary

Have children use each word in a sentence about this week's stories.

charming	conceited
equal	grow
plant	

Review Work with children to review last week's words. Provide a sentence frame for the first word, such as: *It is a _____ day.*

clear	cozy
experience	hibernate
retreat	

Digital Learning

 Fingerplay on **Listening Library Audio CD**

Objective

- Listen and respond to a folktale

Materials

- Read-Aloud Anthology: "The Sticky-Sticky Pine," pp. 109–112

ELL

Reinforce Understanding
Introduce the word *woodcutter* by gesturing the action of a person with an ax cutting down a tree. Point to the tree on the Oral Language chart or point to a tree outside. Have children echo the word *woodcutter* and perform the action of cutting as they do so. If you have brought in realia, say the words *branches, twigs,* and *sap* together.

Readers Theater

BUILDING LISTENING AND SPEAKING SKILLS
Distribute copies of "A Pinch of Pepper," Read-Aloud Anthology pages 191–198. Have children practice performing the play throughout the unit. Assign parts and have children present the play or perform it as a dramatic reading at the end of the unit.

A Pinch of Pepper

Interactive
Read Aloud

Listening Comprehension

GENRE: LITERARY TEXT/FOLKTALE
Remind children that **folktales** are stories that have been told for a long time. *Many of the folktales we have read have been about being kind and helpful to others. Today's folktale will be about being kind to trees and* **plants**.

Read Aloud

CULTURAL PERSPECTIVES
Tell children that today's folktale is from Japan. Pine trees grow in the United States, Japan, and many other parts of the world and stay green all year long. In the United States, some people decorate pine trees at Christmas. In Japan pine tree decorations called *kadomatsu* are hung on doorways on New Year's Day.

READ "THE STICKY-STICKY PINE"

- **MODEL ASKING QUESTIONS ABOUT TEXT STRUCTURE** Use the Think Alouds provided at point of use in the folktale.

- **MODEL FLUENT READING** Read aloud the folktale with fluent expression. Stop occasionally so children can make predictions.

- **EXPAND VOCABULARY** See page 109 of the **Read-Aloud Anthology** to teach new words using the **Define/Example/Ask** routine.

Respond to Literature

TALK ABOUT IT Have children discuss the big idea and important events of the folktale.

- *Why did the pine tree need the kind woodcutter's help?*

- *What is the lesson of this folktale?*

- Guide children to express their opinion of "The Sticky-Sticky Pine."

Write About It
Ask children to draw a favorite part of the folktale. Have them write a label or sentence about their drawing.

Vocabulary

Position Words

REVIEW POSITION WORDS

I am going to read a short story that uses top, middle, *and* bottom. *Each time I say one of those words, nod your head up and down.*

Read the following story:

> *Dale drew a picture for his dad. At the* top *of the piece of paper, he wrote "My Dad." In the* middle *of the page, he drew his dad playing baseball. On the* bottom *of the paper, he wrote "Love, Dale."*

To extend the lesson, have children write friendly notes like the one Dale wrote to his father and read to a friend. After listening to the note, each partner will say what was at the *top, middle,* and *bottom* of the note.

Remind children that many position words are prepositions. When a preposition is used with a naming word, it is called a prepositional phrase. For example, *in the drawer*. The word *in* is the preposition and *drawer* is the naming word.

Story Words: *acorns, roots, stem*

Discuss the meaning of the word *acorn*. Provide a few acorns to pass around, if possible. *Have you seen acorns? Where?*

Display pages 16 and 17 of the **Big Book** *Oak Trees*. Talk about what is similar and what is different in the two pictures.

Repeat with pages 8 and 9 of *Oak Trees*, pointing out the pictures of the *roots* and the *stem*.

TIME TO MOVE!

Play "I Spy," asking children to use *top, middle,* and *bottom. I spy something on top of the table. I spy something in the bottom cubby. I spy something in the middle of the door.*

Objectives

- Use the position words
- Review story words *acorns, roots, stem*

Materials

- Big Book: *Oak Trees*

ELL

Reinforce Meaning Draw a pine tree and point to the top, middle, and bottom. Ask children to echo the words with you. Ask them to draw a bird at the top, a bow in the middle, and a cat at the bottom of the tree.

Objectives

- Sort words with *i, k, n, o, p, s, t*
- Blend sounds to form words with /k/*ck*

Materials

- Puppet
- Word-Building Cards
- pocket chart
- 2 index cards with: *kick, kit*
- Activity Book, pp. 9–10
- Practice Book, p. 165

Phonemic Awareness

✓ Phoneme Blending

Model

Use the **Puppet** to model how to blend the word *kick.*

Repeat with *lick.*

Happy likes to say the sounds in words. Listen to Happy as he says each sound: /k/ /i/ /k/. Happy can blend these sounds together: *kick.* Say the sounds with Happy: /k/ /i/ /k/. Now say the word with Happy: *kick.*

Guided Practice/Practice

Children blend sounds to say the word. Guide practice with the first word.

Happy is going to say the sounds in a word. Listen to Happy as he says each sound. Then blend the sounds to say the word.

/k/ /i/ /t/	/d/ /o/ /k/	/k/ /ē/
/b/ /i/ /t/	/t/ /a/ /b/	/k/ /ē/ /p/

Phonics

✓ Word Sort

k

Model

Display **Word-Building Card** *k*.

This letter is *k*. It stands for the /k/ sound.

Place Word-Building Cards *c* and *k* in the pocket chart.

These are the letters *c* and *k*. Together, they stand for /k/ at the end of a word.

Repeat for *i, l, o, p, s,* and *t*.

This is the letter *i*. It stands for /i/.

Write the words.

kick	kit	pick	lock
lot	sock	pot	sit

Read the words with children. Model sorting the words by initial sound. Group words on the board.

I will group the words *kit* and *kick* because they both begin with /k/. *Pick* and *pot* both begin with /p/.

Guided Practice/Practice

Guide practice with *kick* and *kit*. Have children also sort by final and medial sounds.

Build Fluency: Sound-Spellings

Display the following **Word-Building Cards**: *a, b, c, h, i, l, m, n, s, p, t.* Have children chorally say each sound. Repeat and vary the pace.

✔ Blend with /k/*ck*

Model

Place Word-Building Card *d* in the pocket chart.

This letter is *d.* It stands for the /d/ sound. Say /d/.

Place Word-Building Card *o* next to *d.* Move your hand from left to right.

This letter is *o.* It stands for the /o/ sound. Listen as I blend the two sounds: /dooo/. Now you say it. (/dooo/)

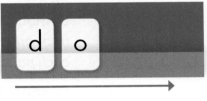

Place Word-Building Cards *c* and *k* next to *do.* Move your hand from left to right.

Repeat for *back.*

These letters are *c* and *k.* They stand for the /k/ sound. Listen as I blend the sounds: /dooook/, *dock.* Now you say it. (/dooook/, *dock*)

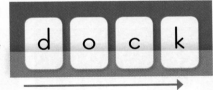

Guided Practice/Practice

Children blend to form words. Guide practice with the first word.

lock	lack	pack	lick	duck
pick	sick	sock	sack	luck

Corrective Feedback

Blending: Sound Error Model the sound that children missed, then have them repeat the sound. For example, for the word *sock,* say: *My turn.* Tap under the letters *ck* in the word *sock* and say: *Sound? What's the sound?* Then return to the beginning of the word. Say: *Let's start over.* Blend the word with children again.

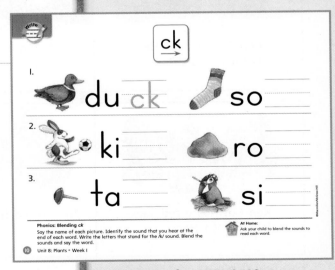

Activity Book, pages 9–10
Practice Book, page 165

Objectives

- Read decodable words with /k/*k* and /k/*ck*
- Read the words *said, little, is, a, we, can,* and *for*
- Reread for fluency

Materials

- Decodable Reader: *Sad Hen*
- High-Frequency Word Cards: *little, said*
- Sound-Spelling Card: *Koala*
- Photo Card: *lock*

Decodable Text

For additional decodable passages, see pages 35–36 of the **Teacher's Resource Book**.

Decodable Reader

Read *Sad Hen*

Sad Hen

 REVIEW Review this week's high-frequency words and phonics skills using the word lists on the inside back cover of *Sad Hen*.

Review the high-frequency words using the **Read/Spell/Write** routine. Then have children chorally read the high-frequency word list.

Review the phonics skills /k/*k* and /k/*ck* using the *Koala* **Sound-Spelling Card** and the **Photo Card** for *lock*. Then have children chorally read the decodable word list. Model blending as needed and take note of children who struggle reading these words. Provide additional instruction and practice during Small Group time.

MODEL CONCEPTS ABOUT PRINT

Demonstrate book handling. *I hold the book so that the cover is on the front and the words are not upside down. I turn the cover. Then I turn each page as I read it.*

 REREAD FOR FLUENCY Have children reread the book with a partner. Circulate and listen in, providing corrective feedback as needed. Then have children reread the book independently.

Ken Cat met Kit Hen.
Is Kit Hen sick?

2

Kit Hen is not sick.
Kit Hen is a little bit sad.

3

Let's sit on the back deck.

4

Kit Hen sits.
Ken Cat sits.

5

Ken Cat has a red sack.
It is for Kit Hen.

6

"It is a red hat!" said Kit.

7

The hat fits.
Kit Hen is not sad.

8

Decodable Reader

Writing

Independent Writing: Steps in a Process

REVISE AND EDIT

Distribute children's writing from yesterday. Have partners reread it and check for the following:

- Did we explain how to do each step in the process?

- Did we use the words *first, next,* and *last* in the right places?

- Did we begin the sentences with a capital letter and end them with a period?

Circulate and help children as they review and revise their sentences, using their knowledge of letter-sound relationships. Have partners share their sentences with another pair of children.

Peter and Miguel

How to Throw a Ball

1. First, pick up the ball.

2. Next, pull your arm back.

3. Next, push your arm forward.

4. Last, let go of the ball.

Write About It

Ask children to draw a picture of a fantasy tree, such as a tree with pizzas or beach balls **growing** on it. Tell them to label their drawings.

Objectives

- Revise and edit sentences
- Use letter knowledge to write letters in a word

Materials

- children's writing from Day 3
- Writer's Checklist; Teacher's Resource Book, p. 205

5-Day Writing

Steps in a Process

DAY 1	Shared: Steps in a Process
DAY 2	Interactive: Steps in a Process
DAY 3	Independent: Prewrite and Draft Steps in a Process
DAY 4	Independent: Revise and Edit Steps in a Process
DAY 5	Independent: Publish and Present

ELL

Use New Language Talk to children about the kinds of things that grow on trees. *Do apples grow on trees? Socks?* Draw a pine tree with something silly, such as goldfish, on it. *Do goldfish grow on trees? What does?*

Transitions That Teach

While lining up, have children name things people do to be **charming**.

Oral Language
- Build Robust Vocabulary

Comprehension
- Strategy: Recognize Text Structure
- Skill: Identify Sequence of Events
- Read Across Texts

Vocabulary
- High-Frequency Words
- Position Words

Phonemic Awareness
- Phoneme Segmentation

Phonics
- Phonics Review
- Read Words
- Dictation

Writing
- Independent Writing: Publish and Present

SMALL GROUP

- Differentiated Instruction, pages 1870–1895

Review and Assess
Oral Language
Build Robust Vocabulary

REVIEW WORDS

Review this week's oral vocabulary words with children. Explain that all of the words will be used to discuss raking leaves. Talk about what it means to rake leaves. *Raking leaves is when you use a tool called a rake to collect the dead leaves in your yard.*

Use the following questions to check children's understanding:

- What type of **plant** does not have leaves to be raked?

- What might **grow** where the leaves and acorns have fallen?

- Would someone **conceited** think they might be too special to rake leaves? Why?

- Would it be fair for two people to each pick up two **equal** piles of leaves? Why?

- Would it be **charming** or annoying for someone to jump in your pile of leaves after you worked hard collecting them? Why?

REVIEW SONGS AND RHYMES ABOUT TREES

Sing the song "Little Red Apple" and ask children to sing along. Have children name and describe the apple tree. Then recite "Nuts in May" with children. Have children name the words that rhyme.

Review and Assess
Comprehension

STRATEGY Recognize Text Structure

REFLECT ON THE STRATEGY Remind children that they have learned that books usually follow a certain structure, or order in which things happen.

Think Aloud I can use the order of how things happen in a nonfiction book to help me remember it.

SKILL Identify Sequence of Events

Lead children in reviewing the photographs and illustrations in *Oak Trees* and "The Sticky-Sticky Pine" to help them recall each selection. Then use the following questions to review sequence.

- *What happens in* Oak Trees *after an acorn is* **planted** *or falls to the ground?*

- *What happens after a stem becomes a small tree?*

- *What happened after the woodcutter repaired the broken branches in "The Sticky-Sticky Pine"?*

Reading Across Texts

Create a chart like the one shown to make connections to the nonfiction book *Oak Trees* and the folktale "The Sticky-Sticky Pine." You may wish to add an additional column for the **Big Book of Explorations** selection.

Oak Trees	The Sticky-Sticky Pine
nonfiction book	folktale
no rhyming lines	some rhyming lines
photographs	illustrations
about a real oak tree and how it **grows**	about a make-believe pine tree
no characters	two woodcutters
acorns fall from the oak tree	money or sticky sap falls from tree

Objectives

- Review the strategy and skill
- Listen to and share information

Materials

- Big Book: *Oak Trees*
- Read-Aloud Anthology: "The Sticky-Sticky Pine"
- Big Book of Explorations, Vol. 2: "Acorn"
- Activity Book, p. 11

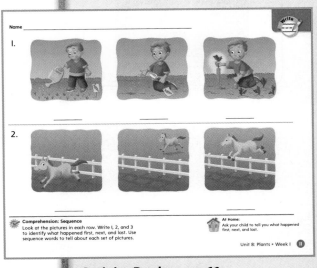

Activity Book, page 11

Objectives

- Review the high-frequency words *little, said, this, do, and, what*
- Review position words
- Develop fluency

Materials

- High-Frequency Word Cards: *little, said, this, do, and, what*
- High-Frequency Word Cards; Teacher's Resource Book, pp. 103–110
- pocket chart
- Photo Cards: *dog, goat, seal*

Fluency

Connected Text Have children reread this week's **Decodable Reader** with a partner. Circulate, listen in, and note those children who need additional instruction and practice reading this week's decodable and sight words.

Review and Assess
Vocabulary

 ## High-Frequency Words

Distribute one of the following **High-Frequency Word Cards** to each child: **little, said, this, do, and,** and **what**. Say: *When you hear the word that is on your card, stand and hold up your Word Card.*

- *Is a kitten* little?
- *I* said, *"Let's* do *a puzzle."*
- *The* little *boy* said, *"*What *is* this*?"*
- This *baby likes puppies* and *kittens.*

Build Fluency: Word Automaticity

Rapid Naming Display the High-Frequency Word Cards *little, said, this, do, and,* and *what*. Point quickly to each card, at random, and have children read the word as fast as they can.

little	said	this
do	and	what

Position Words

Display the pocket chart with one **Photo Card** placed in each row. Ask children: *Where is the dog? The dog is on the* top. Children move the cards around and say the new position of each card.

TIME TO MOVE!

Ask children to follow directions, such as: *Tap the top of your head. Pat the middle of your arm. Stomp with the bottom of your feet.* Tell children to give similar directions to the class.

Review and Assess
Phonemic Awareness

Phoneme Segmentation

Guided Practice

Use the **Puppet**.

Listen to Happy as he breaks the word *kiss* into its sounds: /k/ /i/ /s/. Say the sounds with me: /k/ /i/ /s/.

Happy will break the word *kiss* into sounds again. Count the sounds as Happy says them: /k/ /i/ /s/. There are three sounds in the word *kiss*. Tap as you say the sounds in *kiss* with Happy: /k/ /i/ /s/. Now say the word with Happy: *kiss*.

Repeat the routine with *pack*.

Practice

Have the Puppet say each word. Children say the sounds in the word as they tap them out.

Happy will say a word. Break the word into its sounds and tap them out. Then say the word again.

sock	like	pack	tuck	rack
Ken	neck	lock	Jack	luck

Objective

- Segment sounds in words

Materials

- Puppet

Objectives

- Review sound-spellings for /k/k, /b/b, /l/l, /e/e
- Identify initial sounds in words
- Write simple one-syllable words

Materials

- Word-Building Cards
- 6 index cards with: *Nick, fed, the, little, dog,* period mark
- 7 index cards with: *Ken, said, to, pack, the, kit,* period mark
- Sound Box
- WorkBoard Sound Boxes; Teacher's Resource Book, p. 136
- Activity Book, p. 12

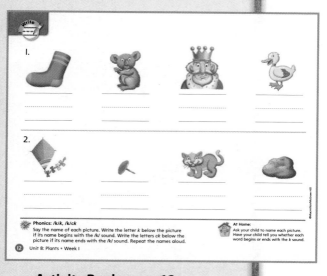

Activity Book, page 12

Review and Assess
Phonics

Build Fluency: Sound-Spellings

Rapid Naming Display the following **Word-Building Cards**: *a, b, c, d, e, f, h, i, k, m, n, o, p, r, s, t.* Have children chorally say each sound as quickly as they can.

 ## Read Words

Apply

Distribute the first set of index cards. Have children stand in sequence.	Let's read the sentence together. Nick fed the little dog.
Repeat, using the other set of index cards.	Let's read the sentence together. Ken said to pack the kit.

 ## Dictation

Dictate sounds for children to spell.	Listen as I say a sound. Repeat the sound, then write the letter that stands for the sound. If a sound can be written two ways, write both. /k/ /b/ /l/ /e/ /d/ /n/
Then dictate words for children to spell. Model for children how to use the **Sound Boxes** to segment the word. Have them repeat.	Now let's write some words. I will say a word. I want you to repeat the word, then think about how many sounds are in the word. Use your Sound Boxes to count the sounds. Then write one letter for each sound you hear.
Write the letters and words on the board for children to self-correct.	den Ken red lock back kit bit pack sack sick

Review and Assess
Writing

Independent Writing: Steps in a Process

PUBLISH

Explain to children that you will gather their writing to make a class bulletin board display.

- Brainstorm ideas for a title, such as "How To."

- Have a few children work on the banner for the display. Write the title on the banner.

- Have children help attach the banner and their illustrated steps in a process to the Big Question portion of the class bulletin board.

PRESENT

Tell partners to take turns reading their steps to the class. Ask them to act out the steps in the process they wrote about.

LISTENING, SPEAKING, AND VIEWING

- Remind children to speak clearly and to be good listeners when classmates are speaking.

- Praise children for their hard work. Children may wish to add copies of their work to their Writing Portfolios.

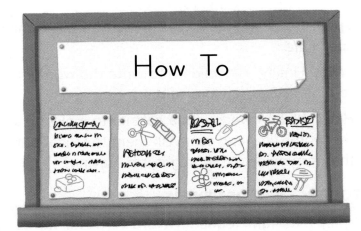

Write About It

Ask children to draw a picture of trees in their favorite season. Tell them to write a caption for their drawing.

Objective

- Publish and present children's sentences

Materials

- sentences from Day 4
- paper for a banner

5-Day Writing	
Procedural Text: Steps in a Process	
DAY 1	Shared: Steps in a Process
DAY 2	Interactive: Steps in a Process
DAY 3	Independent: Prewrite and Draft Steps in a Process
DAY 4	Independent: Revise and Edit Steps in a Process
DAY 5	Independent: Publish and Present

Transitions That Teach

While getting ready for lunch, have children talk about what it means for things to be **equal**.

Approaching Level

Oral Language

Objective Preteach oral vocabulary
Materials • none

THEME WORDS: *grow, plant*

- Tell children the meanings for **grow** and **plant**. *To* grow *means "to live, change, and get bigger."* Animals and people grow *and* change. *A* plant *is a living thing that grows from a seed and cannot move from place to place. When you place a seed in the ground, you* plant *it.*

- Discuss the words with children. Ask: *What* plants *do you see* growing *near your house?*

- Have children use the following sentence frames to generate complete oral sentences using the words: *One thing that grows from a seed is a _____. I would like to plant a _____.*

High-Frequency Words

Objective Preteach high-frequency words
Materials • **High-Frequency Word Cards:** *little, said*

PRETEACH WORDS: *little, said*

- Display the **High-Frequency Word Card** for **little**.

- **Read** Point to and say the word *little. This is the word* little. *It means "small." The puppy is very* little.

- **Spell** *The word* little *is spelled* l-i-t-t-l-e. Have children read and spell *little*.

- **Write** Finally, ask children to write the word *little*. Repeat the routine using the word **said**.

- Have children work with a partner to make up sentences using the words *little* and *said*. Ask them to talk about a little plant that is growing. What might it be saying?

HIGH-FREQUENCY WORDS REVIEW

Tier 2

Display the High-Frequency Word Cards for words previously taught, one card at a time, and have children chorally read and spell the word. Mix and repeat. Note words children need to review.

Approaching Level

Phonemic Awareness

Objective   Identify initial /k/ sound
Materials   • **Photo Cards:** *kangaroo, key, king, kite, kitten, koala*

PHONEME ISOLATION

Model

- Display the **Photo Card** for *key. This is a key. Listen for the beginning sound in* key: */kē/.* Key *begins with /k/. Repeat for* king.

Guided Practice/Practice

- Display the Photo Cards. Have children select a picture, name it, and say the initial sound: *This is a _____. _____ begins with /k/.*

- Have children note the position of their mouths as they say /k/.

Phonics

Objective   Recognize words that begin with /k/*k*
Materials   • **Sound-Spelling Card:** *Koala*   • **Word-Building Cards**
                • **Photo Cards:** *kangaroo, key, king, kitten, koala*

PRETEACH: RECOGNIZE /k/*k*

Model

- Display Photo Cards for *key* and *kangaroo* and the *Koala* **Sound-Spelling Card.** Say: *The name of this letter is* k. K *stands for the /k/ sound that you hear at the beginning of* key. *I will place the* k *card on the picture of the key because* key *begins with /k/. Repeat with* kangaroo.

- Say /k/ and trace the *k* on your **Word-Building Card.**

Guided Practice/Practice

- Display the Photo Cards. Point to the Photo Card for *key* and have children say the name, repeat the initial sound, and identify the letter. Repeat with the remaining Photo Cards for /k/*k*.

- Guide children to trace the letter *k* on their Word-Building Cards.

- Identify objects with names that begin with /k/.

SOUND-SPELLINGS REVIEW

Tier 2

Display Word-Building Cards *m, a, e, s, p, t, i, n, c, o, f, h, d, r,* and *k,* one at a time. Have children chorally say the sound. Repeat and vary the pace.

Corrective Feedback

Mnemonic Display the *Koala* Sound-Spelling Card. Say: *This is the* Koala *Sound-Spelling Card. The sound is /k/. The /k/ sound is spelled with the letter* k. *Say /k/ with me: /k/. This is the sound at the beginning of* koala. *What is the letter? What is the sound? What word begins with /k/?* Koala *is the word we can use to remember the sound for* k, */k/.*

ELL

Extra Practice Provide additional practice in recognizing and naming letters for children whose native languages do not use the symbols of the Latin alphabet.

On Level

High-Frequency Words

Objective Review high-frequency words *little, said, and, what, this, do*

Materials • **High-Frequency Word Cards:** *little, said, and, what, this, do*

REVIEW

- Display the **High-Frequency Word Card** for **little**.

- **Read** Point to and say the word *little. This is the word* little. *It is a word we use when we talk about the size of something. The puppy is little.*

- **Spell** *The word* little *is spelled* l-i-t-t-l-e. Have children read and spell *little. What is the beginning sound in* little? *That's right. The beginning sound is /l/. The letter* l *stands for the /l/ sound. After the /l/ sound, I hear /i/. The letter* i *stands for that sound.*

- **Write** Finally, have children write the word *little.*

- Repeat with **said, and, what, this,** and **do.** Then have partners make up sentences using the words *what, this, and,* and *do.* Ask them to talk about what various things in the classroom, such as a clock, electric pencil sharpener, and calculator, can do.

Phonemic Awareness/Phonics

Objective Review recognizing and blending initial /k/k, final /k/ck, and /i/i

Materials • **Word-Building Cards** • pocket chart
           • **Sound-Spelling WorkBoards**

PHONEME BLENDING

Model

- *Listen as I say the sounds for* kid: /k/ /i/ /d/. *Now I will blend the sounds: /kiiid/,* kid. *I blended /k/ /i/ /d/ together to say the word* kid. Repeat the blending with the word *Kip.*

- Say /k/ /i/ /t/. Have children repeat. *Now you blend the sounds and say the word: /k/ /i/ /t/,* kit. Repeat with /k/ /i/ /k/; /p/ /i/ /k/.

PHONICS: REVIEW /k/k, /k/ck, /i/i

Model

- Display **Word-Building Card** k. *The name of this letter is* k. K *stands for the /k/ sound we hear at the beginning of* kit. *What is the sound? I'll hold up the* k *card because* kit *begins with /k/.* Repeat with *i* and *insect,* and *c* and *k* and *rock.*

Practice

- Have children write *k, i, c,* and *k* several times on their **WorkBoards** as they say /k/ /i/ /k/. Repeat with *pick, Rick, rack.*

ELL

Sound-Letter Relationships Provide additional practice in pronouncing and blending the /k/, /i/ sounds and naming the corresponding letters as children point to them.

Beyond Level

High-Frequency Words/Vocabulary

Objective	Review high-frequency words
Materials	• none

✓ ACCELERATE

- Write *too* and *big* on the board.

- **Read** Point to and say the word *too*. *This is the word* too. *It means "also." I have a red bike, too.*

- **Spell** *The word* too *is spelled* t-o-o. *What's the first sound in* too? *That's right. The first sound is /t/. That's why the first letter is* t. Have children read and spell *too*.

- **Write** Finally, have children write the word *too*.

- Repeat the routine with *big*.

- Have children work with a partner to spell *big* and *too* and to make up oral sentences using the words. Ask them to talk about big things in the classroom.

EXPAND ORAL VOCABULARY

Gifted & Talented

- **Antonyms** Review the meaning of the oral vocabulary word *conceited* with children. Then explain that an *antonym* is a word that means the opposite of another word.

- Say: *An* antonym *for the word* conceited *is* humble. *A conceited person who wins a race might brag, "I'm the best!" A humble runner will be happy but will not brag.*

- Have children take turns using the new word *conceited* in a sentence. Tell children that they will work with a partner to discuss fictional characters who are *conceited* and *humble*.

Phonics

Objective	Read words with *k* and *ck*
Materials	• **Sound-Spelling Card:** *Koala* • **Word-Building Cards**

✓ ENRICH

- Display the *Koala* **Sound-Spelling Card**. Remind children that /k/ can be spelled with *k* at the beginning of a word as in *kit* or with *ck* at the end of a word as in *pick*.

- Write these words on the board for children to read: *pack, jack, rack, quick, quack, chick, thick, kissing, flicker*.

- Display **Word-Building Cards** *a, e, i, o, c, h, k, m, p, n, r, s,* and *t*. Have partners make as many words as they can.

ELL

Partners When pairing children to make up sentences, pair English Language Learners with children who are more proficient. Write their sentences, read them together, and point to the high-frequency words.

ELL — ENGLISH LANGUAGE LEARNERS

Oral Language Warm-Up

Content Objective Learn theme vocabulary
Language Objective Repeat and act out a song to demonstrate understanding
Materials • **Listening Library Audio CD** • **Big Book:** *Oak Trees*

BUILD BACKGROUND KNOWLEDGE

All Language Levels

- Introduce the unit theme "Plants" using the rhyme "Nuts in May." Display a picture of a nut, such as that of the acorn from *Oak Trees*. Teach the word *nut* as you point to the acorn in the picture. Explain that there are many types of nuts. *An acorn is a type of nut. So is a walnut and a pecan. These types of nuts grow on trees. The nuts are seeds.* Have children repeat the words *nut* and *seed* three times.

- Play "Nuts in May" on the **Listening Library Audio CD**. Act out each line as you sing the song; for example, open your arms and pull them in to gesture "gathering" and wrap your arms around your body and shiver for "frosty."

- Then teach children the gestures. Emphasize the key words that connect to each motion, such as *gathering* and *frosty*.

- Ask children to tell what they know about nuts. Build on their responses. For example: *A nut can grow on a tree. A nut grows on a tree, and then it falls to the ground. A nut is a seed.*

Academic Language

Language Objective Use academic language in classroom conversations

All Language Levels

- This week's academic words are **boldfaced** throughout the lesson. Define the word in context and provide a clear example from the selection. Ask children to generate an example.

Academic Language Used in Whole Group Instruction

Oral Vocabulary Words	Vocabulary and Grammar Concepts	Strategy and Skill Words
charming	position words	structure/organized
conceited	describing words	sequence
equal		sentence
grow		describing words
plant		

Cognates

Help children identify similarities and differences in pronunciation and spelling between English words and Spanish cognates:

Cognates

plant	*plantar*

ELL ENGLISH LANGUAGE LEARNERS

Vocabulary

Language Objective Demonstrate understanding and use of key words by discussing trees

Materials • **Visual Vocabulary Resources**

PRETEACH KEY VOCABULARY

All Language Levels

Use the **Visual Vocabulary Resources** to preteach the weekly oral vocabulary words *charming, conceited, equal, grow,* and *plant.* Focus on one or two words per day. Use the following routine that appears in detail on the cards.

- Define the word in English and provide the example given.
- Define the word in Spanish, if appropriate, and indicate if the word is a cognate.
- Display the picture and explain how it illustrates or demonstrates the word.
- Then engage children in structured partner-talk about the image, using the key word.
- Ask children to chorally say the word three times.
- Point out any known sound-spellings or focus on a key aspect of phonemic awareness related to the word.

PRETEACH FUNCTION WORDS AND PHRASES

All Language Levels

Use the Visual Vocabulary Resources to preteach the function phrases *grow from* and *fall to* (the ground). Focus on one phrase per day. Use the detailed routine on the cards.

- Define the phrase in English and, if appropriate, in Spanish. Point out if the phrase is a cognate.
- Refer to the picture and engage children in talk about the phrase. For example, children will partner-talk using sentence frames, or they will listen to sentences and replace a word or phrase with the new function phrase.
- Ask children to chorally repeat the phrase three times.

TEACH BASIC WORDS

Beginning/Intermediate

Use the Visual Vocabulary Resources to teach the basic words *branch, twigs, sap, tree, wood,* and *bark.* Teach these "tree and its parts" words using the routine provided on the card.

Visual Vocabulary Resources

Approaching Level

Oral Language

Objective Reinforce oral vocabulary
Materials • none

THEME WORDS: *grow, plant*

- *We've talked about how living things grow and change. Animals grow. People grow. A plant can grow, too.*

- *How does an animal grow differently than a plant?* Have children speak in complete sentences to answer the questions.

- *What kinds of plants grow in our area? What plants require very little water?*

- *What kinds of plants grow very tall? What kinds stay very low to the ground?*

High-Frequency Words

Objective Reteach high-frequency words
Materials • **High-Frequency Word Cards:** *little, said*
• **Sound-Spelling WorkBoards**

RETEACH WORDS: *little, said*

Tier 2

- Distribute a **WorkBoard** to each child. Then display the **High-Frequency Word Card** for **little**.

- Use the **Read/Spell/Write** routine to reteach the word. Point to and say the word. *This is the word* little. *It is a word that describes the size of something. It means the same as* small. Little *is spelled* l-i-t-t-l-e. Have children read and spell *little*. Then have them write the word on their WorkBoards. Repeat the routine with **said**.

- Have children work with a partner to make up sentences using the words *little* and *said*. Ask them to talk about something little in the classroom.

CUMULATIVE REVIEW

Display the High-Frequency Word Cards for words previously taught, one card at a time, and have children chorally read and spell the word. Mix and repeat. Note words children need to review.

ELL

Partners When pairing children to make up sentences, pair English Language Learners with children who are more proficient. Write their sentences, read them together, and point out the high-frequency words.

Approaching Level

Phonemic Awareness

Objective Identify and blend initial /k/
Materials • **Puppet**

PHONEME BLENDING

Tier 2

Model

■ *Listen as Happy says the sounds in a word: /k/ /i/ /t/. Happy can blend these sounds together: /kiiit/. Now you can say the sounds: /k/ /i/ /t/. Say the word with Happy:* kit.

Practice

■ Have the **Puppet** say /k/ /i/ /m/. Ask children to repeat. *Now you blend the sounds and say the word with Happy: /k/ /i/ /m/,* Kim. Repeat with the following:

/k/ /e/ /n/	/k/ /i/ /k/	/k/ /i/ /d/	/k/ /i/ /t/
/k/ /ī/ /t/	/k/ /i/ /s/	/k/ /i/ /n/	/k/ /ē/ /p/

Phonics

Objective Reinforce letter-sound correspondence for /k/*k*
Materials • **Sound-Spelling Card:** *Koala*   • **Sound-Spelling WorkBoards**
  • **Word-Building Cards**   • **Decodable Reader:** *Sad Hen*

RECOGNIZE /k/*k*

Model

■ Display the *Koala* **Sound-Spelling Card**. *The letter* k *stands for the /k/ sound as in* kite. *What is this letter? What sound does it stand for?* Repeat with *king*.

■ Trace *k* on a **Word-Building Card**. *I will say a sentence. We will trace* k *on the cards when we hear /k/.* Say: *King Karl flies a kite.*

Guided Practice/Practice

■ Distribute a **WorkBoard** to each child. Say: *kid, kit, man, sit, kick, tip, dog, chip, king, kite, jet, kind.* Children write *k* on their WorkBoard when they hear a word with /k/. Guide them with the first two words.

■ **Read the Decodable Reader** Read *Sad Hen* with children. Have them echo-read each page. Chorally reread the story.

CUMULATIVE REVIEW

Display Word-Building Cards *m, a, e, s, p, t, i, n, c, o, f, h, d, r,* and *k,* one at a time. Have children chorally say the sound. Repeat and vary the pace.

Puppet

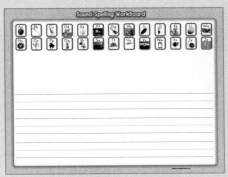

Sound-Spelling WorkBoard

Decodable Reader

Corrective Feedback

Sound Error Say: *My turn. When I say the word* sit, *I hear the sounds /s/ /i/ /t/. I do not hear /k/, so I will not write* k. *Listen again: /s/ /i/ /t/,* sit. *Do you hear the /k/ sound?* Continue with the other words and then repeat *sit*.

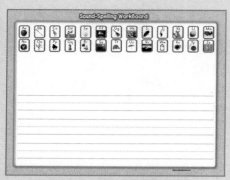

Sound-Spelling WorkBoard

On Level

Phonics

Objective Review recognizing and blending initial /k/k, final /k/ck, and /i/i

Materials • **Word-Building Cards** • pocket chart
• **Sound-Spelling WorkBoards**

REVIEW Kk

- Display **Word-Building Card** k. *The name of this letter is* k. K *stands for the /k/ sound we hear at the beginning of* kit. *What is the sound? I'll hold up the* k *card because* kit *begins with /k/.* Repeat with i and insect, and c and k and rock.

- Say: *king, lick, ink, sack, igloo, luck, koala.* Children hold up their Word-Building Cards and say /k/ for words that begin or end with the /k/ sound and say /i/ for words that begin with /i/. Guide practice with the first two words.

- **Blend Words** Place Word-Building Cards k, i, c, and k in the pocket chart. Point to each letter for children to identify. Move your hand from left to right below the letters as you blend the word. Remind children that ck together stand for one sound: /k/. *Now listen as I blend the three sounds together: /kiiik/,* kick. *What's the word?*

- Have children write k, i, c, and k several times on their **WorkBoards** as they say /k/ /i/ /k/.

Corrective Feedback

If children have difficulty blending words with /k/, demonstrate the /k/ sound while modeling the correct mouth position. *This is the /k/ sound at the end of* pack. *Let's blend* pack *together: /paaak/,* pack. Repeat with kick and check.

Beyond Level

Phonics

Objective Read words with /o/

Materials • **Word-Building Cards**

ACCELERATE

- Display Word-Building Cards r, o, a, d. Point to the letters as you say each sound. *The word* road *has three sounds: /r/ /ō/ /d/, /rrrōōōd/. The /ō/ sound can be spelled with the letters* oa, *as in* road; *with an* o (go); *and with* ow (row).

- Write these words for children to blend: *go, no, toad, bow, row, snow, coat, show, goat, float, tow, grow.*

ELL ENGLISH LANGUAGE LEARNERS

Access to Core Content

Content Objective Develop listening comprehension
Language Objective Discuss text using key words and sentence frames
Materials • **ELL Resource Book**, pp. 208–211 • **Big Book:** *Oak Trees*

PRETEACH BIG BOOK

All Language Levels

Use the Interactive Question-Response Guide on **ELL Resource Book** pages 208–211 to introduce children to *Oak Trees*. Preteach half of the selection on Day 1 and half on Day 2.

- Use the prompts provided in the guide to develop meaning and vocabulary. Use the partner-talk and whole-class responses to engage children and increase student talk. Remind children to listen attentively and face the child speaking.

- When completed, revisit the selection and prompt children to talk about the photographs. Provide sentence starters as needed and build on children's responses to develop language.

ELL Resource Book

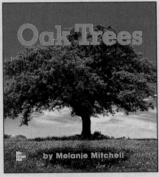

Big Book

Beginning	**Intermediate**	**Advanced**
Use Visuals During the Interactive Reading, select several pictures. Describe them and have children summarize what you said.	**Summarize** During the Interactive Reading, select a few lines of text. After you read them and explain them, have children summarize the text.	**Expand** During the Interactive Reading, select a larger portion of text. After you read it and explain it, have children summarize the text.

Approaching Level

High-Frequency Words

Objective   Recognize high-frequency words *little, said, and, what*

Materials
- **High-Frequency Word Cards:** *little, said, and, what*
- **Word-Building Cards**

REVIEW WORDS: *little, said, and, what*

- Display the **High-Frequency Word Card** for **and**. Say the word and have children repeat it. Point to each letter and have children name it.

- Distribute small **Word-Building Cards** *a, n,* and *d*. Model putting the letters together to form the word *and*. Then have children form *and*.

- Repeat the above routines with the words **little**, **said**, and **what**.

- Ask a question with the word *and*: *Are you and I friends?* Have children use *and* to answer the question. Continue with the other words.

CUMULATIVE REVIEW

Display the High-Frequency Word Cards for words previously taught, one card at a time, as children chorally read and spell the word. Mix and repeat. Note words children need to review.

Phonemic Awareness

Objective   Identify initial /k/k and final /k/ck

Materials
- **Photo Cards:** *kangaroo, key, king, koala, kitten, lock, rock, sock*
- **WorkBoard Sound Boxes; Teacher's Resource Book,** p. 136
- markers

PHONEME ISOLATION

Tier 2

Model
- Use the **Sound Boxes**. Display the **Photo Card** for *key*. *Key begins with /k/. I'll place a marker in the first box to show that I hear /k/ at the beginning of* key.

- Display the Photo Card for *rock*. *Listen for the end sound in* rock. *Rock ends in /k/. I'll place a marker in the last box to show that I hear /k/ at the end of* rock.

Guided Practice/Practice
- Distribute Sound Boxes and markers. Display the Photo Cards. Children select a picture and name it. Have children listen for /k/ and place a marker in the first or last box as they say: *This is a _____. I hear /k/ at the _____ of _____.* Repeat with each picture name. Provide guidance as needed.

ELL

Extra Practice During the Cumulative Review, pair children at different levels of proficiency and have partners take turns reading and spelling the high-frequency words to each other.

Approaching Level

Phonics

Objective	Recognize words that end with /k/ck
Materials	• **Word-Building Cards** • **Photo Cards:** *lock, rock, sock*

RECOGNIZE /k/ck

Tier 2

Model

- Display the **Photo Card** for *sock* and **Word-Building Cards** *c* and *k*. Say: *The letters* ck *together stand for the /k/ sound you hear at the end of* sock. *I will place the letters* c *and* k *on the picture of the sock because* sock *ends with /k/.*

Guided Practice/Practice

- Display the Photo Cards on a table. Say: *This is the picture of a rock. What sound do you hear at the end of* rock? *What letters stand for /k/ at the end of a word? Let's place* c *and* k *on the rock because* rock *ends with /k/.* Repeat with remaining Photo Cards for /k/ck.

- Guide children to trace the letters *c* and *k* on their cards.

Build Fluency

- Have children blend *red, Ken, ten, kit, sick* as quickly as they can.

Decodable Reader

Objective	Reread Decodable Reader *Sad Hen*
Materials	• **Decodable Reader:** *Sad Hen*

REREAD *Sad Hen*

- Display the cover of the book and read the title. Open to the title page and point out the title. *Let's read the title together.* Have children sound out each word as you run your finger under it. *Look at the picture. What is the hen doing? What do you think we will read about in this book? Will it be real or made up?*

- Page through the book. Ask children what they see in each picture. Ask them to find the words *said* and *little*.

- Read the book chorally with children. Have them point to each word as they read it. Provide corrective feedback as needed.

- Ask children to use *little* to talk about the pictures. *Kit Hen is a little sad.*

- After reading, ask children to recall things they read about.

Corrective Feedback

Association Error If children have difficulty identifying initial and final /k/, say: *My turn: /rok/,* rock. *I hear the /k/ sound at the end of rock: /rrroook/. What is the sound? What letters stand for that sound? Let's start over.* Repeat the word *rock* for children to identify the position of /k/.

Decodable Reader

ON YOUR OWN

Make a Card for Hen

Have children create a greeting card to cheer up sad Kit Hen. Have children listen to each other's friendly notes.

On Level

Decodable Reader

Objective Reread *Sad Hen* to develop fluency
Materials • **Decodable Reader:** *Sad Hen*

REREAD FOR FLUENCY

- Ask children to look back at the illustrations in *Sad Hen*. Have them use their own words to retell what the book was about.

- Have children reread a page or two of *Sad Hen*. Work with them to read with accuracy and expression. Model reading a page. Point out how you used your voice to say the words as the bear in the story would say them: *When I read, "Is Kit Hen sick?" my voice went up at the end to show that it was a question.*

- Provide time to listen as children read their page(s). Comment on their accuracy and expression, and provide corrective feedback by modeling proper fluency.

Decodable Reader

Beyond Level

Decodable Reader

Objective Reread *Sad Hen* to reinforce fluency and phonics
Materials • **Decodable Reader:** *Sad Hen*

REREAD FOR FLUENCY

- Have partners reread *Sad Hen*.

- Provide time to listen as children read. Comment on their accuracy and expression and provide corrective feedback as needed.

INNOVATE

- Have children add pages to *Sad Hen* by drawing other things that Ken Cat's red sack contains. The names of the objects should begin or end with /k/. For example, a duck, a kitten, or a kangaroo. Help children write a caption for their drawings.

ENGLISH LANGUAGE LEARNERS

Access to Core Content

Content Objective Develop listening comprehension
Language Objective Discuss text using key words and sentence frames
Materials • **ELL Resource Book,** pp. 212–213

PRETEACH BIG BOOK OF EXPLORATIONS

All Language Levels

Use the Interactive Question-Response Guide on **ELL Resource Book** pages 212–213 to introduce children to "Acorn." Preteach half of the selection on Day 3 and half on Day 4.

Grammar

Content Objective Identify describing words
Language Objective Speak in complete sentences, using sentence frames
Materials • **Listening Library Audio CD** • **Photo Cards**

DESCRIBING WORDS

All Language Levels

- Review that describing words tell more about something. Point to objects in the classroom and name them, including a describing word (red sweater, green plant). Have children repeat the phrases.

- Play "Little Red Apple" from the **Listening Library Audio CD**. Tell children to listen for describing words.

> **Little Red Apple**
> *A little red apple hung high in a tree.*
> Point up high.
> *I looked at it.*
> Look up.
> *And it looked down at me.*
> Look down.
> *"Come down, please," I called.*
> Put hands to mouth as if calling.
> *And what do you suppose?*
> Shrug shoulders.
> *The little red apple fell right on my nose!*
> Put hands on nose.

- Point out the naming word *apple* in the first line and display the **Photo Card** for *apple*. Then say the whole sentence: "A little red apple hung high in a tree." Ask: *What kind of apple is it? What words tell us more about the apple?* (*little, red*)

PEER DISCUSSION STARTERS

All Language Levels

- Distribute Photo Cards of animals, such as *kitten, mouse, dog,* and *horse*.

- Pair children and have them complete sentence frames such as: *Look at this _____ kitten.* Ask them to expand on their sentences by providing as many describing words as they can. For example: *Look at this cute, little kitten.* Circulate, listen in, and take note of each child's language use and proficiency.

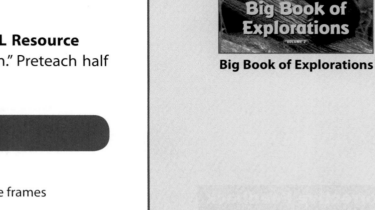
Big Book of Explorations

Puppet

Corrective Feedback

Sound Error If children miss making the letter-sound correspondence, say: *My turn:* lick, /llliiik/. *I hear* /k/ *at the end of* lick, /llliiik/. *I'll hold up my* c *and* k *cards because* /llliiik/ *ends with* /k/. *What is the sound? What letters stand for that sound? Let's start again.*

ELL

Extra Practice Provide additional practice in recognizing and naming letters for children whose native languages do not use the symbols of the Latin alphabet.

Approaching Level

Phonemic Awareness

Objective Blend sounds to form words
Materials • Puppet

PHONEME BLENDING

Tier 2

Model
- *Listen as Happy says the sounds for* rock: /r/ /o/ /k/. *Now Happy will blend the sounds:* /rrroook/, /rok/, rock. *Happy put* /r/ /o/ *and* /k/ *together to say the word* rock. *Now listen again and I'll do another word.* Repeat blending with the words *kick* and *lock*.

Guided Practice/Practice
- Have three children stand side by side. Ask the first child to say the sound /k/. Have the next child say the sound /i/. Have the third child say the sound /t/. Have them say the sounds in order and blend them: /kiiit/, *kit*. Continue with *sock, pack, rack, Kim, Ken,* and *kid*.

Phonics

Objective Blend letter sounds to read words with /k/ck
Materials • **Word-Building Cards** • pocket chart

REVIEW SKILLS: BLEND SOUNDS

Tier 2

Model
- Place **Word-Building Cards** *k, i, c,* and *k* in the pocket chart. *The name of this letter is* k. *The letter* k *stands for the* /k/ *sound. Say* /k/. *The name of this letter is* i. *The letter* i *stands for the* /i/ *sound. Say* /i/. *Remind children that* ck *together at the end of a word stands for one sound:* /k/. *The letters* c *and* k *stand for the* /k/ *sound. Say* /k/.

- Walk by the word and say the sound each letter stands for: /k/ /i/ /k/. *Now I will blend the three sounds together:* /kiiik/, kick.

Guided Practice/Practice
- Keep the Word-Building Cards in the pocket chart. Have children take turns walking by the cards, saying the letter sounds, and blending the word: /k/ /i/ /k/, /kiiik/, *kick*. Repeat with *back, lack, pack, pick,* and *lick*. Guide practice as necessary.

Approaching Level

Leveled Reader Lesson 1

Objective   Read *The Little Tree* to apply skills and strategies
Materials   • **Leveled Reader:** *The Little Tree*

BEFORE READING

- **Preview and Predict** Read the title and the name of the author. *Who do you see on the cover? What is he doing?* Turn to the title page and point out that it also has the title and the name of the author. *What do you think the book is about? Will it be about real things or a made-up story?*

- **Review High-Frequency Words** Write **little**, **said**, **the**, and **see** and read the words aloud. Guide children as they name the letters in each word. Have children find each word in the book and point to the word as they read it.

- **Page Through the Book** Name unfamiliar terms and identify the pictures.

- **Model Concepts About Print** Guide children as they follow along with their books. *This is the top, and this is the bottom of the page. I start reading the left page. Follow my finger. I start at the left and read the lines from left to right.*

- **Set a Purpose for Reading** *Let's find out what the two bears do to grow a little tree.*

DURING READING

- Remind children to use the illustrations to gain information and to look for the high-frequency word *little*.

- Show children how to self-correct if a word doesn't sound right or doesn't make sense in the sentence. *On page 2, I see a word I don't know that starts with* sh. *I look at the picture for a clue and see a shovel. I hear /v/ in the middle and /l/ at the end, just like in the printed word. The word must be* shovel. *It makes sense because I think Little Nick is getting ready to plant a tree.*

- Monitor children's reading and provide help as needed.

AFTER READING

- Ask children to point out words that they had trouble reading and to share strategies they used to help them. Reinforce good behaviors. For example: *Logan, I saw that you paused before reading words and looked for picture clues.*

- Ask children to retell the story and to share personal responses. *Did the story remind you of a plant you have grown? What steps did you take to care for your plant?*

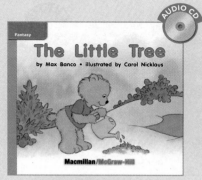

Leveled Reader

Digital Learning

Use the **Leveled Reader Audio CD** for fluency building *after* children read the book with your support during Small Group time.

ON YOUR OWN

Extend *The Little Tree*

Have children extend the story by drawing a picture of the tree fully grown. Have them show what kind of tree it is—a shade tree, a nut tree, a fruit tree, or perhaps an evergreen tree. Tell them to label by adding a word to the sentence: *See the _____ tree.*

See the apple tree.

Leveled Reader

ELL

Retell Use the Interactive Question-Response Guide Technique to help English Language Learners understand *Seeds Make Trees*. As you read, make meaning clear by pointing to pictures, demonstrating word meaning, paraphrasing text, and asking children questions.

ON YOUR OWN

Diagram of a Tree

Have children look at the pictures on pages 2 and 7 of *Seeds Make Trees* and point to the tree, big leaves, and seeds as you name them. Then have children draw a diagram of the maple tree and include the labels *tree, big leaves,* and *little seeds*.

On Level

Leveled Reader Lesson 1

Objective Read *Seeds Make Trees* to apply skills and strategies

Materials • **Leveled Reader:** *Seeds Make Trees*

BEFORE READING

- **Preview and Predict** Read the title and the name of the author. *Who do you see on the cover? What are they doing?* Page through the book and name unfamiliar items.

- **Model Concepts About Print** Demonstrate book handling. *I hold the book so that the cover is on the front and the words are not upside down. I open the book by turning the cover. Then I turn each page as I read it.*

- **Review High-Frequency Words** Write **said**, **I**, **see**, **do**, **you**, **and**, **we**, **like**, and **the** on chart paper. Have children find each word in the book and point to the word as they read it.

- **Set a Purpose for Reading** *Let's find out what plants can grow from seeds.*

DURING READING

- Have children turn to page 2 and begin by whisper-reading the first two pages.

- Remind children to look for the high-frequency words and to use the illustrations.

- Monitor children's reading and provide help. Stop during the reading and ask open-ended questions to facilitate discussion, such as: *What is the author telling us about seeds and trees? What does she tell us at the end about the dad and son?* Build on children's responses to develop deeper understanding of the text.

AFTER READING

- Ask children to point out words they had trouble reading and to share strategies they used. Reinforce good behaviors. For example: *Clara, I noticed that you put your finger under each word as you sounded it out. After you read it, you looked carefully at the picture.*

- **Retell** Ask children to retell the story. Have them share information and help them make a personal connection. *How do trees in your neighborhood change?*

- Have partners take turns asking and answering questions about the text.

Beyond Level

Leveled Reader Lesson 1

Objective   Read *How a Tree Grows* to apply skills and strategies
Materials   • **Leveled Reader:** *How a Tree Grows*

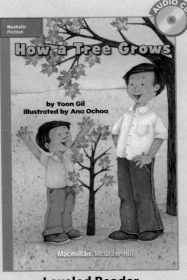

Leveled Reader

BEFORE READING

■ **Preview and Predict** Have children point to the front cover. Read the title and the name of the author. *Who do you see on the cover? What do you think is happening?* Turn to the title page and point out that it also has the title and the name of the author. Page through the book with children and pause to name unfamiliar items.

■ **Introduce Story Words** Point to the word *acorn* on page 2. Read the sentence. Have children explain what an *acorn* is. Repeat with *oak tree*.

■ **Set a Purpose for Reading** Discuss purpose for reading. *Let's find out how an oak tree changes as it grows year after year.*

DURING READING

■ Have children use self-monitoring comprehension strategies to understand text read orally: assess and revise predictions, use picture clues, self-question, and clarify meaning or self-correct. Help them use a picture dictionary to determine the meaning of unknown words.

■ Monitor children's reading and provide help as needed.

AFTER READING

■ Have children point out words they had trouble reading and share the strategies they used to figure them out.

■ Ask children to retell the story and to share personal responses. *Can you tell us about a big tree that you have seen? How do people enjoy it?*

■ **Evaluate** *Do you think planting acorns is a good or bad thing to do? Why?*

■ Have children work in pairs to list things they like about trees. They might list: *fun to climb, colorful leaves, gives shade.*

■ **Model** Tell children they will use their lists to write questions about trees. Write examples on the board: *Does it provide shade? Does it have strong branches for climbing?* These questions will serve as criteria they can use to rate trees. Children may use their answers to the questions to help them determine their favorite kind of tree.

ON YOUR OWN

Relate Personal Experiences

Have children recall how Mack learned about planting and growing an oak tree and then taught his sister. Have children draw and write about something they can do well.

I can build a bridge.

Leveled Reader

Vocabulary

Preteach Vocabulary Use the routine in the **Visual Vocabulary Resources**, pages 343–344, to preteach the ELL Vocabulary listed on the inside front cover of the Leveled Reader.

ELL ENGLISH LANGUAGE LEARNERS

Leveled Reader

Content Objective Read to apply skills and strategies
Language Objective Retell information using complete sentences
Materials • **Leveled Reader:** *We Like Trees*

BEFORE READING

All Language Levels

- **Preview** Read the title *We Like Trees*. Ask: *What's the title? Say it again.* Repeat with the author's name. Point to the cover illustration and say: *I see a man and a boy.* Point to the man and the boy as you name them. *The man is pointing to a tree. Now turn to a partner and tell about this picture.*

- **Page Through the Book** Use simple language to tell about the illustration on each page. Immediately follow up with questions, such as: *What does Dad say? Do you see the seeds? Point to them.*

- **Review Skills** Use the inside front cover to review the phonics skill and high-frequency words.

- **Set a Purpose** Say: *Let's read to find out about trees.*

DURING READING

All Language Levels

- Have children whisper-read each page, or use the differentiated suggestions below. Circulate, listen in, and provide corrective feedback, such as modeling how to decode a word.

- **Retell** Stop after every two pages and ask children to state what they have learned so far. Reinforce language by restating children's comments when they have difficulty using story-specific words. Provide differentiated sentence frames to support children's responses and engage children in partner-talk where appropriate.

Beginning	Intermediate	Advanced
Echo-Read Have children echo-read after you.	**Choral-Read** Have children choral-read with you.	**Read** Have children choral-read.
Check Comprehension Point to pictures and ask questions such as: *Do you see the little trees? Point to a little tree.*	**Check Comprehension** Ask questions/prompts such as: *Describe what you see in this picture. What happens to a little tree?*	**Check Comprehension** Ask: *What did you learn about trees? Read sentences that describe the sizes of trees.*

ELL ENGLISH LANGUAGE LEARNERS

AFTER READING

All Language Levels

Book Talk Children will work with peers of varying language abilities to discuss their books for this week. Display the four **Leveled Readers** read this week: *How a Tree Grows* (Beyond Level), *Seeds Make Trees* (On Level), *The Little Tree* (Approaching Level), and *We Like Trees* (English Language Learners).

Ask the questions and provide the prompts below. Call on children who read each book to answer the questions or respond to the prompt. If appropriate, ask children to find the pages in the book that illustrate their answers.

- Did your book show a big tree or a little tree?
- Describe the trees in the book.
- Do you like trees? Why?
- What did the book tell you about trees?
- What is your favorite tree? Tell about it.

Develop Listening and Speaking Skills Tell children to remember the following:

- Share information in cooperative learning interactions. Remind children to work with their partners to retell the story and complete any activities. Ask: *What happened next in the story?*

- Employ self-corrective techniques and monitor their own and other children's language production. Children should ask themselves: *What parts of this passage were confusing to me? Can my classmates help me clarify a word or sentence that I don't understand?*

- Use high-frequency English words to describe people, places, and objects.

- Narrate, describe, and explain with specificity and detail. Ask: *Where did the story take place? Can you describe the setting? What else did you notice?*

- Express opinions, ideas, and feelings on a variety of social and academic topics. Ask: *What do you think about the characters in the story?*

Puppet

Approaching Level

Phonemic Awareness

Objective Segment sounds in words
Materials • **Puppet**

PHONEME SEGMENTATION

Tier 2

Model
- *Listen as Happy breaks the word* kiss *into its sounds: /k/ /i/ /s/. Happy will repeat the sounds for* kiss. *Track the number and order of the sounds in the word* kiss. *Let's count the sounds as Happy says them: /k/ /i/ /s/. There are three sounds in the word* kiss. *Tap as you say the sounds in* kiss *with Happy: /k/ /i/ /s/. Now say the word with Happy:* kiss. *Repeat the routine with* pack.

Guided Practice/Practice
- Have children practice segmenting words into sounds. *Happy will say a word. Break the word into its sounds and tap them out:* sock, like, pack, tuck, neck, lock, Jack, Ken, kit.

Phonics

Objective Reinforce initial /k/k and final /k/ck and build fluency
Materials • **Photo Cards:** *kangaroo, key, king, kitten, koala, lock, rock, sock*
• **Word-Building Cards** • pocket chart
• **Sound-Spelling WorkBoards**

BUILD FLUENCY

Tier 2

Model
- Place **Word-Building Card** *k* and cards *c* and *k* in the top row of the pocket chart. Place the **Photo Cards** facedown in a stack. Pick the first card, name the picture, and tell whether it begins or ends with the /k/ sound. Then place it in the pocket chart under *k* or *ck*.

Guided Practice/Practice
- Have each child choose a Photo Card, say the name of the picture, identify whether the name begins or ends with /k/, and place it in the pocket chart under *ck* or *k*. Guide practice with the first Photo Card.

Build Fluency
- Display the card for *k*. Have children name the letter as quickly as they can. Then ask them to write the letter *k* on their **WorkBoards** several times as they say /k/.

Approaching Level

Leveled Reader Library

Leveled Reader Lesson 2

Objective Reread *The Little Tree* to reinforce fluency, phonics, and identifying sequence of events

Materials • **Leveled Reader:** *The Little Tree*

FOCUS ON FLUENCY

- Tell children that you will read one page of the book and they should read that page right after you. They should follow along in their books and try to read at the same speed and with the same expression that you use.

SKILL IDENTIFY SEQUENCE OF EVENTS

- Have children identify key events in sequence. *Look at pages 2 and 3. What is the first thing Little Nick does to plant a tree? What happens after Little Nick carefully waters the seeds each day?*

REREAD PREVIOUSLY READ BOOKS

- Distribute copies of the past six **Leveled Readers**. Discuss the purposes of rereading. Tell children that rereading the books will help them develop their skills and enjoy language.

- Circulate and listen in as children read. Stop them periodically and ask them how they are figuring out words or checking their understanding. Tell children to read other previously read Leveled Readers during independent reading time.

High-Frequency Words

Objective Review high-frequency words *little, said, and, what, this, do*

Materials • **High-Frequency Word Cards:** *little, said, and, what, this, do*

BUILD WORD AUTOMATICITY: *little, said, and, what, this, do*

- Distribute copies of the **High-Frequency Word Card** for **little**. Say the word and have children repeat it. Have children name the letters in the word. Repeat with the words **said, and, what, this, do**.

- **Build Fluency** Use the High-Frequency Word Cards to review previously taught words. Repeat, guiding children to read more rapidly.

Fantasy

The Little Tree
by Max Banco • illustrated by Carol Nicklaus

Macmillan/McGraw-Hill

Leveled Reader

Meet Grade-Level Expectations

As an alternative to this day's lesson, guide children through a reading of the On Level Practice Reader. See page 1886. Since both books contain the same vocabulary, phonics, and comprehension skills, the scaffolding you provided will help most children gain access to this more challenging text.

Corrective Feedback

Throughout the lessons, provide feedback based on children's responses. If the answer is correct, ask another question. If the answer is tentative, restate key information to assist the child. If the answer is wrong, provide corrective feedback such as hints or clues, refer to a visual such as a **Sound-Spelling Card** or story illustration, or probe with questions to help the child clarify any misunderstanding.

Leveled Reader

On Level

Leveled Reader Lesson 2

Objective   Reread to apply skills and strategies to retell a story

Materials   • **Leveled Reader:** *Seeds Make Trees*

BEFORE READING

- Ask children to look through *Seeds Make Trees* and recall what the book is about. Reinforce vocabulary by repeating children's sentences using more sophisticated language. For example: *Yes, trees do get big. They can get enormous.* Have children repeat.

DURING READING

- Have children join you in a choral-reading of the story. Model reading with expression. *When I read the sentence on page 5, I read it with a little more excitement. That sentence ends with an exclamation point.* Ask children to use the same kind of expression when they read. Discuss how reading a variety of texts, with expression, can help them enjoy the language.

- Assign each child a page. Have children practice by whisper-reading. *Follow along as other children read, and be ready to come in when it is your turn. Remember, use lots of expression.*

AFTER READING

- Have children retell key events in sequence in their own words.

- *Look at the picture on page 2. How does every tree begin? What comes first after the seeds grow, little trees or big trees?*

- Have children make connections to their own experiences. *Have you ever planted a tree or other plant? How did you take care of it?*

Beyond Level

Leveled Reader Lesson 2

Objective   Reread to apply skills and strategies to retell a story
Materials   • **Leveled Reader:** *How a Tree Grows*

BEFORE READING

- Ask children to look back at *How a Tree Grows* and recall key events in the book. Ask: *How does a tree grow? What are the steps involved?*

DURING READING

- Assign each child a page of the book to read aloud. Have children practice by whisper-reading. *Follow along as each child reads, and be ready to come in when it is your turn. Remember, use lots of expression.* Have children ask questions about the text.

AFTER READING

- Explain that stories have a beginning, a middle, and an end. Remind children of the beginning of *How a Tree Grows*. In the beginning of the story, Mack plants an acorn. Work with children to continue looking through the book to find out what happens in the middle of the story and in the end. Tell them they can think of what they know about the life cycle of a tree, as well as the seasons, to help them.

Expand Vocabulary

Objective   Brainstorm synonyms for *big*
Materials   • **Leveled Reader:** *How a Tree Grows*

ENRICH: synonyms for *big*

Gifted Talented

- Point out the word *big* on page 14.

- Ask children to define the word. Remind them that the sentences on the page as well as the pictures will help them figure out what the word means.

- Draw a word web on the board. Write the word *big* in the center circle and tell children to think of as many other words as they can that mean about the same thing as *big*. Have them think of the big oak tree in the story. Children can also use a dictionary.

- Ask children to use words from the web to describe the oak tree or other big things.

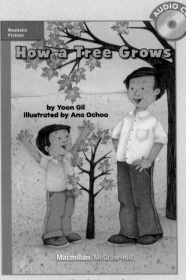

Leveled Reader

ON YOUR OWN

Is It Big or Huge?

Have children write and illustrate sentences about something big that they know. Tell them to use another word for *big* from the web. Ask: *Is a huge tree bigger than a big tree? What would you call a really, really big tree?*

ELL

Partners When children describe the oak tree or other big things, pair English Language Learners with children who are more proficient.

ELL ENGLISH LANGUAGE LEARNERS

Fluency

Content Objectives Reread the Decodable Reader to develop fluency; develop speaking skills

Language Objective Tell a partner what a selection is about

Materials • **Decodable Reader:** *Sad Hen*

REREAD FOR FLUENCY

Beginning

■ Review the high-frequency words **little**, **said**, **this**, **and**, **do**, and **what** using the **Read/Spell/Write** routine.

Intermediate/Advanced

■ Use each word in a sentence that illustrates its use, such as: *This chair is little.* Point to a chair and gesture "little" with your fingers. *What else is little?* Gesture around the class.

■ Then provide sentence starters for children to complete. Where appropriate, act out children's responses. For example: *This ball is little.*

All Language Levels

■ Guide children through a choral-reading of *Sad Hen.* Point to the exclamation mark and the quotation marks on page 7 in *Sad Hen.* Tell children that when a sentence ends in an exclamation mark, we read it as if we are very excited. The quotation marks tell us that someone is talking. Model reading the sentence and have children chorally repeat.

DEVELOP SPEAKING/LISTENING SKILLS

All Language Levels

■ Have children reread *Sad Hen* to a partner. Remind them to listen carefully and follow along in their book as their partner is reading. Work with children to read with accuracy and appropriate intonation.

■ Ask children to tell their partner about the pictures on each page. Then have the other partner describe the pictures. Circulate, listen in, and provide additional language as needed.

Beginning	Intermediate	Advanced
Confirm Understanding Point to the pictures for partners to identify. Ask: *What do you see?* Restate the correct answer in a complete sentence.	**Express Opinions** Ask partners to tell you which is their favorite picture in the book. Prompt them to explain why it is their favorite picture.	**Compare and Contrast** Have partners compare two different pictures and describe them. Prompt them to explain how they are alike and different.

ELL ENGLISH LANGUAGE LEARNERS

High-Frequency Words

Content Objective Spell high-frequency words correctly
Language Objective Write in complete sentences, using sentence frames
Materials • **Sound-Spelling WorkBoards** • **Sound-Spelling Cards** • **Photo Cards**

Beginning/Intermediate

- Write the high-frequency words *little* and *said* on the board. Have children copy the words on their **WorkBoards**. Then help them say, then write, a sentence for each word. Provide the sentence starters *This is a little* _____ and *She said to* _____.

Advanced

- Children should first orally state their sentences. Correct as needed. Then they can draw a picture to complete the sentence. For children who are ready, help them spell words using their growing knowledge of English sound-spelling relationships. Model how to segment the word children are trying to spell and attach a spelling to each sound. Use the **Sound-Spelling Cards** to reinforce the spellings for each English sound.

Writing

All Language Levels

- Dictate the following words for children to write: *kid, rock*. Discuss the meaning of each word before children write it. Have children write the words five times as they say /k/. Demonstrate correct letter formation, as needed.

- Then display a set of **Photo Cards**. Select at least five cards whose picture names begin with /k/k (key, king, kitten, koala, kangaroo) and three whose picture names begin with /l/ (light, leaf, ladder).

- Say the name of each card, stretching or reiterating the initial sound to emphasize it. You may also need to model correct mouth formation when forming the sound. Use the articulation pictures and prompts on the back of the small Sound-Spelling Cards for support. Tell children to write the first letter in each picture name on their WorkBoards.

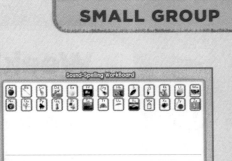

Sound-Spelling WorkBoard

Phonemic Awareness/ Phonics

For English Language Learners who need more practice with this week's phonemic awareness and phonics skills, see the Approaching Level lessons. Focus on minimal contrasts, articulation, and those sounds that do not transfer from the child's first language to English. For a complete listing of transfer sounds, see pages T10–T31.

End-of-Week Assessment

Weekly Assessment

Use your Quick Check observations and the assessment opportunities identified below to evaluate children's progress in key skill areas.

Skills	Quick Check Observations	Pencil and Paper Assessment
✓ **PHONEMIC AWARENESS/ PHONICS** /k/k, /k/ck **k**	1829	Activity Book, pp. 4, 9–10, 12 Practice Book, pp. 161, 165
✓ **HIGH-FREQUENCY WORDS** *little, said* **little**	1850	Activity Book, pp. 7–8 Practice Book, pp. 163–164
✓ **COMPREHENSION** Identify Sequence of Events	1840	Activity Book, pp. 5, 11 Practice Book, p. 162

Quick Check Rubric

Skills	1	2	3
✓ **PHONEMIC AWARENESS/ PHONICS**	Does not connect the /k/ sound with the letter *Kk* and has difficulty blending the CVC and CVCC words *peck, Ken, sick, Nick, tick, sock, back, pack, kick.*	Usually connects the /k/ sound with the letter *Kk* and blends the CVC and CVCC words *peck, Ken, sick, Nick, tick, sock, back, pack, kick* with only occasional support.	Consistently connects the /k/ sound with the letter *Kk* and blends the CVC and CVCC words *peck, Ken, sick, Nick, tick, sock, back, pack, kick.*
✓ **HIGH-FREQUENCY WORDS**	Does not identify the high-frequency words.	Usually recognizes the high-frequency words with accuracy, but not speed.	Consistently recognizes the high-frequency words with speed and accuracy.
✓ **COMPREHENSION**	Does not identify the sequence of events using the pictures and text.	Usually identifies the sequence of events using the pictures and text.	Consistently identifies the sequence of events using the pictures and text.

DIBELS LINK

PROGRESS MONITORING
Use your DIBELS results to inform instruction.

IF...

| Phoneme Segmentation Fluency (**PSF**) | 0–34 |
| Nonsense Word Fluency (**NWF**) | 0–24 |

THEN...
Evaluate for Intervention

TPRI LINK

PROGRESS MONITORING
Use your TPRI scores to inform instruction.

IF...

Phonemic Awareness	Still Developing
Letter Name Identification	Still Developing
Letter to Sound Linking	Still Developing
Listening Comprehension	Still Developing

THEN...
Evaluate for Intervention

Diagnose		Prescribe
Review the assessment answers with children. Have them correct their errors. Then provide additional instruction as needed.		
PHONEMIC AWARENESS/ PHONICS /k/k, /k/ck	**IF...** **Quick Check Rubric:** Children consistently score 1 or **Pencil and Paper Assessment:** Children get 0–2 items correct	**THEN...** Reteach Phonemic Awareness and Phonics Skills using the **Phonemic Awareness** and **Phonics Intervention Teacher's Editions**. SPIRAL REVIEW Use the Build Fluency lesson in upcoming weeks to provide children practice reading words with /k/k and /k/ck.
HIGH-FREQUENCY WORDS little, said	**Quick Check Rubric:** Children consistently score 1 or **Pencil and Paper Assessment:** Children get 0–2 items correct	Reteach High-Frequency Words using the **Phonics Intervention Teacher's Edition**. SPIRAL REVIEW Use the High-Frequency Words lesson in upcoming weeks to provide children practice reading the words little and said.
COMPREHENSION Skill: Identify Sequence of Events	**Quick Check Rubric:** Children consistently score 1 or **Pencil and Paper Assessment:** Children get 0–2 items correct	Reteach Comprehension Skill using the **Comprehension Intervention Teacher's Edition**.

Response to Intervention

To place children in Tier 2 or Tier 3 Intervention use the *Diagnostic Assessment*.

- Phonemic Awareness
- Phonics
- Vocabulary
- Comprehension
- Fluency

Week 2 ★ At a Glance

Priority Skills and Concepts

 Comprehension
- **Genre:** Folktale, Expository
- **Strategy:** Recognize Text Structure
- **Skill:** Retell
- **Skill:** Identify Main Idea and Details

 High-Frequency Words
- *here*, *was*

Oral Vocabulary
- Build Robust Vocabulary: *gradually*, *moist*, *necessary*, *observe*, *seed*

Fluency
- Echo-Read
- Word Automaticity

 Phonemic Awareness
- Phoneme Isolation
- Phoneme Blending
- Phoneme Deletion

 Phonics
- *Uu*

Grammar
- Describing Words (Adjectives)

Writing
- Similes

Key   Tested in Program    Review Skill

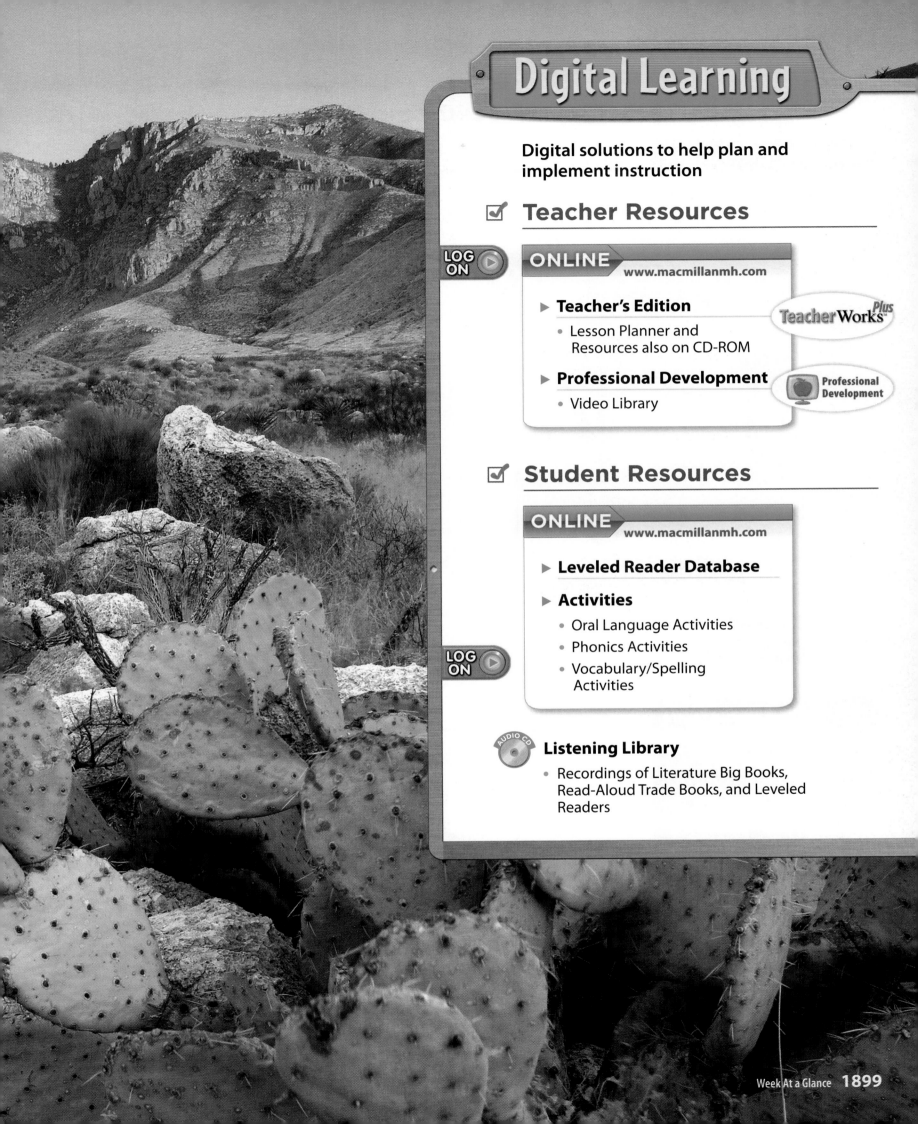

Digital Learning

Digital solutions to help plan and implement instruction

☑ Teacher Resources

LOG ON ▶

ONLINE ▶ www.macmillanmh.com

▶ **Teacher's Edition**
- Lesson Planner and Resources also on CD-ROM

TeacherWorks^Plus

▶ **Professional Development**
- Video Library

Professional Development

☑ Student Resources

LOG ON ▶

ONLINE ▶ www.macmillanmh.com

▶ **Leveled Reader Database**

▶ **Activities**
- Oral Language Activities
- Phonics Activities
- Vocabulary/Spelling Activities

AUDIO CD **Listening Library**
- Recordings of Literature Big Books, Read-Aloud Trade Books, and Leveled Readers

Weekly Literature

Theme: Seeds and Plants

Student Literature

A mix of fiction and nonfiction

Big Book

Genre Expository

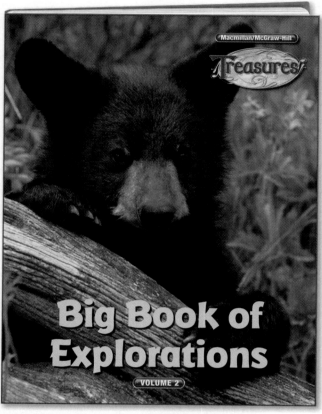

Big Book of Explorations

Genre Poetry

Support Literature

Interactive Read-Aloud Anthology

Genre Folktale

Oral Vocabulary Cards

• Listening Comprehension
• Build Robust Vocabulary

Decodable Reader

Resources for Differentiated Instruction

Leveled Readers: Science

GR Levels A-G

Genre	Expository

- Same Theme
- Same Vocabulary/Phonics
- Same Comprehension Skills

A Approaching Level

C On Level

G Beyond Level

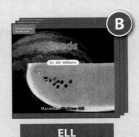

B ELL

LOG ON **Leveled Reader Database**
Go to www.macmillanmh.com.

Practice

Activity Book

Practice Book

English Language Learner Practice Book

ELL Practice Book

Response to Intervention

Tier 2

- Phonemic Awareness
- Phonics
- Vocabulary
- Comprehension
- Fluency

Tier 3

Unit Assessment

Assess Unit Skills

- Phonemic Awareness
- Phonics
- High-Frequency Words
- Listening Comprehension

HOME-SCHOOL CONNECTION

- Family letters in English and Spanish
- Take-home stories and activities

Go to **www.macmillanmh.com** for Online Lesson Planner

TeacherWorks *Plus*
All-In-One Planner and Resource Center

Professional Development
Video Library

Big Book

Seed Secrets by Tom Leonard

WHOLE GROUP

ORAL LANGUAGE

DAY 1

DAY 2

❓ Focus Question What grows from seeds?
Build Background, 1910

Oral Vocabulary *gradually, moist, necessary, observe, seed,* 1910

❓ Focus Question What are some different ways seeds get from here to there?

Oral Vocabulary *gradually, moist, necessary, observe, seed,* 1918

Position Words, 1925

- **Oral Vocabulary**

- **Phonemic Awareness**

✓ **Phonemic Awareness**
Phoneme Isolation, 1913

✓ **Phonemic Awareness**
Phoneme Blending, 1926

WORD STUDY

- **Phonics**

✓ **Phonics**
Introduce: /u/u, 1914
Handwriting: Write *Uu*, 1915
Activity Book, 14
Practice Book, 167

✓ **Phonics**
Review /u/u, /k/k, /l/l, 1926
Blend with /u/u, /k/k, /l/l, 1927

- **High-Frequency Words**

✓ **High-Frequency Words**
here , *was* , 1912

✓ **Review High-Frequency Words**, 1928

READING

- **Listening Comprehension**

- **Apply Phonics and High-Frequency Words**

Share the Big Book
Seed Secrets
Strategy: Recognize Text Structure, 1911
✓ **Skill:** Retell, 1911

Seed Secrets
Big Book

Reread the Big Book
Seed Secrets
Strategy: Recognize Text Structure, 1920
✓ **Skill:** Retell, 1920
Retell, 1924
Decodable Reader: *A Bud Is Up*, 1928
Activity Book, 15–16
Practice Book, 168
Fluency Echo-Read, 1924

Seed Secrets
Big Book

- **Fluency**

LANGUAGE ARTS

- **Writing**

- **Grammar**

Shared Writing
A List, 1917
Grammar
Describing Words (Adjectives), 1916

Interactive Writing
Sentences, 1929

ASSESSMENT

- **Informal/Formal**

Quick Check Phonemic Awareness, 1913

Quick Check Comprehension, 1924

SMALL GROUP Lesson Plan ▷ **Differentiated Instruction 1904–1905**

Priority Skills

| Phonemic Awareness/Phonics /u/u | High-Frequency Words *here, was* | Oral Vocabulary Position Words | Comprehension Strategy: Recognize Text Structure Skill: Retell |

DAY 3

? Focus Question Think of a day when it was very windy. What happened?

Oral Vocabulary *gradually, moist, necessary, observe, seed,* 1930

Oral Vocabulary Cards: "Let's Go to a National Park"

Phonemic Awareness
Phoneme Isolation, 1935

Phonics
Review /u/u, /k/k, /l/l, 1936
Blend with /u/u, 1937
Read Words, 1937

High-Frequency Words
here, was, 1934
Activity Book, 17–18
Practice Book, 169–170
Read for Fluency, 1934

Read the Big Book of Explorations:
"In My Garden," 26–27
"Mary, Mary, Quite Contrary," 28
Literary Element:
Rhyme and Repetition, 1932

Big Book of Explorations

Independent Writing
Prewrite and Draft Similes, 1939
Grammar
Describing Words (Adjectives), 1938

Quick Check High-Frequency Words, 1934

DAY 4

? Focus Question How would you make a vegetable garden here at school?

Oral Vocabulary *gradually, moist, necessary, observe, seed,* 1940

Position Words, 1943

Phonemic Awareness
Phoneme Deletion, 1944

Phonics
Word Sort, 1944
Blend with /u/u, 1945
Activity Book, 19–20
Practice Book, 171
Review High-Frequency Words, 1946

Interactive Read Aloud
Listening Comprehension, 1942
Read Aloud: "The Talking Vegetables"
Decodable Reader: *A Bud Is Up,* 1946

Read Aloud

Fluency Reread for Fluency, 1946

Independent Writing
Revise and Edit Similes, 1947

Quick Check Phonics, 1945

DAY 5
Review and Assess

? Focus Question We read stories about plants and seeds this week. Which story was your favorite?

Oral Vocabulary *gradually, moist, necessary, observe, seed,* 1948

Position Words, 1950

Phonemic Awareness
Phoneme Deletion, 1951

Phonics
Read Words, 1952
Dictation, 1952
Activity Book, 22

High-Frequency Words
here, was, and, what, little, said, 1950

Read Across Texts
Strategy: Recognize Text Structure, 1949
Skill: Retell, 1949
Activity Book, 21

Fluency Word Automaticity, 1950

Independent Writing
Publish and Present Similes, 1953

Weekly Assessment, 1980–1981

Differentiated Instruction

What do I do in small groups?

Teacher-Led Small Groups

Independent Activities

Focus on Skills

IF... children need additional instruction, practice, or extension based on your **Quick Check** observations for the following priority skills

 Phonemic Awareness
Phoneme Isolation, Blending, Deletion

 Phonics
Uu

High-Frequency Words
here , *was*

 Comprehension
Strategy: Recognize Text Structure
Skill: Retell

THEN... | Approaching | Preteach and
| ELL | Reteach Skills
| On Level | Practice
| Beyond | Enrich and Accelerate Learning

 ## Suggested Small Group Lesson Plan

	DAY 1	DAY 2
Approaching Level		
•Preteach/Reteach **Tier 2 Instruction**	• Oral Language, 1954 • High-Frequency Words, 1954 High-Frequency Words Review, 1954 • Phonemic Awareness, 1955 • Phonics, 1955 **ELL** Sound-Spellings Review, 1955	• Oral Language, 1960 • High-Frequency Words, 1960 • Phonemic Awareness, 1961 • Phonics, 1961
On Level		
•Practice	• High-Frequency Words, 1956 • Phonemic Awareness/Phonics, 1956	• Phonics, 1962
Beyond Level		
•Extend/Accelerate **Gifted and Talented**	• High-Frequency Words/Vocabulary, 1957 **ELL** Expand Oral Vocabulary, 1957 • Phonics, 1957	• Phonics, 1962
ELL		
•Build English Language Proficiency **•See ELL in other levels.**	• Oral Language Warm-Up, 1958 • Academic Language, 1958 • Vocabulary, 1959	• Access to Core Content, 1963

Small Group

Focus on Leveled Readers

Levels A–G

Approaching

On Level

Beyond

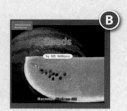
ELL

Additional Leveled Readers

LOG ON ▶ **Leveled Reader Database**
www.macmillanmh.com

Search by

- Comprehension Skill
- Content Area
- Genre
- Text Feature
- Guided Reading Level
- Reading Recovery Level
- Lexile Score
- Benchmark Level

Subscription also available

Manipulatives

Sound-Spelling WorkBoards

Sound-Spelling Cards

Photo Cards

High-Frequency Word Cards

Visual Vocabulary Resources

DAY 3

- High-Frequency Words, 1964 **ELL**
- Phonemic Awareness, 1964
- Phonics, 1965
- Decodable Reader, 1965

- Decodable Reader, 1966 **ELL**

- Decodable Reader, 1966

- Grammar, 1967

DAY 4

- Phonemic Awareness, 1968
- Phonics, 1968 **ELL**
- Leveled Reader Lesson 1, 1969

- Leveled Reader Lesson 1, 1970 **ELL**

- Leveled Reader Lesson 1, 1971
  Analyze, 1971

- Leveled Reader, 1972

DAY 5

- Phonemic Awareness, 1974
- Phonics, 1974 **ELL**
- Leveled Reader Lesson 2, 1975
- High-Frequency Words, 1975

- Leveled Reader Lesson 2, 1976

- Leveled Reader Lesson 2, 1977 **ELL**
- Expand Vocabulary, 1977

- Fluency, 1978
- High-Frequency Words, 1979
- Writing, 1979

Managing the Class

What do I do with the rest of my class?

Teacher-Led Small Groups

Independent Activities

- Activity Book
- Practice Book
- ELL Practice Book
- Leveled Reader Activities
- Literacy Workstations
- Online Activities
- Buggles and Beezy

Classroom Management Tools

Weekly Contract

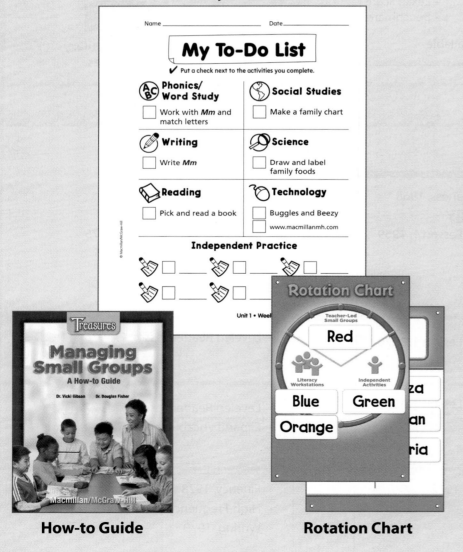

Name _____ Date _____

My To-Do List

✔ Put a check next to the activities you complete.

Phonics/Word Study
☐ Work with *Mm* and match letters

Social Studies
☐ Make a family chart

Writing
☐ Write *Mm*

Science
☐ Draw and label family foods

Reading
☐ Pick and read a book

Technology
☐ Buggles and Beezy
☐ www.macmillanmh.com

Independent Practice

Unit 1 • Week

Treasures
Managing Small Groups
A How-to Guide
Dr. Vicki Gibson   Dr. Douglas Fisher
Macmillan/McGraw-Hill

Rotation Chart

Teacher-Led Small Groups

Red

Literacy Workstations   Independent Activities

Blue   **Green**

Orange

...za
...an
...ria

How-to Guide

Rotation Chart

Digital Learning

Phonics Activities

- Match Letters
- Match Letters to Sounds
- Blend Words

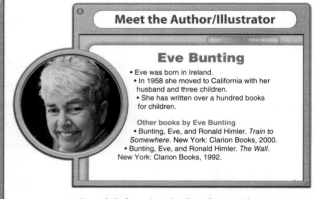

Meet the Author/Illustrator

Eve Bunting

- Eve was born in Ireland.
- In 1958 she moved to California with her husband and three children.
- She has written over a hundred books for children.

Other books by Eve Bunting
- Bunting, Eve, and Ronald Himler. *Train to Somewhere.* New York: Clarion Books, 2000.
- Bunting, Eve, and Ronald Himler. *The Wall.* New York: Clarion Books, 1992.

- Read Other Books by the Author or Illustrator

Practice

Activity Book

Practice Book

ELL Practice Book

Independent Activities

ONLINE INSTRUCTION www.macmillanmh.com

Oral Language Activities

- Focus on Vocabulary and Concepts
- English Language Learner Support

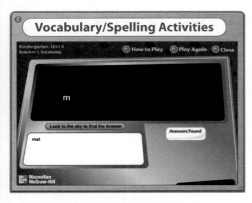

Vocabulary/Spelling Activities

- Differentiated Lists and Activities

Leveled Reader Database

- Leveled Reader Database
- Search titles by level, skill, content area, and more

Available on CD

LISTENING LIBRARY
Recordings of selections
- Literature Big Books
- Read-Aloud Trade Books
- Leveled Readers
- ELL Readers

NEW ADVENTURES WITH BUGGLES AND BEEZY
Phonemic awareness and phonics activities

Leveled Reader Activities

Approaching

On Level

Beyond

ELL

See inside cover of all Leveled Readers.

Literacy Workstations

Reading

Phonics/ Word Study

Writing

Science/ Social Studies

See lessons on pages 1908–1909

Managing the Class

What do I do with the rest of my class?

 Reading

Objectives

- Read and compare books by the same author
- Read a book; write a response to a book

 Phonics/Word Study

Objectives

- Use words that describe position
- Make words that end in -un

Reading — **Read an Author** — 20 Minutes

Read and compare books by one author.

❶ Pick an author. ❷ Read the books. ❸ Talk about them.

Do More
- How are all the books alike?
- Write a new story like the ones you read using the same setting.

For more book titles, go to the Meet the Author/Illustrator page on www.macmillanmh.com

45

© Macmillan/McGraw-Hill

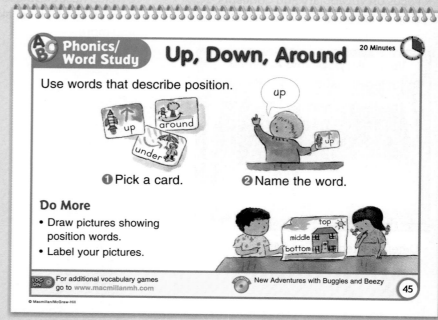

Phonics/Word Study — **Up, Down, Around** — 20 Minutes

Use words that describe position.

❶ Pick a card. ❷ Name the word.

Do More
- Draw pictures showing position words.
- Label your pictures.

For additional vocabulary games go to www.macmillanmh.com

New Adventures with Buggles and Beezy

45

© Macmillan/McGraw-Hill

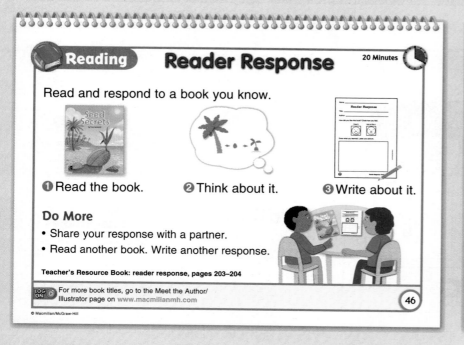

Reading — **Reader Response** — 20 Minutes

Read and respond to a book you know.

❶ Read the book. ❷ Think about it. ❸ Write about it.

Do More
- Share your response with a partner.
- Read another book. Write another response.

Teacher's Resource Book: reader response, pages 203–204

For more book titles, go to the Meet the Author/Illustrator page on www.macmillanmh.com

46

© Macmillan/McGraw-Hill

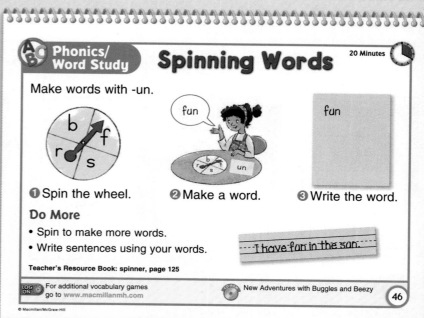

Phonics/Word Study — **Spinning Words** — 20 Minutes

Make words with -un.

❶ Spin the wheel. ❷ Make a word. ❸ Write the word.

Do More
- Spin to make more words.
- Write sentences using your words.

I have fun in the sun.

Teacher's Resource Book: spinner, page 125

For additional vocabulary games go to www.macmillanmh.com

New Adventures with Buggles and Beezy

46

© Macmillan/McGraw-Hill

Literacy Workstations

Reading | **Phonics/Word Study** | **Writing** | **Science/Social Studies**

Literacy Workstation Flip Charts

Writing

Objectives

• Write about something that is happening in the classroom
• Write the letter *Uu*; write words with *Uu*

Content Literacy

Objectives

• Match seeds to plants; illustrate the sequence of seed growth
• Recognize jobs that are related to plants

Writing — **Today's News** — *20 Minutes*

Write about something happening in the classroom.

Jameelah is reading a book.
I see Samira writing.

❶ Look around. ❷ Write sentences. ❸ Draw pictures.

Do More
• Read a partner's sentences.
• Write your name on your pictures.

45

© Macmillan/McGraw-Hill

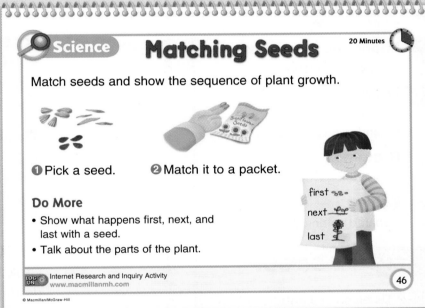

Science — **Matching Seeds** — *20 Minutes*

Match seeds and show the sequence of plant growth.

❶ Pick a seed. ❷ Match it to a packet.

first
next
last

Do More
• Show what happens first, next, and last with a seed.
• Talk about the parts of the plant.

LOG ON Internet Research and Inquiry Activity
www.macmillanmh.com

46

© Macmillan/McGraw-Hill

Writing — **Uu, Up and Under** — *20 Minutes*

Write words with Uu.

up

up
under

❶ Draw a Uu picture. ❷ Write up. ❸ Write under.

It is up.

Do More
• Write a sentence with up.
• Write a sentence with under.

46

© Macmillan/McGraw-Hill

Social Studies — **Jobs With Plants** — *20 Minutes*

Recognize jobs that have to do with plants.

❶ Choose a job. ❷ Think about the job. ❸ Act out the job.

farmer ||||||
florist ||||
gardener ||
chef ||

Do More
• Talk with a partner about your favorite jobs.
• Take a tally of favorite jobs.

Teacher's Resource Book: picture cards, page 88

LOG ON Internet Research and Inquiry Activity
www.macmillanmh.com

45

© Macmillan/McGraw-Hill

WHOLE GROUP

Oral Language
• Build Background

✓ **Comprehension**
• Read *Seed Secrets*
• Strategy: Recognize Text Structure
• Skill: Retell

✓ **High-Frequency Words**
• Introduce *here*, *was*

✓ **Phonemic Awareness**
• Phoneme Isolation

✓ **Phonics**
• Introduce /u/*u*
• Handwriting: Write *Uu*

Grammar
• Describing Words (Adjectives)

Writing
• Shared Writing: A List

SMALL GROUP

• Differentiated Instruction, pages 1954–1979

Oral Vocabulary

Week 2

gradually	moist
necessary	observe
seed	

Review

charming	conceited
equal	grow
plant	

Use the **Define/Example/Ask** routine in the **Instructional Routine Handbook** to review the words.

Oral Language

 Build Background: *Seeds and Plants*

INTRODUCE THE THEME
Tell children that this week they will be talking and reading about **seeds** and plants. Tell children a seed is the part of a plant that grows into a new plant. Ask them what they find when they see an apple cut open. *We can look carefully, or* **observe**, *seeds. What can you observe about seeds in a cut-open apple?*

Write the following question on the board: *What grows from seeds?* Track the print as you read aloud the question. Remind children that we read from left to right and top to bottom. Then prompt children to answer the question.

ACCESS PRIOR KNOWLEDGE
■ Ask children when they have seen seeds. *In which fruits have you seen seeds? Have you ever planted seeds and watched a plant grow? What did you observe?*

Think Aloud Look at this picture. It is a child blowing seeds off a dandelion plant. The seeds are floating in the wind. (Point to the child, the dandelion plant, and the seeds in the air as you describe the picture.) Have you ever picked dandelions and blown the seeds off the plant?

DISCUSS THE PHOTOGRAPH
Look at the photograph and talk about the girl blowing the dandelion seeds. *What do dandelion seeds grow into?*

Teaching Chart 52

Share the Big Book

Listening Comprehension

Big Book

PREVIEW AND PREDICT Display the cover. *I see a **seed** next to an ocean. Let's read about seeds and how they get from one place to another.*

Read the title and the name of the author as you track the print. *What kind of seed is this? What might it grow into?*

GENRE: LITERARY TEXT/EXPOSITORY Tell children that this book is **expository**. Discuss the purposes for reading various genres.

STRATEGY Recognize Text Structure

EXPLAIN/MODEL Remind children that books follow a particular structure and that it is easier to follow and retell the book when we understand how it is organized.

Think Aloud The book is called *Seed Secrets*. I think it will tell what I don't know about seeds.

SKILL Retell

EXPLAIN/MODEL Remind children that they have learned how telling themselves what has happened in a book can help them to understand a book better.

Think Aloud As I read, I will listen to the words and **observe** the illustrations. Then I will remind myself of what I have learned.

Read the Big Book

SET PURPOSE Tell children to remind themselves of the important information in the book as they listen to it. Use the **Define/Example/Ask** routine to teach the story words on the inside back cover.

Respond to Literature

MAKE CONNECTIONS Discuss with children the places in the community where seed are planted. Then have children draw a picture of one of the places and add the drawings to their Writing Portfolios. Ask children to name some of the ways that seeds travel.

Objectives

- Discuss the theme
- Understand and use oral vocabulary words *observe* and *seed*
- Discuss the purposes of reading various texts
- Make connections to the larger community
- Recognize text structure/ retell to understand a book

Materials

- Teaching Chart 52
- Big Book: *Seed Secrets*

ELL

Use the **Interactive Question-Response Guide** for *Seed Secrets*, **ELL Resource Book** pages 214–219, to guide children through a reading of the book. As you read *Seed Secrets*, make meaning clear by pointing to the pictures, demonstrating word meanings, paraphrasing text, and asking children questions.

Digital Learning

Story on **Listening Library Audio CD**

Objectives

- Read the high-frequency words *here, was*
- Identify the words *here* and *was* in speech and text
- Review high-frequency words *and, what, little, said*

Materials

- High-Frequency Word Cards: *here, was, and, what, little, said*
- Teaching Chart 53

ELL

Reinforce Vocabulary
Review the high-frequency words *here, was, and, what, little, said*. Display the **High-Frequency Word Cards** *here, was, and, what, little, said*. Point to areas in the classroom as you ask questions, such as: *What do we do here? Who was sitting here yesterday? What can Maria and Teo do here? Is this chair little or big?* Guide children to answer in complete sentences using the high-frequency words.

High-Frequency Words

 here, was

INTRODUCE Display the **High-Frequency Word Card** for **here** and read the word. Use the **Read/Spell/Write** routine to teach the word.

- **Read** Point to and say the word *here*. *Here is the book.*

- **Spell** *The word* here *is spelled* h-e-r-e. *What's the first sound in* here? *That's right. The first sound in* here *is /h/. That's why the first letter is* h. *Let's read and spell* here *together.*

- **Write** *Now let's write the word* here *on our papers. Let's spell aloud the word as we write it:* here, h-e-r-e.

- Repeat the routine with the word **was**.

SPIRAL REVIEW
REVIEW *and, what, little, said* Display each card and have children read the word.

and   what

READ THE RHYME AND CHIME
Ask children to point to *and, here,* and *was* each time they hear them. Repeat the rhyme together. Then add *here* and *was* to the Word Wall.

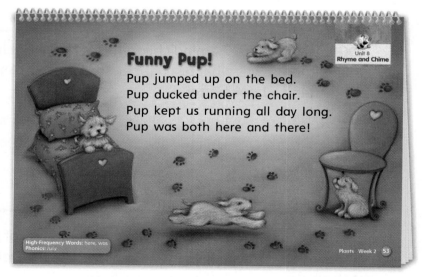

Funny Pup!
Pup jumped up on the bed.
Pup ducked under the chair.
Pup kept us running all day long.
Pup was both here and there!

High-Frequency Words: here, was
Phonics: /u/u

Plants Week 2 53

Teaching Chart 53

For Tier 2 instruction, see page 1954.

 **TIME TO MOVE!**

Give individual children directions, such as: *[Name], please go to the art center. Go to the same place and say: [Name] was here.*

Phonemic Awareness

 ## Phoneme Isolation

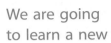

Model

Display the **Photo Card** for *umbrella*.

Repeat with the Photo Card for *up*.

We are going to learn a new sound. Listen for the sound at the beginning of *umbrella*: /u/. *Umbrella* has /u/ at the beginning. Say the sound with me: /u/. What is the sound? Let's pretend to hold up an *umbrella* when we hear a word that begins with /u/.

Read the "Funny Pup!" Rhyme and Chime again. Children pretend to hold an umbrella when they hear /u/.

Pup jumped up on the bed.
Pup ducked under the chair.
Pup kept us running all day long.
Pup was both here and there!

Review /k/ and /l/

 Display the Photo Card for *king*.

Repeat for *lamp*.

This is a *king*. The sound at the beginning of *king* is /k/. What is the sound?

Guided Practice/Practice

Display and name each Photo Card. Children identify words that begin with /u/, /k/, and /l/. Guide practice with the first card. Continue orally with the words *until, kind, uncle, late, keep, like, us*.

Say the name of each picture with me. Tell me the sound you hear at the beginning of the word.

Quick Check

Can children identify the initial sound /u/?

During **Small Group Instruction**

If No → | Approaching Level | Provide additional practice, pages 1955.

If Yes → | On Level | Children blend words with /u/, page 1956.

| Beyond Level | Children blend words with /u/, page 1957.

Objectives

- Identify initial sound /u/
- Review initial /k/ and /l/

Materials

- **Photo Cards:** *umbrella, umpire, up, under, upside down, key, king, kangaroo, kite, kitten, lock, lemon, ladder, leaf, lamp*
- **Teaching Chart 53**

ELL

Pronunciation Display and have children name **Photo Cards** from this and prior lessons to reinforce phonemic awareness and word meanings. Point to a card and ask: *What do you see?* (an umbrella) *What is the sound at the beginning of the word* umbrella? (/u/). Repeat using **Photo Cards** with words that begin with the sounds /k/ and /l/.

- Match the letter *u* to the initial sound /u/
- Form upper- and lowercase *Uu*

Materials

- Sound-Spelling Card: *Umbrella*
- Teaching Chart 53
- Word-Building Cards
- Handwriting
- Handwriting Teacher's Edition, pp. 62–64
- Activity Book, p. 14
- Practice Book, p. 167

ELL

Variations in Languages
Speakers of Spanish, Hmong, Cantonese, Haitian/Creole, and Korean may have difficulty perceiving and pronouncing /u/. Use the Approaching Level Phonics lessons for additional pronunciation and decoding practice.

 Sound Pronunciation

See Sound-Pronunciation CD for a model of the /u/ sound. Play this for the children needing additional models.

Phonics

✔ Introduce /u/*u*

Uu

Model
Display the *Umbrella* **Sound-Spelling Card**.

This is the *Umbrella* card. The sound is /u/. The /u/ sound is spelled with the letter *u*. Say it with me: /u/. This is the sound at the beginning of the word *umbrella*. Listen: /uuu/ . . . *mbrella, umbrella*.

Read the "Funny Pup!" Rhyme and Chime. Reread the first line. Point out that *up* has the letter *u* at the beginning. Model placing a self-stick note below the *u* in *up*.

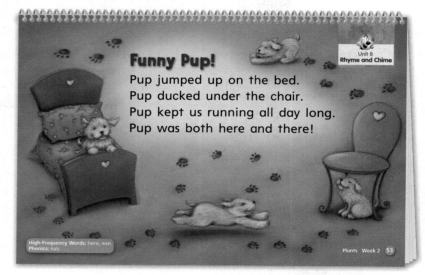

Teaching Chart 53

Guided Practice/Practice
Read the rest of the rhyme. Stop after each line. Children place a self-stick note below words that begin with the letter *u*. Guide practice with *under* in line 2.

Let's put a sticky note below the word in the line that begins with the letter *u*.

Yes, the word *under* begins with *u*.

Corrective Feedback

If children are having difficulty identifying the sound /u/, say the sound and have children repeat it: /u/ /u/ /u/. Have children repeat the following: /u/ /s/, /us/. Repeat with *up*. Then children repeat the words in each pair and tell which word has /u/ in the middle: *sap, mug; mitt, pun; dug, hat.*

Build Fluency: Sound-Spellings

 Display the following **Word-Building Cards**: *a, b, c, d, e, f, h, i, m, n, o, p, r, s, t*. Have children chorally say each sound. Repeat and vary the pace.

Handwriting: Write *Uu*

MODEL Model holding up your writing hand. Say the handwriting cues as you write the capital and lowercase forms of *Uu* on the board. Then trace the letters on the board and in the air as you say the sounds.

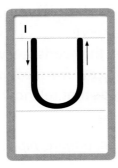

Straight down, curve around, straight up.

Straight down, curve around, and up. Straight down.

PRACTICE Ask children to hold up their writing hand.

- Say the cues together as children trace with their index finger the letters you wrote on the board.

- Have children write *U* and *u* in the air as they say /u/ multiple times.

- Distribute handwriting practice pages. Observe children's pencil grip and paper position, and correct as necessary. Have children say /u/ every time they write the letter *u*.

For Tier 2 instruction, see page 1955.

Daily Handwriting
Check that children form letters starting at the top and moving to the bottom. See **Handwriting Teacher's Edition** for ball-and-stick and slant models.

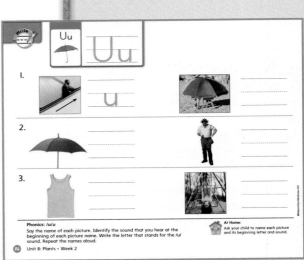

Activity Book, page 14
Practice Book, page 167

- Understand and use descriptive words (adjectives)

Materials

- Big Book: *Seed Secrets*
- Photo Cards: *kitten, pizza, soap, hippo, umpire*

ELL

Basic and Academic Vocabulary Display the **Photo Cards** from the lesson and pair English Language Learners with fluent speakers. Have partners make up sentences using the **Photo Card** for *kitten* and a describing word. Write their sentences, read them chorally, and ask: *What describing word, or adjective, tells about the kitten?*

Grammar
Describing Words (Adjectives)

MODEL Use the **Big Book** *Seed Secrets* to discuss descriptive words. Tell children that descriptive words give more information about somebody or something. Explain that these words can tell about shape, color, size, taste, or how something or somebody feels.

Point to the illustrations on pages 2–3 of the Big Book as you read: *Some **seeds** are little. Some seeds are big.* Tell children that *little* and *big* are descriptive words that tell more about the seeds.

Display and read page 14: *Some sticky seeds travel with animals.* Ask children which word describes the seeds. (*sticky*) Explain that the word *sticky* tells the texture, or how the seeds feel when you touch them. Point out that you can also say: *The seeds are sticky.* Ask children to name other descriptive words that tell how things feel when touched. (*smooth, rough, fuzzy, soft*)

PRACTICE Show **Photo Cards** for *kitten, umpire, hippo, soap,* and *pizza*.

- Model using descriptive words by making up sentences about the pictures.

> *The pizza is round.*
>
> *The pizza is delicious.*
>
> *The pizza is hot.*

- After each sentence, ask children to name the descriptive word. Then have children make up their own sentences about the picture on the Photo Card. Remind them to include descriptive words.

- To extend the lesson, help children write one of the sentences they made up. Ask them to underline the descriptive word.

Writing

Shared Writing: A List

BRAINSTORM

Remind children that in the **Big Book** *Seed Secrets* they **observed** and learned that **seeds** can travel in different ways.

WRITE

Create a list showing how seeds travel. Read the heading with children as you track the print.

- Model by rereading pages 10–11 in the Big Book. *Some seeds travel by air, so I will write that on the chart. Underneath it I will write* Dandelion.

- Display and read pages 12–13. Have children dictate what you should write.

- Display and read pages 18–19. Have children dictate information to add to the list.

- Read the completed list with children.

- Save the list to refer to in other writing activities this week.

How Seeds Travel
Seeds travel by air.
    Dandelion

Seeds travel by water.
    Coconuts

Seeds travel on animals.
    Burrs

Write About It

Ask children to draw and label a picture of a nut, a coconut, or another large seed in their Writer's Notebook.

Objective

- Write a list

Materials

- Big Book: *Seed Secrets*

5-Day Writing

Similes	
DAY 1	Shared: A List
DAY 2	Interactive: Sentences
DAY 3	Independent: Prewrite and Draft Similes
DAY 4	Independent: Revise and Edit Similes
DAY 5	Independent: Publish and Present

ELL

Prewriting Planning
Have children use the Big Book and appropriate **Photo Cards** to name pictures of different kinds of seeds, plants, fruits, and flowers before beginning work on their Writer's Notebook entries.

Transitions That Teach

While lining up, have children describe something they have **observed** in nature.

Oral Language
- Build Robust Vocabulary

✔ Comprehension
- Reread *Seed Secrets*
- Strategy: Recognize Text Structure
- Skill: Retell
- Fluency: Echo-Read

Vocabulary
- Position Words
- Story Words: *sticky, explode*

✔ Phonemic Awareness
- Phoneme Blending

✔ Phonics
- Review /u/u, /k/k, /l/l
- Blend with /u/u, /k/k, /l/l
- Decodable Reader: *A Bud Is Up*

Writing
- Interactive Writing: Sentences

SMALL GROUP

- Differentiated Instruction, pages 1954–1979

Oral Vocabulary

Week 2

gradually	moist
necessary	observe
seed	

Review

charming	conceited
equal	grow
plant	

Use the **Define/Example/Ask** routine in the **Instructional Routine Handbook** to review the words.

Oral Language

 Talk About It

Build Robust Vocabulary

INTRODUCE WORDS

Tell children that today you are going to talk about how seeds travel. Read pages 16–22 from the **Big Book** *Seed Secrets*. *I wondered how seeds were planted. I can observe the different ways by reading the book and looking at the pictures.*

Vocabulary Routine

Use the routine below to discuss the meaning of each word.

Define: A **seed** is a part of a plant from which a new plant will grow. Say the word with me.
Example: We took seeds from a grapefruit and planted them.
Ask: What are some different ways seeds are planted?

Define: To **observe** means "to look and watch carefully." Say the word with me.
Example: On our field trip to the zoo, we observed monkeys playing and grooming each other.
Ask: What did you observe on your way to school today?

CREATE A WORD WEB

Create a word web like the one shown below, or use **Teaching Chart G1**. Add a heading as shown and read the chart together as you track the print. *We can observe ways seeds are planted. Some seeds are planted by people and some by machines. I will write these as two ways that seeds are planted.*

Have children dictate information about other ways seeds are planted. Guide children to take turns and speak one at a time. When the chart is complete, read all words with children and have them repeat.

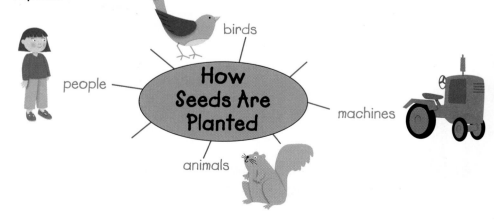

Listen for Rhythm

IDENTIFY RHYTHM

Remind children that a rhythm is a steady or regular beat.

Point out that in this rhyme, there are words with similar sounds that help the rhythm. An example of words with similar word sounds is *hickory, dickory.* Have children identify the beat and similarities in word sounds as they recite the rhyme.

RHYME ABOUT GROWING A GARDEN

Play "Grow a Garden" using the **Listening Library Audio CD.** Teach children the words. Then recite and clap the rhyme together.

Ask children to identify the words with similarities in sounds. (diggity, choppity, uppity, pickity)

Grow a Garden

Dig, diggity, dig! Dig just so.

Plant the seeds and watch them grow.

Chop, choppity, chop! Pull out the weeds.

Warm rain and sunshine my garden needs.

Up, uppity, up! Green stems climb.

Open wide! It's blossom time.

Pick, pickity, pick! The carrots are here!

Pick them all and give a cheer!

Objectives

- Discuss the theme
- Use oral vocabulary words *observe* and *seed*
- Complete a word web
- Identify a beat
- Identify similarities in word sounds

Materials

- **Big Book:** *Seed Secrets*
- **Graphic Organizer; Teaching Chart G1**
- **Listening Library Audio CD**

Digital Learning

Rhyme on Listening Library Audio CD

ELL ENGLISH LANGUAGE LEARNERS

Beginning	Intermediate	Advanced
Confirm Understanding Help children create a drawing to go with each idea in the word web. *This is the word* animals. *Let's look in the Big Book and draw the animals to help you remember the word.*	**Enhance Understanding** Have children gesture an idea from the web for others to figure out. Children can confirm their answer by saying: *Yes, seeds are planted by _____.*	**Extend Knowledge** Have children give more information about how seeds are planted. For example, children can describe how seeds are planted by animals or people.

Objectives

- Recognize text structure
- Retell a book
- Respond to a book
- Develop fluency

Materials

- Big Book: *Seed Secrets*
- Retelling Cards
- Activity Book, pp. 15–16
- Practice Book, p. 168

Big Book

Digital Learning

Story on **Listening Library Audio CD**

ELL

Gesture and Talk Use gestures and other strategies to help make the text comprehensible.

pp. 2–3
little, big: Present children with a collection of small and large objects. Hold up a small object and say: *This is little.* Hold up a large object and say: *This is big.* Continue holding up objects. *Is it big or is it little?*

Reread the Big Book

Listening Comprehension

CONCEPTS ABOUT PRINT Display the cover and read the title and the name of the author aloud with children as you track the print. Have them tell what they remember about the book.

 STRATEGY Recognize Text Structure

Remind children that **observing** how a book is organized can help them to understand it. Seed Secrets *is organized by the different ways that **seeds** travel.*

 SKILL Retell

Remind children that thinking about what happens in each part of a book can help them to remember and understand it. *Today you are going to read the Big Book again and practice retelling what you learned.* Display and read pages 2–3.

Think Aloud What have we learned so far? I see that some seeds are little and others are big. Do you recognize some of these fruits that have seeds?

Read the **Big Book** and use the prompts on the inside covers.

pages 2–3

Some seeds are little.

Some seeds are big.

Develop Comprehension

pages 4–5

ILLUSTRATOR'S CRAFT

■ *How did the illustrator organize the pictures to show how seeds make plants and plants make seeds?* (He used pictures to show a seed growing into a plant and that plant dropping seeds.)

pages 6–7

✴ RETELL

■ *Retell what you learned from these two pages.*

ILLUSTRATOR'S CRAFT
Think Aloud The inset drawing shows a seed under the ground. The illustrator drew this to show how seeds grow underground.

pages 8–9

CONCEPTS ABOUT PRINT

■ *What is the dot at the end of the sentence on page 8? What does it mean?* (It is a period. It shows where the sentence ends.)

pages 10–11

MAIN IDEA AND DETAILS
Think Aloud Each page shows another way that seeds travel. The main idea is that seeds travel. The details are how they travel.

Seeds make plants. ④

Plants can make more seeds. ⑤

Seeds need water and sun to grow. ⑥

How do seeds get from one place to another? ⑦

Some seeds drop down from the plant. ⑧

Some seeds explode away from the plant. ⑨

Some seeds travel by air like helicopters. ⑩

The wind carries them far away from the plant. When the wind stops, the seeds fall down. ⑪

Comprehension

Retell
- (pages 4–5) So far we have learned that seeds can be big or little. They make new plants and plants make more seeds.
- (pages 6–7) These pages tell us that seeds can fall near plants or can shoot away from plants.

Recognize Text Structure
- (pages 10–11) I understand now how this book is organized. Each set of two pages tells me about another way that seeds travel.

Story Word
(page 14) sticky

Names of Plants

p. 2 apple, dandelion, orange, sunflower seeds; p. 3 coconut, avocado, mango, peach seeds; pp. 4-5 sunflower; pp. 6-7 violets, daisies, daffodils, lupines, hollyhock; pp. 8-9 daisies, wild geranium; pp. 10-11 maple tree and seeds, dandelions; pp. 12-13 coconut seeds; pp. 14-15 thistles; pp. 16-17 strawberries; pp. 18-19 oak trees, acorns; pp. 20-21 flowers, corn; pp. 22-23 corn; p. 24 orange, apple, pear, coconut, melon, watermelon

About the Author/Illustrator: Tom Leonard
Tom Leonard has been an illustrator for over 20 years. He is the illustrator of many beautiful children's books with a focus on nature. He lives and teaches in Philadelphia, Pennsylvania.

**Big Book
Inside Back Cover**

ELL

pp. 4–5
seeds, plants: Provide an illustration of the content on these pages. Draw a line to indicate the ground. Draw a seed below the ground. Draw a plant sprouting from it and then add a flower. Next, draw seeds falling from the flower. Use the words *seeds* and *plants* as you draw. Show the cycle again and prompt children to use the words *seeds* and *plants*.

pp. 8–9
drop, explode: Reinforce the action words you introduced yesterday. Use actual seeds or something representing seeds. Show the action of dropping. Then put some in your clenched fist and open your fist forcefully to make the seeds "explode" forth.

pp. 10–11
by air, helicopters: Display the helicopter on page 26 of the **Big Book** *On the Go.* Talk about other things that travel by air and that move in the wind, such as planes and kites.

Develop Comprehension

pages 12–13

RETELL

- *Retell what you have learned from these two pages.* (Possible answer: Water can carry seeds far away.)

Some seeds travel by water.

The seeds float a long way to a new land.

pages 14–15

TEXT STRUCTURE

- *What do these pages tell us?* (Some seeds stick to bears, and then they rub them off.)

- *How are these pages similar to the other pages?* (They show another way that seeds travel.)

Some sticky seeds travel with animals.

The animal can rub the seeds off.

page 16

HIGH-FREQUENCY WORDS

- *Can you find the word* here *on this page?*

TEXT STRUCTURE

- *What way that seeds travel is shown on these pages?* (Birds carry and drop seeds.)

Birds carry some seeds from here to there.

The seeds grow where the birds drop them.

pages 18–19

RETELL

- *What did we learn about how birds and squirrels move seeds?* (Squirrels put seeds in the ground. Birds drop seeds from the air.)

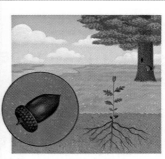

Squirrels put nuts and other seeds in the ground.

This seed was planted by a squirrel. It is now a seedling.

pp. 12–13

float: Draw a boat on water. Say: *The boat is floating.* Have children point to the coconuts floating in the water.

pp. 14–15

sticky: Stick a self-stick note onto your clothing. Point to it and say: *The paper sticks to my shirt.* Brush it off and say *rub off.* Ask children to point to the bears with sticky seeds on them. Then ask them to show you the bear that is rubbing the seeds off on the tree.

pp. 16–17

carry, drop: Carry a pencil and then drop it on the floor. Describe your action, using the words *carry* and *drop.* Have children repeat the actions and words.

pp. 18–19

seedling: Explain that seedlings are small plants that have just sprouted from seeds. Point to the inset of the acorn. *Is this a seed or a seedling?*

page 21

CONCEPT WORDS: POSITION WORDS

■ *I am going to read the sentence. Listen for the word that tells where people put seeds. What word tells where?* (*in*)

People help seeds get from place to place.

20

People get seeds from plants. They put the seeds in the ground.

21

pages 22–23

 RETELL

■ *What is another way people plant seeds? How is this way better than planting by hand?* (Using a machine is another way to plant seeds. It allows you to plant more seeds.)

Some people use machines to put many seeds in the ground.

22

Many seeds make many plants.

23

page 24

CONCEPTS ABOUT PRINT

■ *Where is the beginning of the sentence? How can you tell?* (It starts with a capital letter.) *Where is the end of the sentence? How can you tell?* (The period shows the end of a sentence.)

All these good things to eat come from seeds.

24

Text Evidence

Recognize Text Structure

Explain Remind children that they must support their answers with text evidence.

Discuss Have children listen to pages 8–15. *Which two words are repeated each time the text tells how seeds travel.* (Some seeds) Recognizing text structure helps us find text evidence. Knowing that the words "some seeds" comes before telling how seeds travel, helps me to find information.

ELL

pp. 22–23
machine: Point to the tractor on page 22. Make a motor sound and then say *machine. Is a car a machine?*

p. 24
Point to the seeds in each fruit and say *seeds*. Then ask children to point to all of the seeds on the page as they say *seeds*.

 Activity Book, pages 15–16
Practice Book, page 168

Retelling Rubric

④ Excellent

Retells the selection without prompting, using detailed information, and referring to text structure and features. Clearly describes the main idea.

③ Good

Retells the selection with little guidance, using some details, and occasionally referring to text structure and features. Generally describes the main idea.

② Fair

Retells the selection with some guidance, using limited details. Partially describes the main idea.

① Unsatisfactory

Retells the selection only when prompted, using limited details. Does not describe the main idea.

Respond to Literature

TALK ABOUT IT Ask children to talk about the words and illustrations. Have them share and explain if they liked the book. Have them refer to the book as they answer the questions.

- *What do seeds make?* LOCATE (new plants)

- *What are three ways seeds can get from one place to another?* COMBINE (Possible answers: They can go in the air or wind, on water, or in a bird's beak.)

- *What are some things you have* **observed** *people eating that have seeds?* CONNECT (Possible answers: watermelons and peaches)

Retell

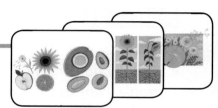

Retelling Cards

GUIDED RETELLING

Remind children that as they listened to *Seed Secrets,* they used the words and the illustrations to understand the text. Now they will use the pictures on these cards to retell the book.

- Display **Retelling Card 1**. Based on children's needs, use either the Guided, Modeled, or ELL prompts. The ELL prompts contain support for English Language Learners based on levels of language acquisition.

- Repeat the procedure with the rest of the Retelling Cards, using the prompts to guide children's retelling.

- Discuss the book.

  What did you learn about seeds?

  What was the most interesting thing in the book?

- Have children act out their favorite parts of the book.

Fluency: Echo-Read

MODEL Reread page 11, pausing between the two sentences. Then reread the page again and have children echo-read as you track the print.

Quick Check

Can children retell to understand expository text?

Vocabulary

Position Words

Chant the following jingle:

The bear goes over *the mountain.*

The fish lives under *the sea.*

The bat flies in *the cave.*

The bird flies out *of the tree.*

- Repeat each line and tell children which word tells a position.

- Give each child a game chip and an envelope. Say directions, such as: *Put the chip* in *the envelope. Take the chip* out *of the envelope. Put the chip* under *the envelope. Put the chip* over *the envelope.*

NAME POSITION WORDS Hide large colored paper circles in obvious places. Ask each child to find a circle and stay in that spot. When all have been found, have children point to and tell where they found their circles. *The red circle was* under *a book.*

PREPOSITIONS Explain that many position words are called prepositions. A preposition is a word that connects naming words and phrases with the rest of the sentence. Some prepositions are not position words, such as *with* or *at*. Examples of prepositions are *over, under, in, from,* and *on*. Chant the jingle line by line and have children name the preposition. Then have children use a preposition in a sentence.

Story Words: *sticky, explode*

Reread the sentence on page 9 of *Seed Secrets*. Say *explode* together. *The flowers look as though they are exploding when they open up. Have you ever **observed** fireworks exploding?*

Display pages 14–15 and point out the word *sticky* and the pictures of seeds on the bears. *The seeds are sticking to the bears. They are attached to the bears. Name some other items that are sticky.*

TIME TO MOVE!

Have children do the "Hokey Pokey." *Put your right foot in and put your right foot out.* Emphasize the position words: *in* and *out*.

Objectives

- **Use position words**
- **Understand and use prepositions**
- **Learn the story words** *sticky, explode*

Materials

- **Big Book:** *Seed Secrets*
- **game chips**
- **envelopes**
- **different-colored paper circles**

Digital Learning

LOG ON For children who need additional language support and oral vocabulary development, use the activities found at **www.macmillanmh.com**.

ELL

Build Vocabulary
Demonstrate several movements while describing what you are doing. Do the actions as you say: *Stand up. Sit down. Reach over. Reach under.* Have children join you in doing the actions and saying the words.

Objectives

- Blend sounds in words with initial /u/*u*, /k/*k*, /l/*l*
- Match letters *u, k, l* to the initial sounds /u/, /k/, /l/

Materials

- Puppet
- Word-Building Cards; Teacher's Resource Book pp. 95–102
- Word-Building Cards
- pocket chart

CVCC, CCVC: DIGRAPHS

Explain Display Word-Building Cards *t, h*. T *and* h *together stand for* /th/ *in* thumb. *What sound do the letters* th *stand for together?* Hold up Word-Building Cards *s, h*. S *and* h *together stand for the* /sh/ *sound as in* shell. *What sound do the letters* sh *stand for together?*

Model Place Word-Building Cards *t, h* inside the first box of the three sound boxes on **Teaching Chart G5**. T *and* h *together say* /th/. Place *i* in the middle box. *Let's blend* th *and* i, /thiii/. *Say it with me:* /thiii/. Place *n* in the last box. Blend /thiiinnn/. Have children repeat. Repeat with *math, shut,* and *fish*.

Guided Practice/Practice Provide children with **Sound Boxes**. Using Word-Building Cards, assist children in placing and blending the word *this*. Change the last two letters to *at,* to make *that*. Continue with *them, thud, path, bath,* and *moth; ship, shop, shack, dish, dash, sash,* and *lash*.

Phonemic Awareness

✓ Phoneme Blending

Model

Use the **Puppet** to model how to blend sounds in the word *up*.

Repeat with *lip*.

Happy is going to say the sounds in a word. Listen to Happy as he says each sound: /u/ /p/. Happy can blend these sounds to say a word: *up*. Now you can say the sounds with Happy: /u/ /p/, /uuup/. Now say the word with Happy: *up*.

Guided Practice/Practice

Use the Puppet to say the sounds.

Children blend the sounds to form words. Guide practice with the first word.

Happy is going to say the sounds in a word. Listen to Happy as he says each sound. Then blend the sounds to say the word.

/u/ /s/	/k/ /i/ /t/	/u/ /p/
/l/ /a/ /p/	/k/ /i/ /k/	/l/ /o/ /t/

Phonics

✓ Review

u	k	l

Model

Hold up **Word-Building Card** *u*. Repeat the routine for letters *k, l*.

This is the letter *u*. The letter *u* stands for the /u/ sound you hear at the beginning of *umbrella*. What is the letter? What sound does this letter stand for?

Say the word. Write the letter *u*.

Listen as I say a word: *umbrella. Umbrella* has /u/ at the beginning.

Repeat with *koala* and *lemon*.

The letter *u* stands for the /u/ sound. I'll write *u*.

Guided Practice/Practice

Children write the letter that stands for the initial sound. Guide practice with the first word.

Listen as I say each word. Write the letter that stands for the beginning sound.

under	lemon	kite	log
king	umpire	lip	undershirt

Build Fluency: Sound-Spellings

 Display the following **Word-Building Cards**: *a, b, c, d, e, f, h, i, k, m, n, o, p, r, s, t, u*. Have children chorally say each sound. Repeat and vary the pace.

Blend with /u/*u*, /k/*k*, /l/*l*

Model

Place Word-Building Card *u* in the pocket chart.

This letter is *u*. The letter *u* stands for the /u/ sound. Say /u/.

Place Word-Building Card *p* next to *u*. Move your hand from left to right.

Repeat with *us*.

This letter is *p*. The letter *p* stands for the /p/ sound. Listen as I blend the two sounds together: /uuup/. Now you say it. (/uuup/)

Guided Practice/Practice

Children blend sounds to form words. Guide practice with the first word.

kick	up	lock	luck
lick	sick	pick	kit
us	bus	bet	let
thin	math	dash	ship

ELL

Build Vocabulary Review the meanings of the words in the Guided Practice portion of the lesson. For example, explain that a *kit* is a group of tools used to fix or to make something. *I took a needle and thread from the sewing kit and sewed the button to the shirt. What else might be in a sewing kit?*

Objectives

- Read decodable words with /u/*u*
- Read the words *here* and *was*
- Reread for fluency

Materials

- Decodable Reader: *A Bud Is Up*
- High-Frequency Word Cards: *here, was, can, a, do, is, the*
- pocket chart

Decodable Text

For additional decodable passages, see pages 37–38 of the **Teacher's Resource Book**.

Decodable Reader

Read *A Bud Is Up*

REVIEW Display the **High-Frequency Word Cards** for **here**, **was**, **can**, **a**, **do**, **is**, and **the** in the pocket chart. Review the words using the **Read/Spell/Write** routine.

MODEL CONCEPTS ABOUT PRINT Demonstrate book handling. *I hold the book so that the cover is on the front.* Point to spaces between words. *Spaces show where one word ends and another word begins. Count the words in the title.*

A Bud Is Up

PREDICT Ask children to describe the cover illustration. *What is the boy looking at? What do you think will happen?*

FIRST READ Have children point to each word, sounding out the decodable words and saying the sight words quickly. Children should chorally read the story the first time through.

DEVELOP COMPREHENSION Ask the following: *What did Nick do with the seed?* (He planted and watered it.) *What happened after he put the cup in the sun?* (First, the seed did not pop up. Then, it did.)

SECOND READ Have partners reread the book together. Circulate, listen in, and provide corrective feedback.

It is fun, fun, fun.
Nick can do it!

2

1. Pick up a cup.
2. Pack it. Fit it in.

3

3. Tap it. Tap it in.
4. Water it on top.

4

5. Set the cup in back.
Set it in the sun.

5

It did not pop up.
The sun was not up.

6

But the sun is hot here.
It can pop up!

7

Nick can see it!
Nick did it!

8

Decodable Reader

Writing

Interactive Writing: Sentences

REVIEW

Display and read aloud the list that children created for yesterday's Shared Writing activity.

WRITE

Today we are going to write sentences about how **seeds** *travel.*

Write the following sentence frames and read aloud.

- _____ *travel by* _____.

- _____ *travel by* _____.

- _____ *travel* on _____.

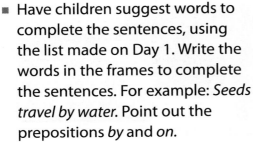

- Have children suggest words to complete the sentences, using the list made on Day 1. Write the words in the frames to complete the sentences. For example: *Seeds travel by water.* Point out the prepositions *by* and *on.*

- Ask children to help by writing all the letters they know.

- Read the completed sentences aloud with children as you track the print.

- Save the sentences to refer to in other writing activities this week.

Write About It

Ask children to draw and label a picture of something they eat that has little seeds, such as a grape or a tomato. Have them write captions using *little* or other adjectives. Have them check that their sentences are grammatically correct.

Objectives

- **Write sentences**
- **Use letter knowledge to write letters**

Materials

- **Shared Writing list from Day 1**

5-Day Writing

Similes	
DAY 1	Shared: A List
DAY 2	Interactive: Sentences
DAY 3	Independent: Prewrite and Draft Similes
DAY 4	Independent: Revise and Edit Similes
DAY 5	Independent: Publish and Present

ELL

Prewriting Planning

Ask children to draw and describe a fruit with seeds that they enjoy eating at home or a fruit from their country of origin. Provide a picture dictionary for reference.

Transitions That Teach

While getting ready for dismissal, have children tell about different types of **seeds** they have eaten, such as sunflower or sesame.

DAY 3
At a Glance

WHOLE GROUP

Oral Language
- Build Robust Vocabulary
- Oral Vocabulary Cards: "Let's Go to a National Park"

Comprehension
- Read "In My Garden" and "Mary, Mary, Quite Contrary"

High-Frequency Words
- Review *here*, *was*

Phonemic Awareness
- Phoneme Isolation

Phonics
- Review /u/*u*, /k/*k*, /l/*l*
- Blend with /u/*u*
- Read Words

Grammar
- Describing Words (Adjectives)

Writing
- Independent Writing: Prewrite and Draft Similes

SMALL GROUP

- Differentiated Instruction, pages 1954–1979

Additional Vocabulary

To provide 15–20 minutes of additional vocabulary instruction, see Oral Vocabulary Cards 5-Day Plan. The pre- and posttests can be found in the **Teacher's Resource Book**, pages 228–229.

Oral Language

Talk About It **Build Robust Vocabulary**

BUILD BACKGROUND
Introduce the selection "Let's Go to a National Park" using **Oral Vocabulary Card 1** and read the title aloud. *What kinds of plants or animals might you see in a national park? What kinds of plants or animals might you see in a park near your home?* Ask children to talk about what they see in the photo. Remind children to speak using complete sentences.

- Read the selection on the cards. Pause at each oral vocabulary word and read the definition. Check children's understanding using the Use Background Knowledge, Compare and Contrast, and Provide Synonyms prompts.

Oral Vocabulary Cards

Vocabulary Routine

Use the routine below to discuss the meaning of each word.

Define: Something that is **necessary** is something that you need or must do. Say the word with me.
Example: It is necessary to eat a healthy diet in order to grow big and strong.
Ask: What is it necessary to do before you cross the street?

Define: Something that is **moist** is not dry; it is a little wet or damp. Say the word with me.
Example: You can clean the table with a moist paper towel.
Ask: What can make the ground moist?

Define: **Gradually** means "slowly over time." Say the word with me.
Example: Over several weeks, seeds grow gradually from sprout to seedling to plant.
Ask: What else grows gradually? How do you grow? Do you grow gradually or all at once?

- Use the routine on Cards 1 and 2 to review the words **seed** and **observe**.

- Review last week's words: *charming, conceited, equal, grow,* and *plant.*

Listen for Alliteration

IDENTIFY ALLITERATION

Remind children that when two or more words begin with the same sound, it is called alliteration.

Tell children that they are going to say a rhyme about a boy who is supposed to be taking care of animals. Play the rhyme and have children join in. Ask children to identify which words begin with the same sound. (boy, blue, blow; cow's corn)

Ask: *Where is Little Boy Blue?* (asleep) *Why is it* **necessary** *to stay awake if you are looking after animals? Where is the cow?* (in the corn)

Little Boy Blue

Little Boy Blue, come blow your horn,

The sheep's in the meadow, the cow's in the corn.

Where is the boy that looks after the sheep?

He's under the haystack fast asleep!

Objectives

- Discuss the theme
- Use oral vocabulary words *gradually, moist, necessary, observe,* and *seed*
- Listen and respond to a nonfiction selection
- Recognize alliteration

Materials

- Oral Vocabulary Cards: "Let's Go to a National Park"

Digital Learning

Rhyme on **Listening Library Audio CD**

Objectives

- Read and respond to a poem
- Identify rhyme and repetition
- Write a poem

Material

- Big Book of Explorations, Vol. 2: "In My Garden" and "Mary, Mary, Quite Contrary," pp. 26–28

Vocabulary

seed the part of a plant that grows into a new plant

quite very or extremely

contrary stubborn or cranky

Poetry

Genre

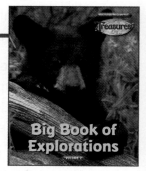

Big Book of Explorations

LITERARY TEXT: POETRY Tell children that today they will listen to two poems. Remind children that poems help us say things in a special way. These two poems will be about seeds and plants.

LITERARY ELEMENT: RHYME AND REPETITION
Explain/Model Tell children that some poems use words that rhyme. Remind them that rhyming words, such as *moon* and *spoon*, have the same sound at the end. *Listen for the rhyming words in each poem.* Review with children that repetition is when the same word or phrase is said more than once. *Listen for the words that repeat in the poem "In My Garden."*

Think Aloud As I read each poem, I will pay attention to the rhyming words I hear. I will also listen for any words and phrases that are repeated. These words can help me understand what the poem is about.

READ "IN MY GARDEN" AND "MARY, MARY, QUITE CONTRARY"

■ **Preview and Predict** Display the page as you read the title "In My Garden" and point to the children in the illustration. *Where are these children?* (in a garden) *What is the boy doing?* (planting seeds) Preview "Mary, Mary, Quite Contrary" by reading the title and tracking the print. Point to Mary. *This is Mary. What is she doing?* (watering her flowers) *What do you think these poems will be about?*

■ **Vocabulary** Introduce and discuss the vocabulary words.

■ **Set Purpose** Tell children to listen for words that rhyme in both poems and for words that repeat in "In My Garden." Read the poems aloud as you track the print. Reread "Mary, Mary, Quite Contrary" and have children join in.

pages 26–27   **page 28**

Retell and Respond

- *Which words rhyme in "In My Garden"? What other words rhyme with* row *and* grow*? What other words rhyme with* too *and* you*?*

- *Which words rhyme in "Mary, Mary, Quite Contrary"? What other words rhyme with* bells *and* shells*? Which rhyming words are in both poems?*

- *Which words are repeated in "In My Garden"?*

- *What two things help seeds and plants grow?*

Write About It

Write a Poem

Remind children that rhyming words have the same ending sounds. Review the rhyming words in "In My Garden" and in "Mary, Mary, Quite Contrary."

Tell children that they are going to write a poem. Help them generate rhyming word pairs, such as *sun/fun*, *seed/need*, and *plant/ant*.

Guide children to create a sentence ending with one of the words from a word pair, and write it on chart paper. Repeat with the other word from the pair. Continue with the remaining word pairs. Read the poem aloud with children.

ELL

Beginning

Gesture and Talk Gesture to show planting seeds in the soil, watering them, and then having them grow. As you gesture to show each action, say: *I plant seeds. I water them. Then the plant grows.* Have children repeat the same actions.

Intermediate

Ask Questions *Where do you plant seeds? What do you do to seeds every morning? What shines on your seeds so they grow?* Provide sentence frames for children's answers.

Advanced

Summarize Have children use their own words to summarize "In My Garden."

Objective

- Read the high-frequency words *here, was*

Materials

- High-Frequency Word Cards: *here, Was, was, A, a*
- pocket chart
- Photo Cards: *bike, bus, car, dog, girl, helicopter*
- index cards with: period mark, question mark
- Activity Book, pp. 17–18
- Practice Book, pp. 169–170

Activity Book, pages 17–18
Practice Book, pages 169–170

High-Frequency Words

✓ *here, was*

 REVIEW Display the **High-Frequency Word Card** for **here**. Review the word using the **Read/Spell/Write** routine.

Repeat the routine for the word **was**.

APPLY Build sentences in the pocket chart using High-Frequency Word Cards and **Photo Cards**. Read each sentence aloud. Then have children chorally read it as you track the print with your finger. Use the sentences below and the following: *Was a bus here? Was a car here? Was a dog here? Was a girl here? Was a helicopter here?*

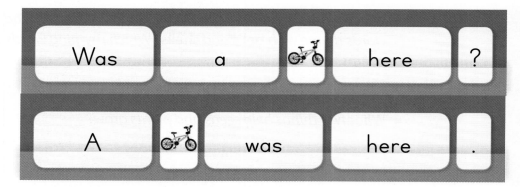

READ FOR FLUENCY Chorally read the Take-Home Book with children. Then have them reread the book to review high-frequency words and build fluency.

Quick Check

Can children read the words *here* and *was*?

During **Small Group Instruction**

If No → **Approaching Level** Provide additional practice with high-frequency words, pages 1964.

If Yes → **On Level** Children are ready to read the Take-Home Book.

Beyond Level Children are ready to read the Take-Home Book.

TIME TO MOVE!

Have children go to an area of the classroom and **observe** it closely. Then have them close their eyes. Remove an item. Have children open their eyes. Point to where the item was. *What was here?*

Phonemic Awareness

Phoneme Isolation

Model

Display the Photo Card for *umbrella* and the **Sound Box**.

This is a picture of an *umbrella*. Say the picture name with me: *umbrella*. *Umbrella* has /u/ at the beginning. I'll put a marker in the first box because /u/ is the first sound in *umbrella*.

Display the Photo Card for *nut*.

This is a picture of a *nut*. Say the picture name with me: *nut*. *Nut* has /u/ in the middle. I'll put a marker in the middle box because *nut* has /u/ in the middle.

Guided Practice/Practice

Distribute Sound Boxes and markers. Say the words. Children identify the position of /u/. Guide practice with the first word.

Listen to the word. Now say the word. Put a marker in the first or middle box to show where you hear /u/.

duck	under	bus	umbrella
run	sun	up	cup
us	fun	cut	umpire

Objective

• Listen for initial and medial /u/

Materials

• Sound Box
• Photo Cards: *umbrella, nut*
• WorkBoard Sound Boxes; Teacher's Resource Book, p. 136
• markers

Objectives

- Review sound-spellings for /u/u, /k/k, /l/l
- Blend sounds in words with /u/u
- Read simple one-syllable words

Materials

- Word-Building Cards
- pocket chart

Phonics

✓ Review

Model

Display **Word-Building Card** *u*.	This is the letter *u*. The letter *u* stands for the /u/ sound you hear at the beginning of *umbrella*. What is the letter? What sound does it stand for?
Repeat for *k* and *l*.	
Say the word *up*. Hold up Word-Building Card *u*.	Now I will say a word: *up*. I will point to the Word-Building Card *u* because I hear the /u/ sound at the beginning of the word.

Guided Practice/Practice

Say a word. Children identify the letter that stands for the initial sound.

Guide practice with the first word.

I am going to say a word. Point to the letter that stands for the beginning sound.

us	key	leaf	kid
let	lap	under	up
kite	lit	king	umbrella

Phoneme Deletion

Model

Place **Word-Building Cards** *c*, *u*, and *p* in the pocket chart. Delete the initial letter *c* to form the word *up*.

I will blend these sounds together: /kuuup/, *cup*.

I will delete the letter *c* to form the word *up*. Blend the sounds with me.

Guided Practice/Practice

Children delete initial letters to form new words. Guide practice with the first word.

Delete the initial letter. Blend the sounds to form new words.

pup   hat   Sam

Build Fluency: Sound-Spellings

 Display the following Word-Building Cards: *a, b, c, d, e, f, h, i, k, m, n, o, p, r, s, t, u*. Have children chorally say each sound. Repeat and vary the pace.

Blend with /u/u

Model

Place **Word-Building Card** *b* in the pocket chart.

This letter is *b*. It stands for the /b/ sound. Say /b/.

Place Word-Building Card *u* next to *b*. Move your hand from left to right.

This is the letter *u*. It stands for the /u/ sound. Listen as I blend the two sounds: /buuu/. Now you blend the sounds. (/buuu/).

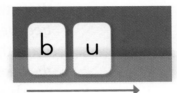

Place Word-Building Card *s* next to *bu*. Move your hand from left to right.

Repeat with *rub*.

This is the letter *s*. It stands for the /s/ sound. Listen as I blend the three sounds: /buuusss/, *bus*. Now you blend the sounds. (/buuusss/, *bus*)

Guided Practice/Practice

Children repeat the blending routine using these words.

run	cup	pup	bud	tuck
nut	bun	up	rut	luck
duck	us	but	sun	cut

 # Read Words

Apply

Write the words and sentences. Guide practice with the first word, using the **Sound-by-Sound Blending Routine**.

Have children read the sentences.

> **rub**
> **bus**
> **Rub the cat here.**
> **The bus was red.**

Corrective Feedback

Blending: Sound Error Model the sound that children missed, then have them repeat the sound. For example, for the word *bus*, say: *My turn.* Tap under the letter *u* in the word *bus* and say: *Sound? What's the sound?* Then return to the beginning of the word. Say: *Let's start over.* Blend the word with children again.

Objective

- Recognize and use describing words (adjectives)

Materials

- Oral Vocabulary Cards: "Let's Go to a National Park"
- Photo Cards: *apple, city, corn, car, globe, lemon, ostrich, snow, umbrella, water, zucchini*

Grammar

Describing Words (Adjectives)

MODEL Use the **Oral Vocabulary Cards** from "Let's Go to a National Park" to review describing words. Remind children that descriptive words tell more about something.

- Write this sentence from Card 1 on the board. *Yet these amazing trees began life as tiny little **seeds** inside a cone the size of an egg.* Track the print as you read it aloud. *The word* amazing *describes the trees. The words* tiny *and* little *describe the seeds.* Underline the words *amazing, tiny*, and *little*. Explain to children that finding naming words, such as *trees* and *seeds*, sometimes helps them to find the describing words.

- Read the following sentence from Card 2 and have children identify the describing words in each sentence. *The climate is hot and the land is dry. Which word describes the climate?* (*hot*) *Which word describes the land?* (*dry*)

PRACTICE Practice recognizing describing words. Read these sentences from "Let's Go to a National Park" and have children identify the describing words.

It is home to the giant sequoia trees. (*giant*)

In the summer the juicy cactus fruit ripens. (*juicy*)

- Practice using describing words. Have children choose a **Photo Card** and make a sentence about the picture using as many describing words as they can. Have them identify the describing words they used.

- Model for children using the Photo Card for *apple.*

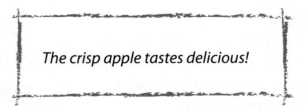

The crisp apple tastes delicious!

Writing

Independent Writing: Similes

Display the lists and sentences from the Shared and Interactive Writing activities.

BRAINSTORM

WRITING TRAIT: IDEAS Display page 10 of the **Big Book** *Seed Secrets. The author says that* **seeds** *travel by air like helicopters.* Explain that children will compare how seeds travel with how other things travel.

Think Aloud I know that seeds also travel by water. What else travels by water? I know that sailboats travel on water. My idea is to compare seeds and sailboats.

PREWRITE

Write the following title and sentence frame and read it aloud.

> How Seeds Travel
>
> Seeds travel by _____ like _____.

- Complete the sentence frame by writing the words *water* and *sailboats*. Read the completed sentence aloud as you track the print.

DRAFT

- Have children write the sentence frame and complete the sentence with one way seeds travel and something else that travels that way.

- Have children draw a picture illustrating one of the ways seeds travel. Collect and save children's work.

- Tell children to write a title for their picture and sentence.

Write About It
Ask children to draw in their Writer's Notebook. Have them draw and label a favorite animal with seeds stuck to its fur.

Objectives
- Write similes
- Use writing trait: ideas

Materials
- lists and sentences from Days 1 and 2
- Big Book: *Seed Secrets*

5-Day Writing

	Similes
DAY 1	Shared: A List
DAY 2	Interactive: Sentences
DAY 3	Independent: Prewrite and Draft Similes
DAY 4	Independent: Revise and Edit Similes
DAY 5	Independent: Publish and Present

ELL

Use New Language Use the **Photo Cards** that show various animals with fur, such as *deer, dog, fox, koala,* and *wolf.* For each animal, ask: *Can a _____ carry seeds in its fur?*

Transitions That Teach

While children pack up, have them tell about something that happens **gradually**.

DAY 4
At a Glance

WHOLE GROUP

Oral Language
- Build Robust Vocabulary

✓ **Comprehension**
- Read Aloud: "The Talking Vegetables"

Vocabulary
- Position Words
- Story Words: *sticky, explode*

✓ **Phonemic Awareness**
- Phoneme Deletion

✓ **Phonics**
- Word Sort
- Blend with /u/*u*
- Decodable Reader: *A Bud Is Up*

Writing
- Independent Writing: Revise and Edit Similes

SMALL GROUP

- Differentiated Instruction, pages 1954–1979

Oral Language

 Talk About It ## Build Robust Vocabulary

WORKING TO PLANT A GARDEN
Discuss the many jobs that need to be done to plant a large garden, such as one you might find on a farm.

- *What things are* **necessary** *to plant vegetables on a farm?*

CREATE A LIST
Write the heading as shown below. Read it as you track the print. Then make a list to record children's ideas.

Think Aloud I have **observed** that a farm field can have row after row of vegetables. The first thing that has to be done is to clear the field to get it ready for planting **seeds**. I will write *Clear the field* first. What can be done next?

Guide children as they suggest the steps, ranging from planting the seeds to eating the vegetables. Remind them that plants grow **gradually**. Add children's ideas to the chart and read the words with them as you track the print.

Planting Vegetables on a Farm

- Clear the field.
- Plant the seeds.
- Water the plants. Keep the ground moist.
- Pull the weeds.
- Pick the vegetables.
- Eat the vegetables.

ELL ENGLISH LANGUAGE LEARNERS

Beginning	Intermediate	Advanced
Confirm Understanding Use gestures to talk about the steps to plant a garden. You may want to have children add pictures to the chart to show each step.	**Enhance Understanding** Ask questions about the steps: *What can you use to clear a field? What kinds of seeds can you plant to grow vegetables? How do you know if the plants need water?*	**Extend Knowledge** Ask children to describe vegetable gardens or farms they have seen. *What is your favorite vegetable to eat? Have you ever seen it growing?*

Listen for Rhythm

IDENTIFY RHYTHM AND RHYME

Remind children that rhythm is a regular beat and that rhyming words have the same end sounds.

RHYME ABOUT GROWING A GARDEN

Let's say the rhyme that we learned on Day 2 about growing a garden. Play "Grow a Garden" using the **Listening Library Audio CD** and have children clap to the beat as they join in.

Ask: *What does the rhyme say that the garden needs?* (warm rain and sunshine) *What kind of plant was planted in the garden?* (carrots)

Have children say the missing rhyming word. Say the rhyme and stop after the word *them* on the second line. Have children say the word that follows and rhymes with *so*. (grow) Continue reciting the rhyme stopping after the words *garden* (needs), *blossom* (time), and *a* (cheer).

Grow a Garden

Dig, diggity, dig! Dig just so.

Plant the seeds and watch them grow.

Chop, choppity, chop! Pull out the weeds.

Warm rain and sunshine my garden needs.

Up, uppity, up! Green stems climb.

Open wide! It's blossom time.

Pick, pickity, pick! The carrots are here!

Pick them all and give a cheer!

Objectives

- Discuss the theme
- Discuss steps for planting vegetables on a farm
- Write a chart
- Identify a regular beat
- Generate rhyme
- Use oral vocabulary words *gradually, moist, necessary, observe,* and *seed*

Materials

- Listening Library Audio CD

Oral Vocabulary

Have children use each word in a sentence about this week's stories.

gradually	moist
necessary	observe
seed	

Review Work with children to review last week's words. Use sentence starters such as: *The seed will _____ into a beautiful leafy _____.*

charming	conceited
equal	grow
plant	

Digital Learning

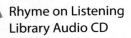

Rhyme on Listening Library Audio CD

Objective

- Listen and respond to a folktale

Materials

- Read-Aloud Anthology: "The Talking Vegetables," pp. 113–116

ELL

Reinforce Understanding
Sketch a few houses, a garden, and a few people. Point to the drawing and explain that a *village* is a very small town, often in the country. Point to the people. Say: *Villagers are people who live in villages.* Ask children to say *village* and *villagers*. *Do you live in a village?*

Readers Theater

BUILDING LISTENING AND SPEAKING SKILLS
Distribute copies of "A Pinch of Pepper," Read-Aloud Anthology pages 191–198. Have children practice reading the play throughout the unit. Assign parts and have children present the play or perform it as a dramatic reading at the end of the unit.

A Pinch of Pepper

Interactive Read Aloud

Listening Comprehension

GENRE: LITERARY TEXT/FOLKTALE
Explain that this story is a **folktale**. Remind children that a folktale is a story told over and over for many years *Many of the stories we have read have been about helping. What happened to the woodcutters in "The Sticky-Sticky Pine"?*

Read Aloud

CULTURAL PERSPECTIVES
Tell children that today they will listen to a folktale from Liberia, a country in Africa. Explain that rice is a very common food in Liberia and many other places all over the world. Remind children that Yoko ate rice with seaweed and fish in the **Big Book** *Yoko*.

READ "THE TALKING VEGETABLES"

- **MODEL ASKING QUESTIONS ABOUT STORY STRUCTURE** Use the Think Alouds provided at point of use in the folktale.

- **MODEL FLUENT READING** Read aloud the folktale with fluent expression. Point out that how you read the dialogue helps the listener understand what the characters say and how they feel.

- **EXPAND VOCABULARY** See page 113 of the **Read-Aloud Anthology** to teach new words, using the **Define/Example/Ask** routine.

Respond to Literature

TALK ABOUT IT Ask children to retell the folktale.

- *Why do the villagers keep coming to Spider? What does he tell them?*

- *What are some of the things the villagers do on the farm?*

- *Do you think Spider should get to pick and eat the vegetables?*

- *What is the lesson of the story? What can you learn from this folktale?*

Write About It

Ask children to draw the talking vegetables. Have them write a label or a sentence about their drawing.

Vocabulary

Position Words

REVIEW POSITION WORDS
I am going to read a short story that uses some words that tell position. Each time I say a word that tells a position, act out what I am saying.

Read the following story.

> *I lost my special pencil. It has my name on it. I looked* in *the drawer. I looked* under *the table. I looked* over *the table. "Ouch!" I said. Something* in *my pocket stuck me. I put my hand* in *my pocket. I took my hand* out of *my pocket. I found my lost pencil!*

For additional practice with prepositions, reread the story and have children identify the prepositions. (on, in, under, over, out, of) Then have them say a sentence using a preposition.

Story Words: *sticky, explode*

Display pages 14–15 of the **Big Book** *Seed Secrets*. Ask children if their hands have ever been sticky. *What made them sticky? Have you ever played with stickers? Why do you think they are called stickers?*

Show children page 9 again and read the sentence. *Have you ever* **observed** *a balloon exploding when it got too full of air?*

Objectives

- Use position words
- Review story words *sticky, explode*

Materials

- Big Book: *Seed Secrets*

ELL

Reinforce Meaning Put a sheet of paper in a book. *Is the paper* in *or under the book?* Put a book under a table. *Is the table* under *or over the book?* Continue to make similar arrangements of classroom items, asking questions about the objects' positions.

Minilesson

Fairy Tales

Explain Tell children that just like folktales and lullabies, many cultures have their own fairy tales. A fairy tale is a story that might have fairies, elves, giants, trolls, or talking animals. There usually is a conflict between good and evil. Most fairy tales have a happy ending. Different cultures around the world have fairy tales with similar good and evil characters as well as recurring phrases.

Discuss: Ask: *Do you know any fairy tales? Who are the characters?*

Apply: Read "Little Ashes" from the Read-Aloud Anthology, page 220. Have children listen and name the good characters and the evil characters. Discuss how this version is similar to a version that they have heard before.

Objectives

- Delete phonemes to form new words
- Sort words by medial, initial, and final letter sounds
- Blend letter sounds to form words with /u/*u*

Materials

- Puppet
- Word-Building Cards
- pocket chart
- Activity Book, pp. 19–20
- Practice Book, p. 171

CVCC, CCVE: Digraphs

Review Remind children that the letters *t* and *h* together stand for the sound /th/ and that the letters *s* and *h* together stand for the sound /sh/.

Practice Using Word-Building Cards *t, h, a, t,* blend the sounds to form *that*. Place your fingers below the *th* and have children repeat /th/. Repeat the routine with *shop*, placing your fingers beneath *sh* and having children repeat /sh/. Then have children blend and build the /th/*th* and /sh/*sh* words *this, shin, ship, then, fish,* and *path.*

Phonemic Awareness

✓ Phoneme Deletion

Model

Use the **Puppet**.

Happy likes to take a sound from a word to make a new word. Listen to Happy say a word: *cup*. Say the word with Happy: *cup*.

Now listen to Happy say *cup* without /k/: *up*. Say the new word with Happy: *up*. *Cup* without /k/ is *up*.

Repeat with *bus/us*.

Guided Practice/Practice

Have children delete the initial sound and say the new word. Guide practice with the first word.

sit/it	bat/at	pup/up
Sam/am	bus/us	kit/it

Phonics

✓ Word Sort

Model

Display **Word-Building Card** *u*.

This is the letter *u*. The letter *u* stands for the /u/ sound.

Repeat for *a* and *i*.

Write the words on the board.

sat	bun	tip	sun	kid
tap	nut	bud	tan	kick

Read the words with children. Begin an initial sort. Children say each word as it is sorted.

Look at the words. Some can go together. I'll group *nut* and *sun* because they have *u* in the middle. I'll group *tip* and *kid* because they both have *i* in the middle. What other words have the same middle sounds?

Guided Practice/Practice

Children do initial and final sounds sorts. Guide practice with final *t* in *sat* and *nut*.

How should we sort the words next? We can group words with the same beginning or ending sounds, too. Tell me how to sort the words.

Build Fluency: Sound-Spellings

 Display the following **Word-Building Cards**: *a, b, c, d, e, f, h, i, k, m, n, o, p, r, s, t, u*. Have children chorally say each sound. Vary the pace.

Blend with /u/u

Model

Place Word-Building Card *r* in the pocket chart.

This letter is *r*. It stands for /r/. Say /rrr/.

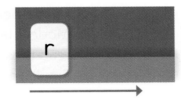

Place Word-Building Card *u* next to *r*. Move your hand from left to right.

This is the letter *u*. It stands for /u/. Listen as I blend the two sounds: /rrruuu/. Now blend the sounds with me. (/rrruuu/)

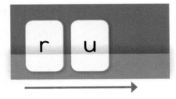

Place Word-Building Card *n* next to *ru*. Move your hand from left to right.

Repeat with *fun*.

This is the letter *n*. The letter *n* stands for /n/. Listen as I blend the three sounds: /rrruuunnn/, *run*. Now you blend the sounds with me. (/rrruuunnn/, *run*)

Guided Practice/Practice

Children blend letter sounds to form words. Guide practice with the first word.

duck	sun	pup
bus	cup	luck
bath,	thin	shut

Corrective Feedback

Blending: Sound Error Model the sound that was missed, then have them repeat the sound. For the word *run*, say: *My turn.* Tap under the letter *u* and say: *What's the sound?* Then return to the beginning of the word. Say: *Let's start over.* Blend the word again.

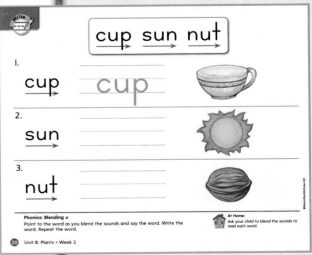

Activity Book, pages 19–20
Practice Book, page 171

Objectives

- Read decodable words with /u/*u*
- Review high-frequency words *here* and *was*
- Reread for fluency

Materials

- Decodable Reader: *A Bud Is Up*
- High-Frequency Word Cards: *here, was, can, a, do, is, the*
- Sound-Spelling Card: *Umbrella*

Decodable Text

For additional decodable passages, see pages 37–38 of the **Teacher's Resource Book**.

Decodable Reader

Read *A Bud Is Up*

 REVIEW Review this week's high-frequency words and phonics skills using the word lists on the inside back cover of *A Bud Is Up*.

A Bud Is Up

Review the high-frequency words **here**, **was**, **can**, **a**, **do**, **is**, and **the** using the **Read/Spell/Write** routine. Then have children chorally read the high-frequency word list.

Review the phonics skill /u/*u* using the *Umbrella* **Sound-Spelling Card**. Then have children chorally read the decodable word list. Model blending as needed and take note of children who struggle to read these words. Provide additional instruction and practice during Small Group time.

MODEL CONCEPTS ABOUT PRINT

Guide children to follow along. *I open the book by turning the cover. Then I turn each page as I read it, starting with the first page and ending with the last page. Now I want you to read the book.*

 REREAD FOR FLUENCY Have children reread the book with a partner. Have partners take turns asking and answering questions from each other. Circulate and listen in, providing corrective feedback. Then have children reread the book independently.

It is fun, fun, fun.
Nick can do it!

2

1. Pick up a cup.
2. Pack it. Fit it in.

3

3. Tap it. Tap it in.
4. Water it on top.

4

5. Set the cup in back.
Set it in the sun.

5

It did not pop up.
The sun was not up.

6

But the sun is hot here.
It can pop up!

7

Nick can see it!
Nick did it!

8

Decodable Reader

Writing

Independent Writing: Similes

REVISE AND EDIT

Distribute children's drawings and sentences from Day 3. Have them reread them and check for the following:

- Did I write a title for my work?

- Does my sentence compare how a **seed** travels with how something else travels?

- Did I begin my sentence with a capital letter and end with a period?

Circulate and help children as they review and revise their sentences. Have them share their sentences with a partner.

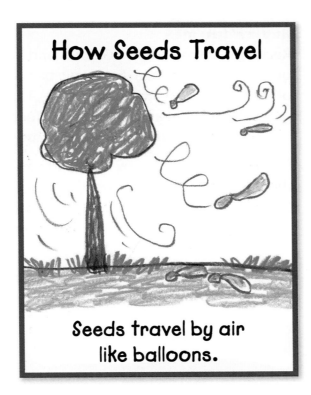

How Seeds Travel

Seeds travel by air like balloons.

Write About It

Have children draw a picture of birds flying and carrying seeds. Help them label their drawings.

Objective
- Revise and edit similes

Materials
- sentences from Day 3
- Writer's Checklist; Teacher's Resource Book, p. 205

5-Day Writing

Similes	
DAY 1	Shared: A List
DAY 2	Interactive: Sentences
DAY 3	Independent: Prewrite and Draft Similes
DAY 4	Independent: Revise and Edit Similes
DAY 5	Independent: Publish and Present

ELL

Use New Language Draw a way that seeds travel and write a caption that compares seeds and something else. Display your picture and read the caption aloud. Explain that the caption uses *like* to describe similarities between seeds and other things.

Transitions That Teach

While children are packing up, have them name something that is **necessary** to take home with them.

WHOLE GROUP

Oral Language
- Build Robust Vocabulary

✔ **Comprehension**
- Strategy: Recognize Text Structure
- Skill: Retell
- Read Across Texts

✔ **Vocabulary**
- High-Frequency Words
- Build Fluency
- Position Words

✔ **Phonemic Awareness**
- Phoneme Deletion

✔ **Phonics**
- Build Fluency
- Read Words
- Dictation

Writing
- Independent Writing: Publish and Present

SMALL GROUP

- Differentiated Instruction, pages 1954–1979

Review and Assess
Oral Language
Build Robust Vocabulary

REVIEW WORDS

Review this week's oral vocabulary words with children. Explain that all of the words will be used to discuss growing plants.

Use the following questions to check children's understanding:

- What things are **necessary** for **seeds** to grow? (water and sun)

- Why might it be better for plants if the ground is **moist** when the weather is very hot?

- Why can't you **observe** flowers the day after you plant the seeds?

- Is it better to water plants **gradually** or to flood the garden? Why?

REVIEW RHYMES

Recite the rhyme "Grow a Garden" and have children join you. Point out that the words *dig, diggity, dig* begin with the same sound. Name other alliterative words in the rhyme. Then work with children to generate different alliterative words for the beginning of the rhyme, such as: *grow, growity, grow* or *cook, cookity, cook*.

Play the rhyme "Little Boy Blue" and have children join in. Have them repeat the group of words that are alliterative: *Boy, Blue, blow*. Guide children to think of other words to fit the rhyme that have alliteration, such as *Little Girl Green, go get your horn*.

Review and Assess
Comprehension

STRATEGY Recognize Text Structure

REFLECT ON THE STRATEGY Remind children that they have already learned that stories and nonfiction pieces are organized in a certain way.

Think Aloud I know that most stories have a beginning, middle, and end. There is also a certain way that the information in a nonfiction book is organized. For example, in *Seed Secrets* the facts about different kinds of **seeds** are all together, and the different ways seeds travel are together.

SKILL Retell

Lead children in reviewing the illustrations in *Seed Secrets* to help them recall the selection. Then use the following questions to review retelling.

- *What does* Seed Secrets *tell us about seeds?*

- *What are the ways seeds travel?*

Reading Across Texts

COMPARE AND CONTRAST GENRES
Create a chart like the one shown to compare and contrast *Seed Secrets* and "The Talking Vegetables."

- *What kind of story is* Seed Secrets? *What kind of story is "The Talking Vegetables"?*

- *Which story could really happen? Which story could not?*

- *Which story happens in a special place? Which story could happen anywhere?*

Seed Secrets	The Talking Vegetables
nonfiction	fiction
could really happen	could not happen
could happen anywhere	happens in a garden

Objectives

- Use oral vocabulary words: *gradually, moist, necessary, observe, seed*
- Review the strategy and skill
- Discuss how authors group information in text
- Compare and contrast genres

Materials

- **Big Book:** *Seed Secrets*
- **Read-Aloud Anthology:** "The Talking Vegetables"
- **Activity Book, p. 21**

Activity Book, page 21

Objectives

- Review high-frequency words *here, was, and, what, little, said*
- Review position words
- Build fluency

Materials

- High-Frequency Word Cards: *here, was, and, what, little, said*
- position words on index cards with picture clues: *over, under, in, out*
- ball

Fluency

Connected Text Have children reread this week's **Decodable Reader** with a partner. Circulate, listen in, and note those children who need additional instruction and practice reading this week's decodable and sight words.

Review and Assess
Vocabulary

 ## High-Frequency Words

Distribute one of the following **High-Frequency Word Cards** to each child: **here**, **was**, **and**, **what**, **little**, and **said**. *When you hear the word that is on your card, hold up your Word Card.*

- *Mom* and *Dad are* here.

- *Do you like to play* here?

- *The* little *girl* said, *"Hello."*

- What *book* was here?

- *I* was *looking for you.*

Build Fluency: Word Automaticity

Rapid Naming Display the High-Frequency Word Cards. Point quickly to each card. Have children read the word as fast as they can.

here	was	and
what	little	said

Position Words

Write position words on index cards and illustrate their meanings.

- Have children pick a card. Read the word together. Ask each child to act out the word meaning and say what they did. For example, a child with the card *in* might look in a drawer and say *I looked in a drawer*. Point out the prepositional phrases in the sentences.

TIME TO MOVE!

Children stand in a circle. Hand a ball to a child and say: *Roll the ball under the table.* Give the ball to another child and say: *Put the ball in the basket.*

Review and Assess
Phonemic Awareness

 Phoneme Deletion

Guided Practice

Say the word *pup.* Guide practice with *bus, pin,* and *cup.*

I will say a word. Let's take away the beginning sound from the word to make a new word. Listen as I say a word: *pup.* Say the word with me: *pup.*

Now take /p/ from the beginning of *pup: up.* What is *pup* without the beginning /p/? (*up*)

Practice

Repeat the routine with these words. Children delete the initial sound to form new words.

I will say a word. Take away the beginning sound and tell me the word.

kit/it	hat/at	Pam/am
ran/an	bus/us	tin/in
cup/up	can/an	pin/in

Objective

- Delete phonemes to form new words

Objective

- Read and write simple one-syllable words

Materials

- Word-Building Cards
- 5 index cards with: *We, can, run, here,* period mark
- 5 index cards with: *This, run, was, fun,* period mark
- WorkBoard Sound Boxes; Teacher's Resource Book, p. 136
- Activity Book, p. 22

Phonics: /u/u
Say the name of each picture. Write the letter below the picture if its name begins with the /u/ sound. Repeat the names aloud.

At Home:
Ask your child to name each picture that begins with the same sound as umbrella.

22   Unit 8: Plants • Week 2

Activity Book, page 22

Review and Assess
Phonics

Build Fluency: Sound-Spellings

Rapid Naming Display the following **Word-Building Cards**: *a, b, c, d, e, f, h, i, k, m, n, o, p, r, s, t, u*. Have children chorally say each sound as quickly as they can.

✔ Read Words

Apply

Distribute the first set of cards. Have children stand in sequence.	Let's read the sentence together. *We can run here.*
Repeat, using the other set of cards.	Let's read the sentence together. *This run was fun.*

✔ Dictation

Dictate sounds for children to spell.

Listen as I say a sound. Repeat the sound, then write the letter that stands for the sound.

/k/   /a/   /b/   /i/   /h/   /u/
/d/   /e/   /r/   /i/   /l/   /o/

Then dictate words for children to spell. Model for children how to use the **Sound Boxes** to segment the sounds in the word. Have them repeat.

Write the letters and words on the board for children to self-correct.

Now let's write some words. I will say a word. I want you to repeat the word, then think about how many sounds are in the word. Use your Sound Boxes to count the sounds. Then write one letter for each sound you hear.

run   deck   tick   cut   sun
nut   bat   rock   duck   luck

Review and Assess
Writing

Independent Writing: Similes

PUBLISH

Explain to children that you will gather their illustrated sentences to make a class book.

- Brainstorm ideas for a title, such as "A **Seed** Is Like . . ."

- Have a few children make the cover for the book. Write the title on the cover.

- Make holes along the edges of the cover and pages.

- Bind the pages together with yarn.

PRESENT

Have children take turns displaying their drawings and reading their sentences to the class.

LISTENING, SPEAKING, AND VIEWING

- Remind children to speak clearly and to be good listeners when a classmate is speaking.

- Praise children for their hard work and display the finished book for everyone to enjoy. Children may wish to add a copy of their work to their Writing Portfolios.

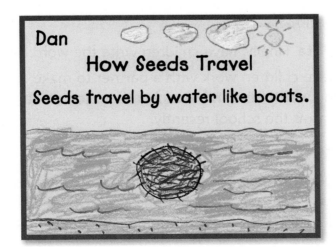

Dan
How Seeds Travel
Seeds travel by water like boats.

Write About It
Have children draw a picture of things that travel in the air. Help them label their drawing.

Objective
- Publish and present children's sentences

Materials
- sentences from Day 4

5-Day Writing	
Similes	
DAY 1	Shared: A List
DAY 2	Interactive: Sentences
DAY 3	Independent: Prewrite and Draft Similes
DAY 4	Independent: Revise and Edit Similes
DAY 5	Independent: Publish and Present

Transitions That Teach

While children are waiting in line, have them describe how to keep a plant's soil **moist** and why it's important.

ON YOUR OWN

Seeds Grow

Have children draw plants in different stages of growth. They can start with seeds, then a small plant, and then show the plant growing taller.

ELL

Partners When pairing children to make up sentences, pair English Language Learners with children who are more proficient. Write their sentences, read them together, and point out the high-frequency words.

Approaching Level

Oral Language

Objective Preteach oral vocabulary
Materials • none

THEME WORDS: *observe, seed*

- Tell children the meanings for **observe** and **seed**. *To observe means "to look and watch carefully." I like to observe how bees go from flower to flower. A seed is a part of a plant from which a new plant will grow. I took a seed from an apple and planted it.*

- Discuss the words with children. Ask: *When you plant a seed, what can you observe happening after a month?*

- Have children use sentence frames to generate complete oral sentences using the words: *When I have quiet time, I like to observe _____. A seed that I would like to plant is _____.*

High-Frequency Words

Objective Preteach high-frequency words
Materials • **High-Frequency Word Cards:** *here, was*

PRETEACH WORDS: *here, was*

- Display the **High-Frequency Word Card** for **here**.

- **Read** Point to and say the word *here*. *This is the word* here. *It means "this place." I will plant a flower here.*

- **Spell** *The word* here *is spelled* h-e-r-e. Have children read and spell *here*.

- **Write** Finally, have children write the word *here*.

- Have children work with a partner to make up sentences using the words *here* and **was**. Ask them to talk about someone that **was** at the school recently.

HIGH-FREQUENCY WORDS REVIEW

Tier 2

Display the High-Frequency Word Cards for words previously taught, one card at a time, and have children chorally read and spell the word. Mix and repeat. Note words children need to review.

Approaching Level

Phonemic Awareness

Objective Identify initial sound /u/

Materials
- **Photo Cards:** *umbrella, umpire, under, undershirt, up, upside down*
- **Sound-Spelling Card:** *Umbrella*

✔ PHONEME ISOLATION

Model

- Display the **Photo Card** for *up. This is* up. *Listen for the beginning sound in* up: /uuup/. Up *begins with* /u/. *Repeat for* umpire.

- Distribute the *Umbrella* **Sound-Spelling Card**. Point out the articulation picture. *Notice how the lips are open but not round. When I say /u/, my tongue is in the middle of my mouth.*

Guided Practice/Practice

- Display the Photo Cards. Have children take turns selecting a picture, naming it, and saying the initial sound of the picture name: *This is (an) _____. _____ begins with /u/.*

- Have children note the position of their lips as they say /u/.

Phonics

Objective Recognize words that begin with /u/*u*

Materials
- **Sound-Spelling Card:** *Umbrella* • **Word-Building Cards**
- **Photo Cards:** *umbrella, undershirt, umpire, up, under*

✔ PRETEACH: RECOGNIZE /u/*u*

Model

- Display Photo Cards for *umbrella* and *undershirt* and the *Umbrella* Sound-Spelling Card. Say: *The name of this letter is* u. U *stands for the /u/ sound that you hear at the beginning of* umbrella. *I will place a* u *on the picture of the umbrella because* umbrella *begins with /u/. Repeat with* undershirt.

Guided Practice/Practice

- Display the Photo Cards on a table. Say: *This is the picture of an* umpire. *What sound do you hear at the beginning of* umpire? *What letter stands for /u/? Let's place Word-Building Card* u *on the umpire because* umpire *begins with /u/. Repeat with remaining Photo Cards for* u.

SOUND-SPELLINGS REVIEW

Display Word-Building Cards *m, a, s, p, t, i, n, c, o, f, h, d, r, e, b, l, k,* and *u,* one at a time. Have children chorally say the sound. Repeat and vary the pace.

Tier 2

Corrective Feedback

Mnemonic Display the *Umbrella* Sound-Spelling Card. Say: *The sound is /u/. The /u/ sound is spelled with the letter* u. *Say /u/ with me: /u/. This is the sound at the beginning of* umbrella. *What is the letter? What is the sound? What word begins with /u/?* Umbrella *is the word we can use to remember the sound for* u, /u/.

On Level

High-Frequency Words

Objective Review high-frequency words *here, was, little, said, and, what*

Materials • **High-Frequency Word Cards:** *here, was, little, said, and, what*

REVIEW

- Display the **High-Frequency Word Card** for **little**.

- **Read** Point to and say the word *little. This is the word* little. *It is a word we use when we talk about the size of something. It means "small." The bud is little.*

- **Spell** *The word* little *is spelled* l-i-t-t-l-e. Have children read and spell *little*.

- **Write** Finally, have children write the word *little*.

- Repeat with **here, was, and, said,** and **what**. Then have partners make up questions and answers using the words *what* and *said*. Ask them to talk about what someone in the classroom said: *What did Tina say? Tina said it was time for lunch.*

Phonemic Awareness/Phonics

Objective Blend sounds to form words and review /k/*k*, /k/*ck*, and /u/*u*

Materials • **Word-Building Cards** • pocket chart
• **Sound-Spelling WorkBoards**

PHONEMIC BLENDING

Model
- Listen as I *say the sounds in a word: /d/ /u/ /k/. Now I'm going to blend the sounds: /duuuk/,* duck. *Say the sounds with me: /d/ /u/ /k/, /duuuk/,* duck. *Now say the word:* duck.

Practice
- Say: *Listen to the sounds, then blend the sounds to say the word:*

/l/ /u/ /k/	/b/ /u/ /s/	/n/ /u/ /t/	/f/ /u/ /n/
/k/ /u/ /p/	/r/ /u/ /n/	/k/ /u/ /t/	/h/ /u/ /g/

REVIEW /k/*k*, /k/*ck*, /u/*u*

- Display **Word-Building Card** *k. The name of this letter is* k. K *stands for the /k/ sound we hear at the beginning and end of* kick. *What is the sound? I'll hold up the* k *card because* kick *begins and ends with /k/. Repeat with* ck *and* pick *and* u *and* up.

Practice
- Have children write *k, i, t,* and *k* several times on their **WorkBoards** as they say /k/ /i/ /t/. Repeat with *sock, lock, tuck,* and *luck*.

ELL

Sound-Letter Relationships Provide additional practice in pronouncing and blending the sounds /k/, /k/, /u/ and naming the corresponding letters as children point to them.

Beyond Level

High-Frequency Words/Vocabulary

Objective Review high-frequency words
Materials • **none**

✔ **ACCELERATE**

- Write *do* and *be* on the board.

- **Read** Point to and say the word *do. This is the word* do. *We use it to talk about something that will happen. What will you do tomorrow?*

- **Spell** *The word* do *is spelled* d-o. Have children read and spell *do.*

- **Write** Finally, have children write the word *do.*

- Repeat the routine with *be. Then* Have children work with a partner to make up oral sentences using the words *do* and *be.*

EXPAND ORAL VOCABULARY

- **Suffixes** Review the meaning of the oral vocabulary word *gradually* with children. Then explain that a *suffix* is a word part added to the end of a word to form a new word.

- Say: *The suffix* -ly *at the end of* gradually *means "in a certain way." Something that happens* gradually *happens in a slow, steady way. Another word with* -ly *is* gladly. Gladly *means "in a happy way." I will* gladly *take a break from running around the track.*

- Have children take turns using the new word *gladly* in a sentence. Then tell children that they will work with a partner to name and define other words with the suffix *-ly.*

Phonics

Objective Read words with *u*
Materials • **Sound-Spelling Card:** *Umbrella* • **Word-Building Cards**
• pocket chart

✔ **ENRICH**

- Display the *Umbrella* **Sound-Spelling Card.** Remind children that the /u/ sound is spelled with the letter *u. Uncle begins with the /u/ sound. Truck has /u/ in the middle.*

- Write these words on the board for children to read: *must, luck, tuck, stuck, rust, crust, trust, truck, pluck, plug, plum, plus.*

- Display **Word-Building Cards** *u, c, h, k, m, p, n, r, s,* and *t.* Have partners make as many words as they can. Provide time for children to share their lists.

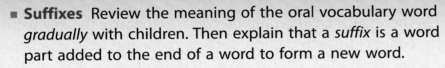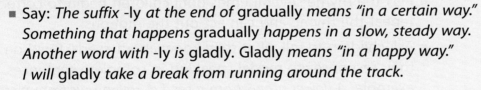

ELL   ENGLISH LANGUAGE LEARNERS

Oral Language Warm-Up

Content Objective Learn theme vocabulary
Language Objective Repeat and act out a rhyme to demonstrate understanding
Materials • **Listening Library Audio CD** • **Big Book:** *Seed Secrets*

BUILD BACKGROUND KNOWLEDGE

All Language Levels

■ Continue developing vocabulary around the unit theme "Plants" using the rhyme "Little Boy Blue." Display a picture of corn from *Seed Secrets*. Teach the word *corn* as you point to the corn in the picture. Explain that corn grows from seeds. Other fruits and vegetables grow from seeds, too. Have children repeat the word *corn* three times.

■ Play "Little Boy Blue" on the **Listening Library Audio CD**. Act out each line as you chant the rhyme; for example, gesture "come" and mime blowing a horn.

■ Then teach children the gestures. Emphasize the key words that connect to each motion, such as *come* and *blow your horn*.

■ Play the rhyme several times until children begin to correctly repeat the rhyme and can act out the motions.

■ Ask children to tell what they know about seeds. Build on their responses to model speaking in complete sentences. For example: *A flower grows from a seed. A tree grows from a seed. All plants grow from seeds.*

Academic Language

Language Objective Use academic language in classroom conversations

All Language Levels

■ This week's academic words are **boldfaced** throughout the lesson. Define the word in context and provide a clear example from the selection. Ask children to generate an example.

Academic Language Used in Whole Group Instruction

Oral Vocabulary Words	Vocabulary and Grammar Concepts	Strategy and Skill Words
gradually **moist** **necessary** **observe** **seed**	**position words** **describing words**	**retell** **structure/organization** **describing words** **capital letter**

Cognates

Help children identify similarities and differences in pronunciation and spelling between English words and Spanish cognates:

Cognates

gradually	*gradualmente*
necessary	*necessario*
observe	*observar*

ELL ENGLISH LANGUAGE LEARNERS

Vocabulary

Language Objective Demonstrate understanding and use of key words by discussing plants and animals

Materials • Visual Vocabulary Resources

Visual Vocabulary Resources

PRETEACH KEY VOCABULARY

All Language Levels

Use the **Visual Vocabulary Resources** to preteach the weekly oral vocabulary words *gradually, moist, necessary, observe,* and *seed.* Focus on one or two words per day. Use the following routine that appears in detail on the cards.

- Define the word in English and provide the example given.
- Define the word in Spanish, if appropriate, and indicate if the word is a cognate.
- Display the picture and explain how it illustrates or demonstrates the word.
- Then engage children in structured partner-talk about the image, using the key word.
- Ask children to chorally say the word three times.
- Point out any known sound-spellings or focus on a key aspect of phonemic awareness related to the word.

PRETEACH FUNCTION WORDS AND PHRASES

All Language Levels

Use the Visual Vocabulary Resources to preteach the function words and phrases *travel with* (someone) and *travel by* (plane, train, etc.). Focus on one word per day. Use the detailed routine on the cards.

- Define the word in English and, if appropriate, in Spanish. Point out if the word is a cognate.
- Refer to the picture and engage children in talk about the word. For example, children will partner-talk using sentence frames, or they will listen to sentences and replace a word or phrase with the new function word.
- Ask children to chorally repeat the word three times.

TEACH BASIC WORDS

Beginning/Intermediate

Use the Visual Vocabulary Resources to teach *squash, coconut, strawberry, pepper, watermelon,* and *pear.* Teach these words for "plants we can eat" using the routine provided on the card.

Approaching Level

Oral Language

Objective Reinforce oral vocabulary
Materials • none

THEME WORDS: *observe, seed*

Preteach

- Say: *We've talked about **seeds** and how you can **observe** them grow.*

- *What can you observe if you look carefully at a flower? What do some different flower seeds look like?* Have children respond using complete sentences.

- *Have you ever eaten seeds? What kinds of seeds can you eat?*

- *If you observe the soil the moment that you plant a seed, will you see anything? How long must you wait before you can observe anything?*

High-Frequency Words

Objective Reteach high-frequency words
Materials • **High-Frequency Word Cards:** *here, was*
• **Sound-Spelling WorkBoards**

RETEACH WORDS: *here, was*

Tier 2

- Distribute a **WorkBoard** to each child. Then display the **High-Frequency Word Card** for **here**.

- Use the **Read/Spell/Write** routine to reteach the word. Point to and say the word. *This is the word* here. *It means "in this place or spot."* Here *is spelled* h-e-r-e. Have children read and spell *here*. Then have them write the word on their WorkBoards. Repeat the routine with **was**.

- Have children work with a partner to make up sentences using the words *here* and *was*. Ask them to talk about objects that were in the classroom.

CUMULATIVE REVIEW

Display the High-Frequency Word Cards for words previously taught, one card at a time, and have children chorally read and spell the word. Mix and repeat. Note words children need to review.

ELL

Partners When pairing children to make up sentences, pair English Language Learners with children who are more proficient. Write their sentences, read them together, and point out the high-frequency words.

Approaching Level

Phonemic Awareness

Objective Blend sounds to form words
Materials • **Puppet**

Puppet

PHONEME BLENDING

Tier 2

Model

- Hold up the **Puppet**. *Happy is going to say the sounds in a word: /u/ /p/. Happy can blend these sounds together: /uuup/. Now you say the sounds: /u/ /p/. Say the word with Happy: /uuup/,* up.

Practice

- Have the Puppet continue to give sounds using words with initial /u/. *Now you blend the sounds and say these words with Happy.* Use the following words: /u/ /s/; /u/ /p/; /u/ /n/ /t/ /i/ /l/. Guide practice with the first word.

Phonics

Objective Reinforce sound/letter correspondence for /u/*u*
Materials • **Sound-Spelling Card:** *Umbrella* • **Sound-Spelling WorkBoards**
  • **Word-Building Cards** • **Decodable Reader:** *A Bud Is Up*

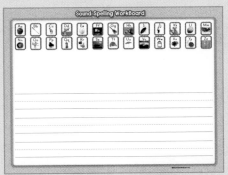

Sound-Spelling WorkBoard

RECOGNIZE /u/*u*

Model

- Display the *Umbrella* **Sound-Spelling Card**. *The letter* u *stands for the /u/ sound as in* umbrella. *What is this letter? What sound does it stand for?* Repeat with *umpire*.

- Trace *u* on a small **Word-Building Card** *u*. *I will say a sentence. We will trace* u *on the card when we hear /u/.* Say: *My umbrella goes up, and I stand under it.*

Guided Practice/Practice

- Distribute a **WorkBoard** to each child. Say: *unzip, kit, under, sit, uncle, uptown, dog, chip, umpire.* Children write *u* on their WorkBoard when they hear a word with /u/. Guide them with the first two words.

Decodable Reader

- **Read the Decodable Reader** Read *A Bud Is Up* with children. Have them echo-read each page. Chorally reread the story.

CUMULATIVE REVIEW

Display Word-Building Cards *m, a, s, p, t, i, n, c, o, f, h, d, r, e, b, l, k,* and *u,* one at a time. Point to the letters in random order. Have children chorally say the sound. Repeat and vary the pace.

Corrective Feedback

Sound Error Say: *My turn. When I say the word* kit, *I hear the sounds /k/ /i/ /t/. I do not hear /u/, so I will not write* u. *Listen again: /k/ /i/ /t/,* kit. *Do you hear the /u/ sound?* Continue with the other words.

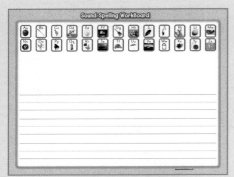

Sound-Spelling WorkBoard

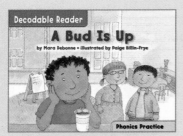

Decodable Reader

On Level

Phonics

Objective Review recognizing and blending initial /t/*t*, /u/*u*, and /n/*n*

Materials
- **Word-Building Cards** • pocket chart
- **Sound-Spelling WorkBoards** • **Decodable Reader:** *A Bud Is Up*

 REVIEW /u/*u*, /t/*t*, /n/*n*

- Display **Word-Building Card** *t. The name of this letter is* t. T *stands for /t/ at the beginning of* tiger. *I'll hold up the* t *card because* tiger *begins with /t/.* Repeat with *u* and *up*, *n* and *nest*, and *b* and *bird*.

- Distribute small Word-Building Cards. Say: *umpire, bud, new, beach, noodle, umbrella, top, nest, table.* Children repeat the initial sound and hold up the card that stands for that sound. Guide practice with the first two words.

- **Blend Words** Place Word-Building Cards *n, u, t* in the pocket chart. Point to each letter for children to identify. Move your hand from left to right under the letters as you blend the sounds: /nnnuuut/, *nut.* Repeat with *bun* and *tub.*

- Have children write *n, u, t* several times on their **WorkBoards** as they say /n/ /u/ /t/. Repeat with *b, u, n* and *t, u, b.*

- **Read the Decodable Reader** Read *A Bud Is Up.* Have children reread each page. Then chorally reread the story.

Beyond Level

Phonics

Objective Read words with long *e*

Materials
- **Word-Building Cards**
- pocket chart

 ACCELERATE

- Display Word-Building Cards *b, e* in the pocket chart. Point to the letters as you say each sound. *The word* be *has two sounds: /b/ /ē/. Listen as I blend the sounds: /bēēē/. The /ē/ sound can be spelled with one* e *or two.*

- Write these words on the board: *bee, she, teen, seem, be, me, we, weed, seed, feet, feed, we, green, teeth.* Model blending as needed.

ELL ENGLISH LANGUAGE LEARNERS

Access to Core Content

Content Objective Develop listening comprehension

Language Objective Discuss text using key words and sentence frames

Materials • **ELL Resource Book**, pp. 214–219 • **Big Book:** *Seed Secrets*

PRETEACH BIG BOOK

All Language Levels

Use the Interactive Question-Response Guide on **ELL Resource Book** pages 214–219 to introduce children to *Seed Secrets*. Preteach half of the selection on Day 1 and half on Day 2.

- Use the prompts provided in the guide to develop meaning and vocabulary. Use the partner-talk and whole-class responses to engage children and increase student talk.

- When completed, revisit the selection and prompt children to talk about the photographs. Provide sentence starters as needed and build on children's responses to develop language.

ELL Resource Book

Big Book

Beginning	Intermediate	Advanced
Use Visuals During the Interactive Reading, select several pictures. Describe them and have children summarize what you said.	**Summarize** During the Interactive Reading, select a few lines of text. After you read them and explain them, have children summarize the text.	**Expand** During the Interactive Reading, select a larger portion of text. After you read it and explain it, have children summarize the text.

Approaching Level

High-Frequency Words

Objective Recognize high-frequency words *here, was, little, said*

Materials • **High-Frequency Word Cards:** *here, was, little, said*

REVIEW WORDS: *here, was, little, said*

- Display the **High-Frequency Word Card** for **here**. Say the word and have children repeat it. Point to each letter and have children name it.

- Distribute small **Word-Building Cards** *h, e, r,* and *e*. Model putting the letters together to form the word *here*. Then have children form *here*.

- Repeat the above routines with the words **was**, **little**, and **said**.

- Have children take turns asking a question with the words *here, was, little,* and *said*. Others answer using the words: *What was here? She said a little car was here.*

CUMULATIVE REVIEW

Display High-Frequency Word Cards for words previously taught, one card at a time, and have children chorally read and spell the word. Mix and repeat. Note words children need to review.

Phonemic Awareness

Objective Identify medial /u/*u*

Materials • **Photo Cards:** *bus, duck, nut, sun, up, undershirt*

• **WorkBoard Sound Boxes; Teacher's Resource Book** • markers

PHONEME ISOLATION

Tier 2

Model

- Use **Sound Boxes**. Display the **Photo Card** for *bus*. *Listen for the middle sound. Bus has /u/ in the middle. I'll place a marker in the middle box to show that I hear /u/ in the middle of* bus.

- Display the Photo Card for *up*. *Listen for the beginning sound in* up: */uuup/,* up. *Up begins with /u/. I'll place a marker in the first box to show that I hear /u/ at the beginning of* up.

Guided Practice/Practice

- Distribute Sound Boxes and markers. Display the Photo Cards. Children take turns selecting a picture and naming it. Have them listen for /u/ and place the marker in the first or middle box as they say: *This is a(n) _____. I hear /u/ at the beginning/middle of _____.*

- Repeat with each picture name. Provide guidance as needed.

Approaching Level

Phonics

Objective   Blend letter sounds with /u/*u* and build fluency
Materials   • **Word-Building Cards**   • pocket chart

RECOGNIZE /u/*u*

Tier 2

Model

■ Place **Word-Building Card** *u* in the pocket chart. *The name of this letter is* u. *The letter* u *stands for the /u/ sound. Say /u/. What is the letter? What is the sound?*

■ Place *s* next to *u*. *The name of this letter is* s. *The letter* s *stands for the /s/ sound. Say /s/. What is the letter? What is the sound?*

■ Move your hand from left to right below the letters. *Now listen as I blend the two sounds together: /uuusss/, us. What's the word? Let's blend the word together: /u/ /s/, /uuusss/, us.*

Guided Practice/Practice

■ Give the *b, u, s* cards to three children. Each child says the sound for the letter on his or her card: /b/ /u/ /s/. Have children blend the sounds to say the word *bus*. Repeat with *sub, run, cut, sun.*

Build Fluency

■ Have children blend *bus, sub, run, cut,* and *sun* as quickly as they can.

Decodable Reader

Objective   Reread Decodable Reader *A Bud Is Up*
Materials   • **Decodable Reader:** *A Bud Is Up*

REREAD *A Bud Is Up*

■ Display the cover of the book and read the title. Open to the title page and point out the title. *Let's read the title together.* Have children sound out each word as you run your finger under it. *Look at the picture. What is the boy doing? What do you think we will read about in this book?*

■ Page through the book. Ask children what they see in each picture. Ask children to find the words *can, here,* and *the.*

■ Read the book chorally with children. Have them point to each word or rebus as they read it. Provide corrective feedback as needed.

■ Ask children to use *can, here,* and *the* to talk about the pictures. *Nick can see the bud here.*

■ After reading, ask children to recall things they read about.

Corrective Feedback

Association Error If children have difficulty identifying initial and medial /u/, say: *My turn: /b/ /u/ /s/, /buuusss/, bus. I hear the /u/ sound in the middle of bus: /buuusss/. What is the sound? What is the letter? Let's start over.* Repeat with the word *bus* for children to identify the position of /u/.

Decodable Reader

ON YOUR OWN

Draw Nick's Plant

Have children draw a picture and write a sentence to tell what kind of plant Nick is growing.

Things That Go Up

Have children draw and label a list of things that go up. They can start with the bud from the story. Have them share their lists with their group.

On Level

Decodable Reader

Objective Reread *A Bud Is Up* to develop fluency
Materials • **Decodable Reader:** *A Bud Is Up*

REREAD FOR FLUENCY

■ Ask children to look at the illustrations in *A Bud Is Up* and use their own words to retell what the book was about.

■ Have children reread a page or two of *A Bud Is Up*. Work with them to read with accuracy and expression. Model reading a page. Point out how you used your voice to say the words: *When I read page 8, I see that the sentence ends with an exclamation point. I read that sentence excitedly. I want to show that Nick is happy.*

■ Provide time to listen as children read their page(s). Comment on their accuracy and expression and provide corrective feedback by modeling proper fluency.

Decodable Reader

Beyond Level

Decodable Reader

Objective Reread *A Bud Is Up* to reinforce fluency and phonics
Materials • **Decodable Reader:** *A Bud Is Up*

REREAD FOR FLUENCY

■ Have partners reread *A Bud Is Up*. Provide time to listen as children read. Comment on their accuracy and expression and provide corrective feedback by modeling proper fluency.

■ Have partners take turns asking each other a question about the text. Have the other partner respond.

INNOVATE

■ Have children create a new story by replacing the word *Bud* in the title. For example, the story could be *A Duck Is Up*. Have children draw a new cover illustration for the story.

ELL ENGLISH LANGUAGE LEARNERS

Access to Core Content

Content Objective Develop listening comprehension
Language Objective Discuss text using key words and sentence frames
Materials • **ELL Resource Book,** pp. 220–221

PRETEACH BIG BOOK OF EXPLORATIONS

> **All Language Levels**

Use the Interactive Question-Response Guide on **ELL Resource Book** pages 220–221 to introduce children to *In My Garden* and *Mary, Mary, Quite Contrary*. Preteach half of the selection on Day 3 and half on Day 4.

Grammar

Content Objective Identify describing words
Language Objective Speak in complete sentences, using sentence frames
Materials • **Big Book:** *Seed Secrets* • **Photo Cards**

DESCRIBING WORDS

> **All Language Levels**

- Review describing words. Tell children that describing words tell more about something. Point to objects in the classroom and describe them: *My sweater is brown. The chair is small.* Have children repeat the sentences.

- Display the cover of *Seed Secrets*. Say sentences about the illustration. For example: *The water is blue. The trees are tall.* Have children repeat. Tell children to listen for describing words. Remind them that a describing word tells more about something.

- Point out the naming word in each sentence: *water, trees.* Ask: *What word tells the color of the water? What word tells us about how big the trees are?* (*blue, tall*)

PEER DISCUSSION STARTERS

> **All Language Levels**

- Distribute **Photo Cards** of fruits, such as *banana, lemon, strawberry,* and *watermelon*.

- Pair children and have them complete sentence frames such as: *This banana is _____.* Ask them to expand on their sentences by providing as many describing words as they can. For example: *This banana is yellow and sweet.* Circulate, listen in, and take note of each child's language use and proficiency.

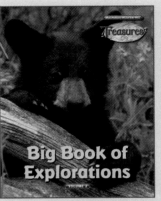

Big Book of Explorations

Puppet

Approaching Level

Phonemic Awareness

Objective Delete sounds to form new words
Materials • **Puppet**

PHONEME DELETION

Tier 2

Model

■ Hold up the **Puppet**. *Happy is going to say a word:* cup. *Cup has three sounds: /k/ /u/ /p/. Listen as Happy says only the second and third sounds of cup: /u/ /p/. When Happy takes off the first sound of cup, he says the word up: /k/ /u/ /p/, cup; /u/ /p/, up.* Repeat with *lit/it*.

Guided Practice/Practice

■ Use the Puppet to provide the following clues for children to respond to: *Say* pat *without /p/, and what do you have?* (at) *Say* bus *without /b/.* (us) *Say* fin *without /f/.* (in) *Say* pup *without /p/.* (up) Guide practice as needed.

■ Continue with *bus/us, lox/ox, tan/an, sit/it, bat/at,* and *pup/up.*

Phonics

Objective Blend with medial /u/u to read words
Materials • **Word-Building Cards** • pocket chart

BLEND WORDS WITH /u/u

Tier 2

Model

■ Place **Word-Building Cards** *f, u, n* in the pocket chart. *The name of this letter is* f. *The letter f stands for the /f/ sound. Say /f/. The name of this letter is* u. *The letter stands for the /u/ sound. Say /u/. The name of this letter is* n. *The letter stands for the /n/ sound. Say /n/.*

■ Walk by the word and say the sound each letter stands for: */f/ /u/ /n/. Now I blend the three sounds together: /ffffuuunnn/,* fun.

Guided Practice/Practice

■ Keep the Word-Building Cards in the pocket chart. Have children take turns walking by the cards, saying the letter sounds, and blending the word: */f/ /u/ /n/, /ffffuuunnn/,* fun. Repeat with *sun, run, bun, bud,* and *mud.*

Leveled Reader Library

Approaching Level

Leveled Reader Lesson 1

Objective Read *Seeds* to apply skills and strategies
Materials • **Leveled Reader:** *Seeds*

Leveled Reader

BEFORE READING

- **Preview and Predict** Read the title and the author's name. *What do you see on the cover? What do you think the book is about?* Turn to the title page and point out the title and author's name.

- **Model Concepts About Print** Demonstrate book handling. *I hold the book so that the cover is on the front and the words are not upside down. I open the book and turn each page as I read it, starting with the first page and ending with the last page of the book.*

- **Review High-Frequency Words** Write **here**, **is**, **a**, **was** and read the words aloud. Guide children as they name the letters in each word. Have children find each word in the book and read it.

- **Page Through the Book** Name unfamiliar terms and identify the pictures.

- **Set a Purpose for Reading** *Let's find out how plants change as they grow.*

DURING READING

- Remind children to use the illustrations to gain information and to look for the high-frequency words *here, is, a,* and *was.*

- Show children how to self-correct if a word doesn't sound right or doesn't make sense in the sentence. *On page 2, I see a picture of a flower, so I think the sentence is "Here is a flower." But then I see that the word begins with an* s. Flower *doesn't begin with* s. *It looks like a sunflower.* Sunflower *starts with* s. *I go back and reread the sentence: "Here is a sunflower."*

- Monitor children's reading and provide help as needed.

AFTER READING

- Ask children to point out words that they had trouble reading and to share strategies they used. Reinforce good behaviors: *Isabel, I noticed you pointed to the word* here *each time you read it.*

- Ask children to retell important facts in the text and to share personal responses. *How do plants change as they grow? Have you planted a seed and watched it change and grow? What did the seed become?*

Digital Learning

Use the **Leveled Reader Audio CD** for fluency building *after* children read the book with your support during Small Group time.

ON YOUR OWN

Before and After

Children can think of another living thing, such as another kind of plant or an animal, and write sentences to tell how living things change. Provide the sentence frames: *Here is a _____. It was a _____.* Have children include drawings to show the change.

Here is a cat.
It was a kitten.

Leveled Reader

ELL

Retell Use the Interactive Question-Response Guide Technique to help English Language Learners understand *From Seed to Plant*. As you read, make meaning clear by pointing to pictures, demonstrating word meaning, paraphrasing text, and asking children questions.

ON YOUR OWN

Create a Seeds and Plants Chart

Provide a two-column chart. Label one column *Seeds* and the other column *Plants*. Have children draw and label pictures for each column.

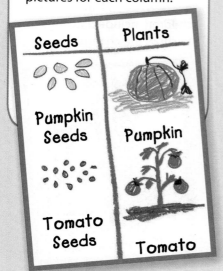

On Level

Leveled Reader Lesson 1

Leveled Reader Library

Objective   Read *From Seed to Plant* to apply skills and strategies

Materials   • **Leveled Reader:** *From Seed to Plant*

BEFORE READING

- **Preview and Predict** Read the title and the name of the author. *What do you see on the cover? What do you think the book will be about?* Open and page through the book. Name unfamiliar items and identify the pictures.

- **Model Concepts About Print** Demonstrate book handling. *I hold the book so that the cover is on the front and the words are not upside down. I open the book by turning the cover. Then I turn each page as I read it.*

- **Review High-Frequency Words** Write **here**, **are**, **this**, **was**, and **a** on chart paper. Have children find each word in the book and point to the word as they read it.

- **Set a Purpose for Reading** *Let's find out about different types of seeds.*

DURING READING

- Have children turn to page 2 and begin by whisper-reading the first two pages.

- Remind children to look for the new high-frequency word and to use the illustrations.

- Monitor children's reading and provide help. Stop during the reading and ask open-ended questions to facilitate discussion, such as: *What is the author telling us about seeds? How do the photographs help you?* Build on children's responses to develop deeper understanding of the text.

AFTER READING

- Ask children to point out words they had trouble reading and to share strategies they used. Reinforce good behaviors, such as: *Clara, I noticed that you put your finger under each word as you sounded it out. After you read it, you looked carefully at the picture.*

- **Retell** Ask children to retell important facts from the book. Help them make a personal connection. *Have you ever planted seeds? What kind of seeds were they?*

- Have partners take turns asking and answering questions about the text.

Beyond Level

Leveled Reader Lesson 1

Objective Read *Seeds, Seeds, Seeds!* to apply skills and strategies
Materials • **Leveled Reader:** *Seeds, Seeds, Seeds!*

BEFORE READING

■ **Preview and Predict** Read the title and the name of the author. *What do you see on the cover? Have you ever eaten these kinds of seeds?* Turn to the title page and point out that it also has the title and the name of the author. Page through the book with children and pause to name unfamiliar items.

■ **Introduce Story Words** Point to the word *sprout* on page 4. Read the sentence. Have children tell what *sprout* means. Ask them to think of another action word with the same meaning.

■ **Set a Purpose for Reading** *Let's find out how plant seeds are the same and different.*

DURING READING

■ Remind children that when they come to an unfamiliar word, they can look for familiar chunks in the word, break the word into syllables and sound out each part, or think about what the word might mean. If the word does not sound right or make sense in the sentence, children can self-correct.

■ Monitor children's reading and provide help as needed.

AFTER READING

■ Ask children to point out words they had trouble reading and to share the strategies they used.

■ Ask children to retell the story and to share personal responses. *What did you learn about how seeds are different?*

■ Have partners take turns asking and answering questions about the text.

■ **Analyze** *Identify the parts of a plant that are named in the selection.*

■ List the following vegetable categories on the board: *bulb, root, leaf, stalk.* Have partners research and list vegetables that fall into each category. Under *leaf*, for example, children might list *lettuce, spinach,* and *cabbage.*

■ **Model** Tell children they will use their research to create a five-question multiple-choice quiz, which they may share with a family member. Write an example: *1. Which vegetable is a root? a) carrot; b) lettuce; c) potato.* Have them write an answer key.

Leveled Reader

Create Seed Booklets

Have each child create a little book of seeds. For each page, have them glue a seed on the page and write the caption: *Here is a _____ seed.* Then have them draw what the seed becomes and write the caption: *A _____ plant will grow.*

Leveled Reader

Vocabulary

Preteach Vocabulary Use the routine in the **Visual Vocabulary Resources**, pages 345–346, to preteach the ELL Vocabulary listed on the inside front cover of the Leveled Reader.

ELL ENGLISH LANGUAGE LEARNERS

Leveled Reader

Content Objective Read to apply skills and strategies
Language Objective Retell information using complete sentences
Materials • **Leveled Reader:** *Seeds*

BEFORE READING

All Language Levels

- **Preview** Read the title *Seeds*. Ask: *What's the title? Say it again.* Repeat with the author's name. Point to the cover photo and say: *Look at the seeds in this watermelon.* Point to the seeds as you name them. *The seeds are black. Now turn to a partner and tell about this picture.*

- **Page Through the Book** Use simple language to tell about the photo on each page. Immediately follow up with questions, such as: *Where are the tomato seeds? Is the tomato on the plant?*

- **Review Skills** Use the inside front cover to review the phonics skill and high-frequency words.

- **Set a Purpose** Say: *Let's read to find out about seeds and plants.*

DURING READING

All Language Levels

- Have children whisper-read each page, or use the differentiated suggestions below. Circulate, listen in, and provide corrective feedback, such as modeling how to decode a word.

- **Retell** Stop after every two pages and ask children to state what they have learned so far. Reinforce language by restating children's comments when they have difficulty using story-specific words. Provide differentiated sentence frames to support children's responses and engage children in partner-talk where appropriate.

Beginning	Intermediate	Advanced
Echo-Read Have children echo-read after you.	**Choral-Read** Have children choral-read with you.	**Choral-Read** Have children choral-read.
Check Comprehension Point to pictures and ask questions such as: *Do you see the seeds inside the tomato? Point to the seeds.*	**Check Comprehension** Ask questions/prompts such as: *Describe what you see in this picture. What kind of plant is this?*	**Check Comprehension** Ask: *What did you learn about seeds and plants? Read sentences that tell about seeds.*

ENGLISH LANGUAGE LEARNERS

AFTER READING

All Language Levels

Book Talk Children will work with peers of varying language abilities to discuss their books for this week. Display the four **Leveled Readers** read this week: *Seed, Seeds, Seeds!* (Beyond Level), *From Seed to Plant* (On Level), *Seeds* (Approaching Level), and *Seeds* (English Language Learners).

Ask the questions and provide the prompts below. Call on children who read each book to answer the questions or respond to the prompt. If appropriate, ask children to find the pages in the book that illustrate their answers.

> • What kinds of seeds did your book tell about?
>
> • Describe the seeds in the book.
>
> • What seeds can you eat?
>
> • How are all the seeds alike? How are they different?
>
> • Tell how a seed becomes a plant.

Develop Listening and Speaking Skills Tell children to remember the following:

- Share information in cooperative learning interactions. Remind children to work with their partners to retell the story and complete any activities. Ask: *What happened next in the story?*

- Employ self-corrective techniques and monitor their own and other children's language production. Children should ask themselves: *What parts of this passage were confusing to me? Can my classmates help me clarify a word or sentence that I don't understand?*

- Use high-frequency English words to describe people, places, and objects.

- Narrate, describe, and explain with specificity and detail. Ask: *Where did the story take place? Can you describe the setting? What else did you notice?*

- Express opinions, ideas, and feelings on a variety of social and academic topics. Ask: *What do you think about the characters in the story?*

ON YOUR OWN

Under the Umbrella

Have children draw pictures of children under an umbrella. They can include other *u* words in their picture, including someone standing *upside down*. Have them label all *u* words with the letter *u*.

ELL

Sound-Letter Relationships Provide additional practice in pronouncing the sounds /u/, /k/, /l/ and naming the corresponding letters, as children point to them.

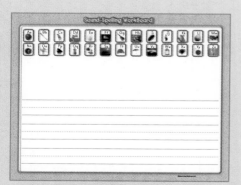

Sound-Spelling WorkBoard

Approaching Level

Phonemic Awareness

Objective Delete sounds to form new words
Materials • none

PHONEME DELETION

Tier 2

Model

- *Listen as I say a word:* pup. *Say the word with me:* pup. *Now let's take away the beginning sound to make a new word. We'll take the /p/ from the beginning of* pup: up. *What is the new word?* (up) Repeat with *bus/us, pin/in,* and *cup/up.*

Guided Practice/Practice

- Have children practice deleting the initial sound to form new words. *Now I will say a word. Take away the beginning sound and tell me the word.* Use the following words:

| kit/it | hat/at | Pam/am | bus/us | fit/it |
| ran/an | Gus/us | tin/in | sat/at | cup/up |

Phonics

Objective Identify initial /u/u, /k/k, and /l/l and build fluency
Materials
- **Photo Cards:** *umbrella, umpire, under, up, upside down, koala, kangaroo, key, king, kitten, lock, ladder, lemon, ladybug, lamp*
- **Word-Building Cards** • pocket chart
- **Sound-Spelling WorkBoards**

BUILD FLUENCY

Tier 2

Model

- Place **Word-Building Cards** *u, k,* and *l* in the top row of the pocket chart. Place the **Photo Cards** facedown in a stack. Pick the first card, name the picture, and identify the initial sound. Then place it in the pocket chart under the corresponding letter.

Guided Practice/Practice

- Have each child choose a Photo Card, say the name of the picture, identify its initial sound, and place it in the pocket chart under *u, k,* or *l.* Guide practice with the first Photo Card.

Build Fluency

- Display the Word-Building Cards. Have children name each letter as quickly as they can. Then ask them to write the letters *u, k,* and *l* on their **WorkBoards** several times as they say the letter names.

Approaching Level

Leveled Reader Lesson 2

Objective   Reread *Seeds* to reinforce fluency, phonics, and retelling

Materials   • **Leveled Reader:** *Seeds*

FOCUS ON FLUENCY

- Tell children that you will read one page of the book and they should read that page right after you. They should follow along in their books and try to read at the same speed and with the same expression that you use.

 SKILL   **RETELL**

- *Look at pages 2 and 3. What plants do you see? Name the other plants that started out as seeds.*

READ PREVIOUSLY READ BOOKS

- Distribute copies of the past six **Leveled Readers**. Tell children that rereading the books will help them develop their skills and enjoy language.

- Circulate and listen in as children read. Stop them periodically and ask them how they are figuring out words or checking their understanding. Tell children to read other previously read Leveled Readers during independent reading time.

High-Frequency Words

Objective   Review high-frequency words *here, was, little, and, said,* and *what*

Materials   • **High-Frequency Word Cards:** *here, was, little, said, and, what*

BUILD WORD AUTOMATICITY: *here, was, little, said, and, what*

- Distribute copies of the **High-Frequency Word Card** for **here**. Say the word and have children repeat it. Have children name the letters in the word. Repeat with the words **was**, **little**, **and**, **said**, and **what**.

- **Build Fluency** Use the High-Frequency Word Cards to review previously taught words. Repeat, guiding children to read more rapidly.

Leveled Reader

Retell

Children can draw pictures to retell what the seeds became. Ask children to display and discuss their pictures.

Meet Grade-Level Expectations

As an alternative to this day's lesson, guide children through a reading of the On Level Leveled Reader. See page 1970. Since both books contain the same vocabulary, phonics, and comprehension skills, the scaffolding you provided will help most children gain access to this more challenging text.

Leveled Reader

Create an Idea Web

Children can create their own idea webs to show things that were once seeds. Have them write the sentence *It was a seed* inside a circle. Then have them draw pictures showing things that grew from seeds to form an idea web.

On Level

Leveled Reader Lesson 2

Objective   Reread *From Seed to Plant* to apply skills and strategies to retell a story

Materials   • **Leveled Reader:** *From Seed to Plant*

BEFORE READING

- Ask children to look through *From Seed to Plant* and recall what the book is about. Reinforce vocabulary by repeating children's sentences using more sophisticated language. For example: *Yes, tomato seeds are small. They are smaller than melon seeds, aren't they?*

- Discuss the purposes for reading various texts. Have students compare what they learned in this book to what they learned in *Seed Secrets.*

DURING READING

- Have children join you in a choral-reading of the story. Model reading with expression. *I read the sentence on page 8 with a little more excitement. That sentence ends with an exclamation point. I want to say that sentence with more emphasis.* Ask children to use the same kind of expression when they read.

- Assign each child a page. Have children practice by whisper-reading. *Follow along as other children read, and be ready to come in when it is your turn. Remember, use lots of expression.*

AFTER READING

- Have children retell the important facts from the text.

- *Look at pages 2 and 3. What kind of seeds do you see? What do they turn into? What can you tell me about pumpkin or melon seeds?*

- Have children make connections to their own experiences. *Have you ever planted a seed? Did it grow into a plant? How did you care for it?*

Beyond Level

Leveled Reader Lesson 2

Objective   Reread *Seeds, Seeds, Seeds* to apply skills and strategies to retell a story

Materials   • **Leveled Reader:** *Seeds, Seeds, Seeds!*

BEFORE READING

- Ask children to look back at *Seeds, Seeds, Seeds!* and recall what the book is about. Ask: *How are pumpkin seeds and sunflower seeds the same? How are they different?*

- Discuss the purposes for reading various texts.

DURING READING

- Assign each child a page of the book to read aloud. Have children practice by whisper-reading. *Follow along as each child reads, and be ready to come in when it is your turn. Remember, use lots of expression.*

AFTER READING

- Explain that some stories have special pictures and labels that tell more information. Turn to pages 4 and 5. Point out the photos of plants and the inset photos that show the seeds of a pumpkin, an apple, and an oak tree. Model using special text features.

Expand Vocabulary

Objective   Brainstorm words for places to grow seeds

Materials   • **Leveled Reader:** *Seeds, Seeds, Seeds!*

ENRICH: *words for places to grow seeds*

Gifted & Talented

- Reread the sentence on page 6: *Seeds need sun, water, and soil. They need a place to grow. Seeds can grow in a field. They can grow in your backyard!* Have children find the words that describe the places seeds can grow. (*field, backyard*)

- Draw a word web on the board. Write *Where to grow seeds* in the center circle and write the words *field* and *backyard* in surrounding circles.

- Reread the sentences on page 12: *Here is a cornfield. The corn grew from corn seeds.* Have children find the word that describes where corn grows. (*cornfield*) Add *cornfield* to the word web.

- Browse through the book with children. Ask them to name more words for places seeds can grow and write them on the word web. Have children make up sentences using words in the web.

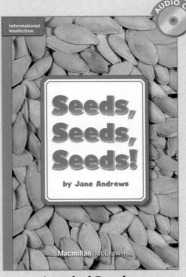

Leveled Reader

ON YOUR OWN

Make a Math Chart

Provide a three-column chart. Have children label one column *No Seeds,* the second column *Some Seeds,* and the third column *Many Seeds.* Children can draw and label pictures of fruits or vegetables in each column.

ELL

Partners When children make up sentences, pair English Language Learners with children who are more proficient.

ELL ENGLISH LANGUAGE LEARNERS

Fluency

Content Objectives Reread the Decodable Reader to develop fluency; develop speaking skills

Language Objective Tell a partner what a selection is about

Materials • **Decodable Reader:** *A Bud Is Up*

REREAD FOR FLUENCY

Beginning

- Review the high-frequency words **here**, **was**, **and**, **what**, **little**, and **said** using the **Read/Spell/Write** routine.

Intermediate/Advanced

- Use each word in a sentence that illustrates its use, such as: *Here is my desk*. Point to your desk. *What else is here?* Gesture around your desk and name items.

- Then provide sentence starters for children to complete. Where appropriate, act out children's responses. For example: *Here are Jaime and Marta.*

All Language Levels

- Guide children through a choral-reading of *A Bud Is Up*. Point to the numbers on page 3. Tell children that these numbers tell us we are reading the steps in a process. Model reading the sentences and have children chorally repeat.

DEVELOP SPEAKING/LISTENING SKILLS

All Language Levels

- Have children reread *A Bud Is Up* to a partner. Remind them to listen carefully and follow along in their book as their partner is reading. Work with children to read with accuracy and appropriate expression.

- Ask children to tell their partner about the pictures on each page. Then have the other partner describe the pictures. Circulate, listen in, and provide additional language as needed.

Beginning	Intermediate	Advanced
Confirm Understanding Point to the pictures for partners to identify. Ask: What do you see? Restate the correct answer in a complete sentence.	**Express Opinions** Ask partners to tell you which is their favorite picture in the book. Prompt them to explain why it is their favorite picture.	**Compare and Contrast** Have partners compare two different pictures and describe them. Prompt them to explain how they are alike and different.

ELL ENGLISH LANGUAGE LEARNERS

High-Frequency Words

Content Objective Spell high-frequency words correctly.
Language Objective Write in complete sentences, using sentence frames
Materials • **Sound-Spelling WorkBoards** • **Sound-Spelling Cards** • **Photo Cards**

Beginning/Intermediate

■ Write the high-frequency words **here** and **was** on the board. Have children copy the words on their **WorkBoards**. Then help them say, then write a sentence for each word. Provide the sentence starters *Here is a* _____ and *It was* _____.

Advanced

■ Children should first orally state each sentence. Correct as needed. Then they can draw a picture to complete the sentence. For children who are ready, help them spell words using their growing knowledge of English sound-spelling relationships. Model how to segment the word children are trying to spell and attach a spelling to each sound. Use the **Sound-Spelling Cards** to reinforce the spellings for each English sound.

Writing

All Language Levels

■ Say the word *up* and ask children to write it. Point upward as you say *up*. Then use the word in context: *Look up!* Have children write the word five times as they say *up*. Demonstrate correct letter formation, as needed.

■ Then display a set of **Photo Cards**. Select at least five cards whose picture names begin with /u/ (*umpire, under, undershirt, up, upside down*) and three whose picture names begin with /k/ (*koala, key, kitten*).

■ Say the name of each card, stretching or reiterating the initial sound to emphasize it. You may also need to model correct mouth formation when forming the sound. Use the articulation pictures and prompts on the back of the small **Sound-Spelling Cards** for support. Tell children to write the first letter in each picture name on their **WorkBoards**.

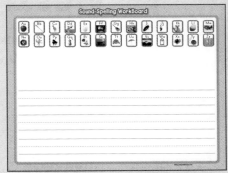

Sound-Spelling WorkBoard

Phonemic Awareness/ Phonics

For English Language Learners who need more practice with this week's phonemic awareness and phonics skills, see the Approaching Level lessons. Focus on minimal contrasts, articulation, and those sounds that do not transfer from the child's first language to English. For a complete listing of transfer sounds, see pages T10–T31.

Weekly Assessment

Use your Quick Check observations and the assessment opportunities identified below to evaluate children's progress in key skill areas.

Skills		Quick Check Observations	Pencil and Paper Assessment
PHONEMIC AWARENESS/ PHONICS /u/u	u	1913	Activity Book, pp. 14, 19–20, 22 Practice Book, pp. 167, 171
HIGH-FREQUENCY WORDS *here, was*	here	1934	Activity Book, pp. 17–18 Practice Book, pp. 169–170
COMPREHENSION Retell		1924	Activity Book, pp. 15–16, 21 Practice Book, p. 168

Quick Check Rubric

Skills	1	2	3
PHONEMIC AWARENESS/ PHONICS	Does not connect the sound /u/ with the letter *Uu* and has difficulty blending the CVC words *run, but, pup, bun, sun, pat, top, cap, sip, big, bad.*	Usually connects the sound /u/ with the letter *Uu* and blends the CVC words *run, but, pup, bun, sun, pat, top, cap, sip, big, bad* with only occasional support.	Consistently connects the sound /u/ with the letter *Uu* and blends the CVC words *run, but, pup, bun, sun, pat, top, cap, sip, big, bad.*
HIGH-FREQUENCY WORDS	Does not identify the high-frequency words.	Usually recognizes the high-frequency words with accuracy, but not speed.	Consistently recognizes the high-frequency words with speed and accuracy.
COMPREHENSION	Does not retell using the pictures and text.	Usually retells using the pictures and text.	Consistently retells using the pictures and text.

DIBELS LINK

PROGRESS MONITORING
Use your DIBELS results to inform instruction.
IF...
Initial Sound Fluency (ISF)   0–34

THEN...
Evaluate for Intervention

TPRI LINK

PROGRESS MONITORING
Use your TPRI scores to inform instruction.
IF...
Phonemic Awareness   Still Developing
Graphophonemic Knowledge   Still Developing
Listening Comprehension   Still Developing

THEN...
Evaluate for Intervention

Diagnose		Prescribe
Review the assessment answers with children. Have them correct their errors. Then provide additional instruction as needed.		
PHONEMIC AWARENESS/ PHONICS /u/*u*	**IF...** **Quick Check Rubric:** Children consistently score 1 or **Pencil and Paper Assessment:** Children get 0–2 items correct	**THEN...** Reteach Phonemic Awareness and Phonics Skills using the **Phonemic Awareness** and **Phonics Intervention Teacher's Editions**. Use the Build Fluency lesson in upcoming weeks to provide children practice reading words with /u/*u*.
HIGH-FREQUENCY WORDS *here, was*	**Quick Check Rubric:** Children consistently score 1 or **Pencil and Paper Assessment:** Children get 0–2 items correct	Reteach High-Frequency Words using the **Phonics Intervention Teacher's Edition**. Use the High-Frequency Words lesson in upcoming weeks to provide children practice reading the word *here* and *was*.
COMPREHENSION Skill: Retell	**Quick Check Rubric:** Children consistently score 1 or **Pencil and Paper Assessment:** Children get 0–2 items correct	Reteach Comprehension Skill using the **Comprehension Intervention Teacher's Edition**.

Response to Intervention

To place children in Tier 2 or Tier 3 Intervention use the *Diagnostic Assessment*.

Tier 2

- Phonemic Awareness
- Phonics
- Vocabulary
- Comprehension
- Fluency

Tier 3

Week 3 ★ At a Glance

Priority Skills and Concepts

 Comprehension
- **Genre:** Folktale, Fiction, Expository
- **Strategy:** Recognize Story Structure
- **Skill:** Draw Conclusions

 Skill: Identify Sequence of Events

 High-Frequency Words
- *little*, *said*, *here*, *was*

Oral Vocabulary
- Build Robust Vocabulary: *arrange*, *basic*, *garden*, *senses*, *tend*

Fluency
- Echo-Read
- Word Automaticity

 Phonemic Awareness
- Phoneme Isolation
- Phoneme Segmentation
- Phoneme Deletion
- Phoneme Blending

 Phonics
- *Uu, Kk, Ll*

Grammar
- Describing Words (Adjectives)

Writing
- Poems

Key    Tested in Program   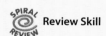 Review Skill

Digital Learning

Digital solutions to help plan and implement instruction

☑ Teacher Resources

LOG ON ▶

ONLINE www.macmillanmh.com

▶ **Teacher's Edition**
- Lesson Planner and Resources also on CD-ROM

TeacherWorks™ Plus

▶ **Professional Development**
- Video Library

Professional Development

☑ Student Resources

LOG ON ▶

ONLINE www.macmillanmh.com

▶ **Leveled Reader Database**

▶ **Activities**
- Oral Language Activities
- Phonics Activities
- Vocabulary/Spelling Activities

Listening Library
- Recordings of Literature Big Books, Read-Aloud Trade Books, and Leveled Readers

Weekly Literature

Theme: What's in My Garden?

A mix of fiction and nonfiction

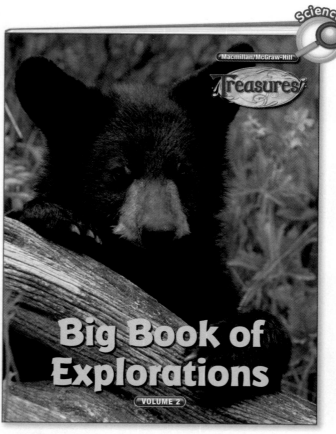

Trade Book

Genre Fiction

Big Book of Explorations

Genre Expository

Support Literature

**Interactive
Read-Aloud Anthology**

Genre Folktale

Oral Vocabulary Cards

• Listening Comprehension
• Build Robust Vocabulary

Decodable Reader

Resources for Differentiated Instruction

Leveled Readers

GR Levels A-G

Genre	Fiction

- Same Theme
- Same Vocabulary/Phonics
- Same Comprehension Skills

A

Approaching Level

C

On Level

G

Beyond Level

B

ELL

Leveled Reader Database
Go to www.macmillanmh.com.

Practice

Activity Book

Practice Book

ELL Practice Book

Response to Intervention

Tier 2

- Phonemic Awareness
- Phonics
- Vocabulary
- Comprehension
- Fluency

Tier 3

Unit Assessment

Assess Unit Skills

- Phonemic Awareness
- Phonics
- High-Frequency Words
- Listening Comprehension

HOME-SCHOOL CONNECTION

- Family letters in English and Spanish
- Take-home stories and activities

Go to **www.macmillanmh.com** for Online Lesson Planner

Professional Development Video Library

Trade Book

WHOLE GROUP

ORAL LANGUAGE

- **Oral Vocabulary**
- **Phonemic Awareness**

WORD STUDY

- **Phonics**
- **High-Frequency Words**

READING

- **Listening Comprehension**
- **Apply Phonics and High-Frequency Words**
- **Fluency**

LANGUAGE ARTS

- **Writing**
- **Grammar**

ASSESSMENT

- **Informal/Formal**

DAY 1

? Focus Question If you had a little garden here, what would you grow?

Build Background, 1994

Oral Vocabulary *arrange, basic, garden, senses, tend*, 1994

✓ **Phonemic Awareness**
Phoneme Isolation, 1997

✓ **Phonics**
Review: /k/k, /u/u, /l/l, /b/b, 1998
Handwriting: Review *Uu, Kk*, 1999
Activity Book, 24
Practice Book, 173

✓ **High-Frequency Words**
little , said , here , was , 1996

Share the Trade Book
Sunflower House
Strategy: Recognize Story Structure, 1995
✓ **Skill:** Draw Conclusions, 1995

Trade Book

Shared Writing
A List, 2001
Grammar
Describing Words (Adjectives), 2000

Quick Check Phonemic Awareness, 1997

DAY 2

? Focus Question If you had a little sunflower house here, what would you do in it?

Oral Vocabulary *arrange, basic, garden, senses, tend*, 2002

Position Words, 2009

✓ **Phonemic Awareness**
Phoneme Segmentation, 2010

✓ **Phonics**
Cumulative Review: /u/u, /k/k, /b/b, /l/l, 2010
Blend with -*ot*, 2011

✓ **Review High-Frequency Words**, 2012

Reread the Trade Book
Sunflower House
Strategy: Recognize Story Structure, 2004
✓ **Skill:** Draw Conclusions, 2004
Retell, 2008
Decodable Reader: *Pick It!*, 2012
Activity Book, 25–26
Practice Book, 174
Fluency Echo-Read, 2008

Trade Book

Interactive Writing
A Poem, 2013

Quick Check Comprehension, 2008

SMALL GROUP Lesson Plan ⟩ Differentiated Instruction 1988–1989

Priority Skills

Half-Day Kindergarten

Teach Core Skills
Focus on tested skill lessons, other lessons, and small group options as your time allows.

Phonemic Awareness/Phonics	High-Frequency Words	Oral Vocabulary	Comprehension
Review /u/u, /k/k, /l/l, /b/b	*little, said, here, was*	Position Words	**Strategy:** Recognize Story Structure **Skill:** Draw Conclusions

DAY 3

❓ **Focus Question** A tomato plant was once a little seed. Was an apple tree a seed?

Oral Vocabulary *arrange, basic, garden, senses, tend,* 2014

Oral Vocabulary Cards: "Anansi and the Melon"

✔ **Phonemic Awareness**
Phoneme Deletion, 2019

✔ **Phonics**
Cumulative Review, 2020

Blend with -*op*, 2021

Read Words, 2021

✔ **High-Frequency Words**
little, *said*, *here*, *was*, 2018

Activity Book: "Little Red," 27–28

Practice Book, 175–176

Read for Fluency, 2018

Read the Big Book of Explorations:
"How Does a Garden Grow?," 29–32

Text Feature: Photographs, 2016

Big Book of Explorations

Independent Writing
Prewrite and Draft Poems, 2023

Grammar
Describing Words (Adjectives), 2022

Quick Check High-Frequency Words, 2018

DAY 4

❓ **Focus Question** What tools do you use in a little garden?

Oral Vocabulary *arrange, basic, garden, senses, tend,* 2024

Position Words, 2027

✔ **Phonemic Awareness**
Phoneme Blending, 2028

✔ **Phonics**
Review, 2028

Blend with -*ick* and -*uck*, 2029

Activity Book, 29–30

Practice Book, 177

✔ **Review High-Frequency Words**, 2030

Interactive Read Aloud
Listening Comprehension, 2026

Read Aloud: "The Rabbit and the Elephant"

Decodable Reader: *Pick It!,* 2030

Read Aloud

Fluency Reread for Fluency, 2030

Independent Writing
Revise and Edit Poems, 2031

Quick Check Phonics, 2029

DAY 5
Review and Assess

❓ **Focus Question** Which story about gardens was the best?

Oral Vocabulary *arrange, basic, garden, senses, tend,* 2032

Position Words, 2034

✔ **Phonemic Awareness**
Phoneme Segmentation, 2035

✔ **Phonics**
Read Words, 2036

Dictation, 2036

Activity Book, 32

✔ **High-Frequency Words**
little, *said*, *here*, *was*, *and*, *what*, 2034

Read Across Texts
Strategy: Recognize Story Structure, 2033

✔ **Skill:** Draw Conclusions, 2033

Activity Book, 31

Fluency Word Automaticity, 2034

Independent Writing
Publish and Present Poems, 2037

✔ **Weekly Assessment, 2064–2065**

Differentiated Instruction

What do I do in small groups?

Teacher-Led Small Groups

Independent Activities

Focus on Skills

IF... children need additional instruction, practice, or extension based on your **Quick Check** observations for the following priority skills

 Phonemic Awareness
Phoneme Isolation, Segmentation, Deletion, Blending

 Phonics
Uu, Kk, Ll

 High-Frequency Words
little, *said*, *here*, *was*

 Comprehension
Strategy: Recognize Story Structure
Skill: Draw Conclusions

THEN...
Approaching	Preteach and
ELL	Reteach Skills
On Level	Practice
Beyond	Enrich and Accelerate Learning

 LOG ON ▶ **Suggested Small Group Lesson Plan**

	DAY 1	DAY 2
Approaching Level		

Tier 2 • **Preteach/Reteach** **Tier 2 Instruction**	• Oral Language, 2038
	• High-Frequency Words, 2038 **ELL**
	  High-Frequency Words Review, 2038
	• Phonemic Awareness, 2039
	• Phonics, 2039 **ELL**
	  Sound-Spellings Review, 2039
		• Oral Language, 2044
		• High-Frequency Words, 2044 **ELL**
		  Phonemic Awareness, 2045
		• Phonics, 2045

On Level • **Practice**	• High-Frequency Words, 2040 • Phonemic Awareness/Phonics, 2040 **ELL**	• Phonics, 2046
Beyond Level • **Extend/Accelerate** **Gifted and Talented**	• High-Frequency Words/Vocabulary, 2041 **ELL** Expand Oral Vocabulary, 2041 • Phonics, 2041	• Phonics, 2046
ELL • **Build English Language Proficiency** • See **ELL** in other levels.	• Oral Language Warm-Up, 2042 • Academic Language, 2042 • Vocabulary, 2043	• Access to Core Content, 2047

Focus on Leveled Readers

Levels A–G

Approaching

On Level

Beyond

ELL

Additional Leveled Readers

LOG ON **Leveled Reader Database**
www.macmillanmh.com

Search by
- Comprehension Skill
- Content Area
- Genre
- Text Feature
- Guided Reading Level
- Reading Recovery Level
- Lexile Score
- Benchmark Level

Subscription also available

Manipulatives

Sound-Spelling WorkBoards

Sound-Spelling Cards

Photo Cards

like
bike
High-Frequency Word Cards

Visual Vocabulary Resources

DAY 3

- High-Frequency Words, 2048 **ELL**
- Phonemic Awareness, 2048
- Phonics, 2049
- Decodable Reader, 2049

- Decodable Reader, 2050

- Decodable Reader, 2050

- Access to Core Content, 2051
- Grammar, 2051

DAY 4

- Phonemic Awareness, 2052
- Phonics, 2052 **ELL**
- Leveled Reader Lesson 1, 2053

- Leveled Reader Lesson 1, 2054 **ELL**

- Leveled Reader Lesson 1, 2055
  Synthesize, 2055

- Leveled Reader, 2056–2057

DAY 5

- Phonemic Awareness, 2058
- Phonics, 2058 **ELL**
- Leveled Reader Lesson 2, 2059
- High-Frequency Words, 2059

- Leveled Reader Lesson 2, 2060

- Leveled Reader Lesson 2, 2061
- Expand Vocabulary, 2061 **ELL**

- Fluency, 2062
- High-Frequency Words, 2063
- Writing, 2063

Managing the Class

What do I do with the rest of my class?

- Activity Book
- Practice Book
- ELL Practice Book
- Leveled Reader Activities
- Literacy Workstations
- Online Activities
- Buggles and Beezy

Classroom Management Tools

Weekly Contract

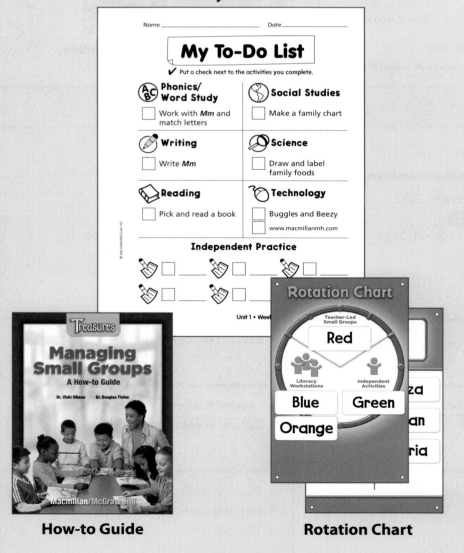

Name _____ Date _____

My To-Do List

✔ Put a check next to the activities you complete.

(ABC) Phonics/ Word Study
☐ Work with *Mm* and match letters

🌐 Social Studies
☐ Make a family chart

✏ Writing
☐ Write *Mm*

🔬 Science
☐ Draw and label family foods

📖 Reading
☐ Pick and read a book

🌰 Technology
☐ Buggles and Beezy
☐ www.macmillanmh.com

Independent Practice

Unit 1 • Week

How-to Guide

Treasures
Managing Small Groups
A How-to Guide
Dr. Vicki Gibson   Dr. Douglas Fisher
Macmillan/McGraw-Hill

Rotation Chart

Rotation Chart
Teacher-Led Small Groups
Red
Literacy Workstations   Independent Activities
Blue   **Green**
Orange

Digital Learning

Phonics Activities

- Match Letters
- Match Letters to Sounds
- Blend Words

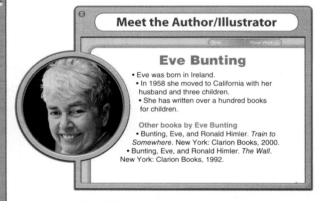

Meet the Author/Illustrator

Eve Bunting

- Eve was born in Ireland.
- In 1958 she moved to California with her husband and three children.
- She has written over a hundred books for children.

Other books by Eve Bunting
- Bunting, Eve, and Ronald Himler. *Train to Somewhere*. New York: Clarion Books, 2000.
- Bunting, Eve, and Ronald Himler. *The Wall*. New York: Clarion Books, 1992.

- Read Other Books by the Author or Illustrator

Practice

Activity Book

Treasures
Practice Book

Practice Book

Treasures
English Language Learner Practice Book

ELL Practice Book

Independent Activities

 LOG ON

ONLINE INSTRUCTION www.macmillanmh.com

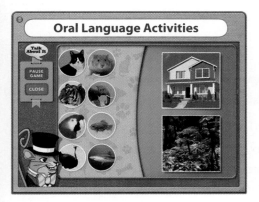

Oral Language Activities

- Focus on Unit Vocabulary and Concepts
- English Language Learner Support

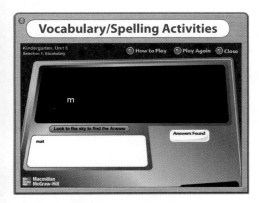

Vocabulary/Spelling Activities

- Differentiated Lists and Activities

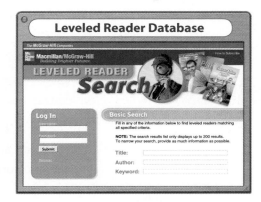

Leveled Reader Database

- Leveled Reader Database
- Search titles by level, skill, content area, and more

Available on CD

LISTENING LIBRARY
Recordings of selections
- Literature Big Books
- Read-Aloud Trade Books
- Leveled Readers
- ELL Readers

NEW ADVENTURES WITH BUGGLES AND BEEZY
Phonemic awareness and phonics activities

Leveled Reader Activities

Approaching

On Level

Beyond

ELL

See inside cover of all Leveled Readers.

Literacy Workstations

See lessons on pages 1992–1993.

Managing the Class

What do I do with the rest of my class?

 Reading

Objectives

- Read and discuss a book with a group
- Read a magazine aloud

 Phonics/Word Study

Objectives

- Use Word Cards to make and read sentences
- Read and sort words

Reading — Book Club — 20 Minutes

Read and talk about a book with friends.

❶ Sit in a circle.　❷ Read the book together.　❸ Talk about it.

Do More
- Listen to the CD of *Sunflower House*.
- Talk about the characters.

For more book titles, go to the Meet the Author/Illustrator page on www.macmillanmh.com

© Macmillan/McGraw-Hill

47

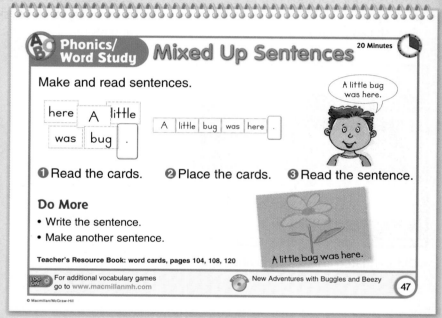

Phonics/Word Study — Mixed Up Sentences — 20 Minutes

Make and read sentences.

here　A　little　was　bug　.

A little bug was here .

A little bug was here.

❶ Read the cards.　❷ Place the cards.　❸ Read the sentence.

Do More
- Write the sentence.
- Make another sentence.

Teacher's Resource Book: word cards, pages 104, 108, 120

A little bug was here.

For additional vocabulary games go to www.macmillanmh.com

New Adventures with Buggles and Beezy

© Macmillan/McGraw-Hill

47

Reading — Book Buddies — 20 Minutes

Read a magazine to a puppet friend.

❶ Make a buddy.　❷ Read to your buddy.

Do More
- Read a book to a partner's buddy.
- Draw the beginning, middle, and end of the book.

For more book titles, go to the Meet the Author/Illustrator page on www.macmillanmh.com

© Macmillan/McGraw-Hill

48

Phonics/Word Study — Word Sort — 20 Minutes

Read and sort words.

sick　pop　hip　pick　sip　hop

hop　sick　sip　pop　pick　hip

❶ Read the words.　❷ Sort the words.

Do More
- Sort the words another way.
- Write new words and sort them.

Teacher's Resource Book: word family cards, pages 116–118

For additional vocabulary games go to www.macmillanmh.com

New Adventures with Buggles and Beezy

© Macmillan/McGraw-Hill

48

Literacy Workstations

 **Reading**  **Phonics/ Word Study**  **Writing**  **Science/ Social Studies**

Literacy Workstation Flip Charts

 ## Writing

Objectives

- Write a story about things that grow
- Write sentences about seeds and plants

 ## Content Literacy

Objectives

- Draw and label a flower
- Draw a simple map of a garden

Writing — Living Things — 20 Minutes

Write a story about a living thing.

❶ Draw a character.
❷ Finish the sentence.
❸ Write another sentence.

Do More
- Add more sentences to the story.

47

© Macmillan/McGraw-Hill

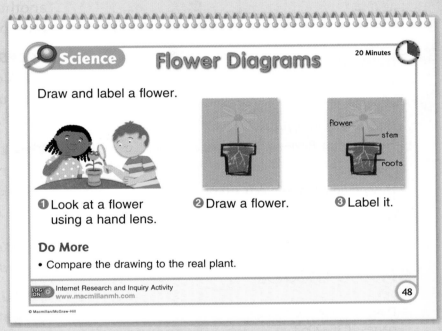

Science — Flower Diagrams — 20 Minutes

Draw and label a flower.

❶ Look at a flower using a hand lens.
❷ Draw a flower.
❸ Label it.

Do More
- Compare the drawing to the real plant.

Internet Research and Inquiry Activity
www.macmillanmh.com

48

© Macmillan/McGraw-Hill

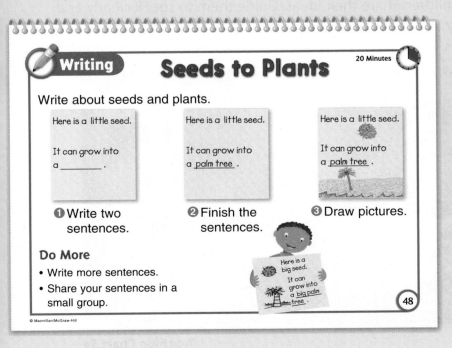

Writing — Seeds to Plants — 20 Minutes

Write about seeds and plants.

Here is a little seed.
It can grow into a _____.

Here is a little seed.
It can grow into a _palm tree_.

Here is a little seed.
It can grow into a _palm tree_.

❶ Write two sentences.
❷ Finish the sentences.
❸ Draw pictures.

Do More
- Write more sentences.
- Share your sentences in a small group.

48

© Macmillan/McGraw-Hill

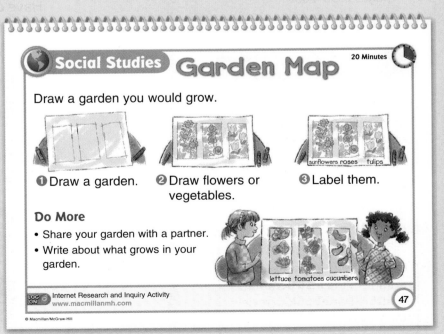

Social Studies — Garden Map — 20 Minutes

Draw a garden you would grow.

❶ Draw a garden.
❷ Draw flowers or vegetables.
❸ Label them.

Do More
- Share your garden with a partner.
- Write about what grows in your garden.

Internet Research and Inquiry Activity
www.macmillanmh.com

47

© Macmillan/McGraw-Hill

WHOLE GROUP

Oral Language
- Build Background

✓ **Comprehension**
- Read *Sunflower House*
- Strategy: Recognize Story Structure
- Skill: Draw Conclusions

✓ **High-Frequency Words**
- Review *here*, *little*, *said*, *was*

✓ **Phonemic Awareness**
- Phoneme Isolation

✓ **Phonics**
- Review /k/k, /u/u, /l/l, /b/b
- Handwriting: Review *Uu, Kk*

Grammar
- Describing Words (Adjectives)

Writing
- Shared Writing: A List

SMALL GROUP

- Differentiated Instruction, pages 2038–2063

Oral Vocabulary

Week 3

arrange	basic
garden	senses
tend	

Review

gradually	moist
necessary	observe
seed	

Use the **Define/Example/Ask** routine in the **Instructional Routine Handbook** to review the words.

Oral Language

 Talk About It ## Build Background: *What's in My Garden?*

INTRODUCE THE THEME

Tell children that this week they will be reading and talking about what grows in **gardens**, such as roses, apple trees, or grass.

Write the following question on the board: *If you had a little garden here, what would you grow?* Frame the word *you*. Point to each letter as you name it. *This is the first letter in the word* you. *The letter is* y. *This is the last letter in the word* you. *The letter is* u. Have a child choose another word and point to and name the first and last letters. Then prompt children to answer the question.

ACCESS PRIOR KNOWLEDGE

- Ask children to imagine that they are walking through a garden. *We use our* **senses** *to learn about the world. We touch, taste, smell, hear, and see things.*

Think Aloud Let's look at the picture. I see a girl with a butterfly on her hand. (**Point to the girl, butterfly, and hand.**) She is looking at the butterfly and can feel it on her hand. I wonder if she can hear the butterfly move its wings.

- *Picture a garden in your mind. How would you use your senses? What would you see, hear, taste, touch, or smell in the garden?*

DISCUSS THE PHOTOGRAPH

Look at and discuss the photograph of the girl with the butterfly. Have children share their ideas. Guide them to speak clearly and audibly. Ask them if they have ever planted a garden with their families. *What flowers, fruits, or vegetables might grow in a garden?*

Teaching Chart 54

Share the Trade Book

Listening Comprehension

PREVIEW Display the cover. *I see a boy looking at big flowers. I wonder if these are sunflowers.* Point to the flowers and boy as you talk. *Let's read about a boy who plants flowers in his **garden**.*

Read the title and the names of the author and illustrator. *What are some words that describe these flowers?*

Trade Book

GENRE: LITERARY TEXT/FICTION
*This story is **fiction**, which means it did not really happen.*

 STRATEGY **Recognize Story Structure**

EXPLAIN/MODEL Tell children that stories follow a structure. They have a beginning, middle, and end.

Think Aloud The book is called *Sunflower House*. There is a picture of a boy looking at huge sunflowers. Maybe the beginning of the book tells about planting the flowers. Let's read to find out.

 SKILL **Draw Conclusions**

EXPLAIN/MODEL Tell children that they can use the **key events** in a story and their own experiences to learn things that may not be stated in the story.

Think Aloud I'll pay attention to all of the information in the beginning, middle, and end of the story to see if there are things I can learn that are not said in the words.

Read the Trade Book

SET PURPOSE Have children pay attention to the story's beginning, middle, and end as they draw conclusions. Use the **Define/Example/Ask** routine to teach the story words on the inside back cover.

Respond to Literature

MAKE CONNECTIONS *What is a main event in the story? Will the boy have a sunflower house next year? Where do sunflowers grow in your community?* Have children draw and write their opinion of the story.

Objectives

- Discuss the theme
- Identify first and last letters in words
- Use oral vocabulary words *senses* and *garden*
- Listen and respond to a story
- Recognize story structure/ draw conclusions

Materials

- Teaching Chart 54
- Read-Aloud Trade Book: *Sunflower House*

ELL

Use the Interactive Question-Response Guide for *Sunflower House*, **ELL Resource Book** pages 222–229, to guide children through a reading of the book. As you read *Sunflower House*, make meaning clear by pointing to the pictures, demonstrating word meanings, paraphrasing text, and asking children questions.

Digital Learning

Story on **Listening Library Audio CD**

Objectives

- Read the high-frequency words *here, little, said, was*
- Review the high-frequency words *and, what*
- Identify the words *little, said, here, was* in text and speech

Materials

- High-Frequency Word Cards: *little, said, here, was, and, what*
- Teaching Chart 55

ELL

Reinforce Vocabulary
Review the high-frequency words *here, little, said, was, and, what*. Display the High-Frequency Words Cards *here, little, said, was, and, what*. Point to or hold classroom objects as you ask questions, such as: *What do you see here? Which is little, the pencil or the table? Who said the pencil was little? Where do we keep the pens and pencils?* Guide children to answer in complete sentences using the high-frequency words.

High-Frequency Words

 here, little, said, was

here

REVIEW Display the **High-Frequency Word Cards** for **here, little, said, was**. Use the **Read/Spell/Write** routine to teach the words.

■ **Read** Point to and say the word *here. I found a penny* here.

■ **Spell** *The word* here *is spelled* h-e-r-e. *What's the first sound in* here? *The first sound is /h/, and the first letter is* h. *There is an* r *in the middle of the word, but I hear the /r/ sound last because the last* e *is silent. Let's read and spell* here *together.*

■ **Write** *Now let's write the word* here *on our papers. Let's spell aloud the word as we write it:* here, h-e-r-e.

Repeat the routine with *little, said,* and *was*.

REVIEW *and, what* Display each High-Frequency Word Card and have children read the word. Repeat several times.

READ THE RHYME AND CHIME Have children point to the words *little, said, here,* and *was* each time they see them. Repeat the rhyme together for fluency.

Kick the Little Ball

Uncle Bob said, "Kick it here."
Uncle Rick said, "Kick it far."
Little Kate said, "Kick it up."
Where was the ball?
I kicked it under the car!

High-Frequency Words: little, said, here, was
Phonics: /k/k, /k/ck, /u/u

Unit 8
Rhyme and Chime

Plants · Week 3 55

Teaching Chart 55

For Tier 2 instruction, see page 2038.

TIME TO MOVE!

Have children sit in a circle. Place a few small items in the middle and point to an item. *Here is a little car.* Have children repeat the sentence, pointing to the item. Take the item away. Have children point to the empty space and say: *The little car was here.*

Phonemic Awareness

Phoneme Isolation

Model

Display the Photo Card for kite.

The sound at the beginning of kite is /k/. What is the sound?

Display the Photo Card for umbrella.

The sound at the beginning of umbrella is /u/. What is the sound?

Listen to the rhyme. Let's use a key when we hear a word that begins with /k/.

Say the "Kick the Little Ball" Rhyme and Chime again. Have children pretend to use a key in a lock every time they hear /k/.

Uncle Bob said, "Kick it here."
Uncle Rick said, "Kick it far."
Little Kate said, "Kick it up."
Where was the ball?
I kicked it under the car!

Repeat the rhyme.

Now let's point up when we hear a word that begins with /u/.

SPIRAL REVIEW

Review /b/, /l/

Display the Photo Card for ladybug.

This is a *ladybug*. The beginning sound in *ladybug* is /l/. What is the sound?

Repeat for balloon.

Guided Practice/Practice

Display and name the remaining Photo Cards. Children identify initial sounds. Guide practice with the first card using the same routine.

Say each picture name with me. Tell me the sound you hear at the beginning of the word.

Quick Check

Can children identify the initial /k/ and /u/ sounds?

During **Small Group Instruction**

If No → Approaching Level Provide additional practice, page 2039.

If Yes → On Level Children blend words with /k/ and /u/, page 2040.

Beyond Level Children read words with /k/ and /u/, page 2041.

Objective

• **Review initial /b/, /l/, /k/, /u/**

Materials

• **Photo Cards:** *baby, balloon, banana, bat, bike, boat, book, box, kangaroo, key, king, kite, kitten, koala, ladder, ladybug, lamp, leaf, lemon, lightning, lock, umbrella, umpire, under, undershirt, up, upside down*

ELL

Pronunciation Display and have children name Photo Cards from this and prior lessons to reinforce phonemic awareness and word meanings. Point to a card and ask: *What do you see?* (a kite) *What is the sound at the beginning of the word* kite? (/k/) Repeat using Photo Cards with words that begin with the /b/, /l/, and /u/ sounds.

Objectives

- Match letters to the initial sound for /k/k, /u/u, /l/l, /b/b
- Form uppercase and lowercase *Uu, Kk*

Materials

- Sound-Spelling Cards: *Bat, Koala, Lemon, Umbrella*
- Teaching Chart 55
- Word-Building Cards
- Handwriting
- Handwriting Teacher's Edition
- Activity Book, p. 24
- Practice Book, p. 173

Phonics

✔ Review /k/k, /u/u, /l/l, /b/b

Model

Display the *Umbrella* **Sound-Spelling Card**.

Repeat the routine for *Koala, Lemon, Bat*.

This letter is *u*. It stands for the /u/ sound you hear in *umbrella*. Say the sound with me: /u/. What is the name of this letter? What sound does this letter stand for?

Read "Kick the Little Ball." Reread the title. Point out that *Kick* begins with /k/. Model placing a self-stick note below the *K* in *Kick*.

Kick the Little Ball

Uncle Bob said, "Kick it here."
Uncle Rick said, "Kick it far."
Little Kate said, "Kick it up."
Where was the ball?
I kicked it under the car!

High-Frequency Words: little, said, here, was
Phonics: /k/k, /l/ck, /u/u

Plants Week 3   55

Unit 8
Rhyme and Chime

Teaching Chart 55

Guided Practice/Practice

Read the rest of the rhyme. Stop after each line. Children place self-stick notes below words that begin with *k*. Guide practice with *Kick* in line 1. Repeat with *u, l, b*.

Let's place a sticky note below the word in the line that begins with the letter *k*.

The word *kick* begins with the letter *k*.

Corrective Feedback

If children have difficulty with the letter-sound correspondence for /k/k, have them take turns writing or tracing the letter on the board. Have them name the letter, say the sound it stands for, and name a word that ends with that sound.

Build Fluency: Sound-Spellings

 Display the following **Word-Building Cards**: *a, b, c, d, e, f, h, i, k, l, m, n, o, p, r, s, t, u*. Have children chorally say each sound. Repeat and vary the pace.

Handwriting: Review *Uu, Kk*

MODEL Model holding up your writing hand. Say the handwriting cues from **Handwriting Teacher's Edition** pages 62–64 as you write the capital and lowercase forms of *Uu* and *Kk* on the board. Then trace the letters on the board and in the air as you say the sounds.

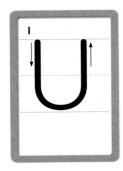  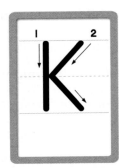 

PRACTICE Ask children to hold up their writing hand.

- Say the cues together as children trace with their index finger the letters you wrote on the board.

- Have children write *U and u* in the air as they say /u/. Then have children write *K and k* in the air as they say /k/ multiple times.

- Distribute handwriting practice pages. Observe children's pencil grip and paper position, and correct as necessary. Have children say /u/ every time they write the letter *u* and /k/ every time they write the letter *k*.

For Tier 2 instruction, see page 2039.

See page 2039.

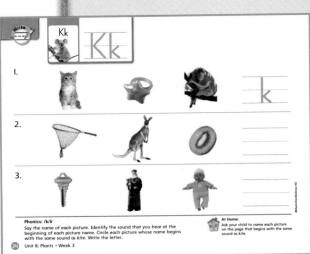

Activity Book, page 24
Practice Book, page 173

Objective

- Understand and use descriptive words (adjectives)

Materials

- Read-Aloud Trade Book: *Sunflower House*
- Photo Cards: *apple, banana, berries, butter, carrots, celery, cheese, cherry, corn, egg, grapes, juice, lemon, nut, olive, pea, peach, pear, pie, pizza, pumpkin, sandwich, soup, strawberry, vegetables, watermelon, yogurt, zucchini*
- chart paper with a drawing of an eye, nose, hand, ear, and mouth on it

ELL

Basic and Academic Vocabulary Display the Photo Cards from the lesson and pair English Language Learners with fluent speakers. Have partners make up sentences using the Photo Card for *pie* and a describing word. Write their sentences, read them chorally, and ask: *What describing word in your sentence tells about pie?*

Grammar
Describing Words (Adjectives)

MODEL Use the **Trade Book** *Sunflower House* to discuss descriptive words. Point to the illustrations on pages 12–13 of the Trade Book as you say: *The sunflowers in the garden are big and yellow.* Tell children that the sentence has two describing words that tell more about the sunflowers. Explain that you can use more than one word to tell more about something.

■ Explain that describing words help us tell what we learn from using our **senses**. *We see that the sunflowers are big and yellow.*

Ask children what other describing words they can use.

■ *What words might describe how the leaves of the sunflowers feel?*

■ *What words might describe how the leaves sound on a windy day?*

■ *What words might describe how the sunflowers smell?*

■ *What words might describe how the sunflower seeds taste?*

PRACTICE Show children the **Photo Card** for *soup* and name it. Tell children that you will think of ways to describe soup. Explain that you will use the senses chart to help you remember all of the senses and use the senses to help you describe soup.

I don't know what kind of soup this is, so I will think of a soup that I have had. That way, I can use my experience to describe the soup. I like tomato soup. Point to the eye on the senses chart. *Tomato soup is red.* Point to the nose. *It smells like tomatoes.* Point to the hand. *It feels warm and creamy.* Point to the ear. *I can hear it bubbling in the pot.* Point to the mouth. *It tastes salty. Which words did I use to describe soup?* (*red, warm, creamy, bubbling, salty*)

■ Distribute the remaining Photo Cards to children. Ask children to name the card and to use their senses to describe the pictured item. Tell them to use the senses chart to help them remember all of the senses. Have children share their descriptive words with the class.

Writing

Shared Writing: A List

BRAINSTORM

■ Remind children that in the **Trade Book** *Sunflower House,* they read a story about a boy who planted sunflower seeds in his **garden**. *What did the sunflowers look like? What might you learn about them with your other* **senses**?

WRITE

Make a list as shown. Read the title aloud with children.

■ Explain that children will list descriptive words to paint a picture of sunflowers in the reader's mind.

■ Model by describing the flowers on page 13. *The sunflowers are yellow, big, and bright. I'll write those words on the list.*

■ Continue displaying the book. Ask children to name other words to describe the sunflowers. Add their ideas to the list. Have children contribute by writing the letters and words they know.

■ Read the completed list together as you track the print.

■ Save the list to refer to in other writing activities this week.

Sunflowers are

| bright |
| yellow |
| big |
| mammoth |
| wide |
| golden |
| tall |
| puffy |
| brown |

Write About It

Ask children to draw a picture of something else that grows. Help them to write a caption.

Objective

• Write a list

Materials

• Read-Aloud Trade Book: *Sunflower House*

5-Day Writing

Poems	
DAY 1	Shared: A List
DAY 2	Interactive: A Poem
DAY 3	Independent: Prewrite and Draft Poems
DAY 4	Independent: Revise and Edit Poems
DAY 5	Independent: Publish and Present

ELL

Prewriting Planning Page through the Trade Book with children. Point to and describe the pictures. Check children's understanding of descriptive words by asking questions such as: *What in our classroom is yellow? Is a flagpole tall?*

Transitions That Teach

While packing up, have children name things that grow in a **garden**.

WHOLE GROUP

Oral Language
- Build Robust Vocabulary

✓ **Comprehension**
- Reread *Sunflower House*
- Strategy: Recognize Story Structure
- Skill: Draw Conclusions
- Fluency: Echo-Read

Vocabulary
- Position Words
- Story Words: *mammoth, castle*

✓ **Phonemic Awareness**
- Phoneme Segmentation

✓ **Phonics**
- Cumulative Review
- Blend with *-ot*
- Decodable Reader: *Pick It!*

Writing
- Interactive Writing: A Poem

SMALL GROUP

- Differentiated Instruction, pages 2038–2063

Oral Vocabulary

Week 3

arrange	basic	
garden	senses	tend

Review

gradually	moist	
necessary	observe	seed

Use the **Define/Example/Ask** routine in the **Instructional Routine Handbook** to review the words.

Oral Language

 Talk About It

Build Robust Vocabulary

INTRODUCE WORDS

Tell children that they are going to talk about the **Trade Book** *Sunflower House*. Display and read aloud pages 2–14. *I see the boy and his father planting a garden. A garden is a plot of land where plants such as flowers, fruits, and vegetables grow. What is the first thing the boy says he will do in his garden?* (pull out the weeds) *What is the next thing he does?* (sow seeds) Explain that the word *sow* means "to plant." *How do you use your senses in a garden?*

Vocabulary Routine

Use the routine below to discuss the meaning of each word.

Define: You have five **senses**: eyes to see, ears to hear, nose to smell, skin to touch and feel, and mouth to taste. Say the word with me.
Example: We use our sense of smell to enjoy the scent of flowers.
Ask: What senses do you use when you eat?

Define: A **garden** is a plot of land where plants such as flowers, fruits, and vegetables grow. Say the word with me.
Example: We planted sunflower seeds in the school garden.
Ask: If you had a garden, what would you grow in it?

CREATE A CHART

Create a three-column chart, or use **Teaching Chart G4**. Label and read the columns as you track the print. *I am thinking of the steps to growing a sunflower house. I know what happens first. I'll write the words* Pull out weeds *and* Sow the seeds *under* First. Tell children that the words *first, next,* and *last* are sequence words. Have them use these words as they add their ideas to the chart.

Continue by asking children what happens next and last and adding their ideas to the chart. Remind children to use complete sentences when speaking. Read the completed chart with children as you track the print.

Growing a Sunflower House

First	Next	Last
Pull out weeds.	Water the plants.	The stems grow.
Sow the seeds.	Shoo away the birds.	The petals open.

Listen for Rhyme

IDENTIFY RHYME

Remind children that rhyming words have the same ending sounds.

RHYME ABOUT A SEED

Let's say a rhyme about a seed from a big tree. Play the rhyme "I'm a Little Acorn Brown," using the **Listening Library Audio CD**. Then teach children the words and recite the rhyme together.

Tell children that acorns are nuts that contain seeds. They come from oak trees. If they are planted, they will grow into oak trees.

What are some other garden plants that have seeds? If children have difficulty answering the question, remind them that seeds are inside fruits and vegetables.

Recite the rhyme again. Ask children to name words that rhyme with *brown.* (*town, down, clown, frown*) Then ask children to name words that rhyme with *nut.* (*rut, hut, cut*)

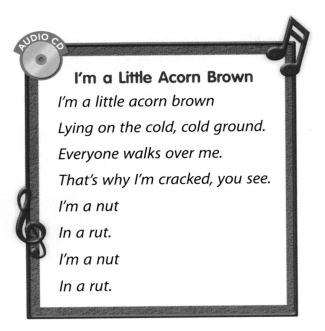

I'm a Little Acorn Brown

I'm a little acorn brown

Lying on the cold, cold ground.

Everyone walks over me.

That's why I'm cracked, you see.

I'm a nut

In a rut.

I'm a nut

In a rut.

ELL — ENGLISH LANGUAGE LEARNERS

Beginning

Confirm Understanding Have children use the illustrations to help them talk about the book. *This is the boy in his yard. Point to what the boy is holding. Is it a watering can? What do you think the boy will do with it?*

Intermediate

Enhance Understanding Ask children to use words on the chart to retell the story in sequence. Ask questions such as: *What did the boy do first, water the plants or sow the seeds? What happened after the stems grew?*

Advanced

Continue the Story Ask children to continue the story by adding to the chart what happens after the petals open.

Objectives

- Recognize story structure
- Draw conclusions
- Respond to a story
- Retell a story
- Develop fluency

Materials

- Read-Aloud Trade Book: *Sunflower House*
- Activity Book, pp. 25–26
- Practice Book, p. 174

Trade Book

Digital Learning

Story on **Listening Library Audio CD**

ELL

Gesture and Talk Use gestures and other strategies to make the text comprehensible.

pp. 4–7
Guide children to look at the pictures and act out the steps of *pulling weeds, planting seeds, watering plants,* and *shooing away birds.* Use the vocabulary from the story during this activity.

Reread the Trade Book

Listening Comprehension

CONCEPTS ABOUT PRINT Display the cover and read the title aloud with children as you track the print.

 STRATEGY **Recognize Story Structure**

Tell children that paying attention to how a book is organized can help them to understand it. Ask children to recall what happened in the beginning, middle, and end of the story.

 SKILL **Draw Conclusions**

Tell children that they can figure something out, such as a **key event**, that is not explained in the book, by following the **plot,** or what happens in a story, as well as their own experiences to draw conclusions.

Think Aloud The author doesn't tell us why the sunflowers are dying. I'll look for clues to see if I can figure out why they die.

Read the story and use the prompts on the inside back cover.

pages 4–5

 STORY STRUCTURE
Think Aloud In the beginning the boy and his father plant sunflower seeds. Seeds are how flowers begin.

pages 6–7

 DRAW CONCLUSIONS
Think Aloud The words do not tell us why the boy is shooing the birds away. He tells them to eat berries. I think the birds must be trying to eat the seeds.

Develop Comprehension

pages 8–9

pages 10–11

⭐ STORY STRUCTURE

Think Aloud In the beginning of the story, the sunflower plants are small. On these pages they are growing bigger. I think by the middle of the story, they will be taller than the boy.

pages 12–13

VOCABULARY

Think Aloud The sunflowers are *mammoth*. I wonder what that means? Let's read the sentence again. The sunflowers are really big. I think *mammoth* must mean "really big."

pages 14–15

⭐ STORY STRUCTURE

■ *In the beginning of the story, the boy planted sunflower seeds. What have the seeds turned into?* (They turned into a sunflower house.)

Comprehension

Recognize Story Structure

● *(pages 9–15)* At the beginning of the story, the boy planted sunflower seeds. Then the seeds grew bigger and bigger. Now the seeds have turned into a sunflower house.

Draw Conclusions

● *(pages 24–25)* The sunflower plants are falling over, but the author does not say why. I think it is probably the end of summer, when many plants start to fall over and die.

Story Word

(page 12) mammoth   *(page 17)* castle

About the Author: Eve Bunting

When Eve Bunting was growing up in Ireland, storytellers went from house to house telling folktales. After moving to California, she wrote her first children's book about an Irish giant and a Scottish giant. Since then, Eve has written lots of books about a variety of different subjects.

Trade Book
Inside Back Cover

ELL

pp. 10–11

circle, growing: Have each child draw a sunflower plant. Then have children crouch in a circle around you holding their pictures of sunflowers. Use your index finger to sweep around, indicating the circle of plants around you. *I am inside a circle. You are making the circle.* Then have children gradually stand to simulate their plants growing.

pp. 12–13

big, mammoth: Indicate the height of a life-size sunflower by placing a self-stick note on a wall 6 feet from the floor. Then point to the sunflowers on these pages. Say *big, very big, MAMMOTH!*

pp. 14–15

sunflower house: Have children repeat what they did for pages 10–11, but now hold their pictures high over their heads to indicate the flowers' growth. Look around and say: *I am inside the circle of sunflowers just like I am inside a house.*

Draw Conclusions

Explain Remind children that when they answer a question, they must support their answer with text evidence.

Discuss Have children look at and listen to pages 16–23. Ask them to follow the plot and use the story's pictures and what they already know to figure out what the sunflowers have become (a sunflower house Have children point to clues in the book that helped them draw this conclusion.

ELL

pp. 18–19

sleep out: Draw a simple cross-section view of a house. Point to the bedroom and say: *I sleep here. It is inside the house.* Then indicate the area outside of the house by drawing a tree and clouds in the sky. Point to this area and tell children that it is *outside.* Draw a sleeping bag and pillow and say: *Sometimes I sleep outside of the house.*

pp. 22–23

tumbling down: Pile up some blocks. Knock them down and say: *The blocks tumble down.*

Develop Comprehension

pages 16–17

PHONEMIC AWARENESS

- *Listen as I say a word from this page:* house. *What is the beginning sound in* house? (/h/)

pages 18–19

AUTHOR'S PURPOSE

- *The author used the words* bundled up *and* snuggled *to tell about the boys' night in the sunflower house. Did the author want to make the sunflower house sound scary or safe?* (safe) *How do you know?*

pages 20–21

⭐ **DRAW CONCLUSIONS**

- *The boy makes a wish that cannot come true. What do you think he might be wishing for?* (Possible answer: He wishes that the sunflower house lasts forever.)

pages 22–23

⭐ **DRAW CONCLUSIONS**

- *The sunflowers are turning brown and bending over. What do you think is happening?* (Possible answer: They are beginning to die.)

pages 24–25

 DRAW CONCLUSIONS

Think Aloud The sunflower plants are falling over, but the author does not say why. We said they might be dying. I think it is the end of summer, when many plants start to die.

pages 26–27

MAKE PREDICTIONS

- *The boy says* wait. *He must have had an idea. What do you think it is?* (Possible answer: to get the seeds from the sunflowers)

pages 28–29

 SEQUENCE OF EVENTS

- *When will there be another sunflower house?* (The sunflower house will grow back in the spring.)

pages 30–31

AUTHOR'S CRAFT

Think Aloud Listen as I reread the sentences and count the beats, or parts of words, in each line. Each line has eight beats. The author chose words very carefully so that there would be rhythm.

ELL

pp. 28–29

seeds: Call attention to the picture on page 29. If possible, show children some actual sunflower seeds.

Retelling Rubric

4 Excellent

Retells the selection without prompting, in sequence, and using supporting details. Clearly describes the setting, main characters, and complete plot.

3 Good

Retells the selection with little guidance, in sequence, and using some details. Generally describes the setting, main characters, and plot.

2 Fair

Retells the selection with some guidance, mostly in sequence, and using limited details. Partially describes the setting, main characters, and plot.

1 Unsatisfactory

Retells the selection only when prompted, out of sequence, and using limited details. Does not describe the main characters or plot.

page 32

 DRAW CONCLUSIONS

■ *How did the boy feel about his sunflower house?* (The author tells us that he is happy that he can have another one next year. I think that the boy really loved his sunflower house.)

Respond to Literature

TALK ABOUT IT Have children discuss the words and illustrations that they liked. Help them to speak audibly and in complete sentences. Refer to the book as they answer the following questions.

■ *What do the children take from the puffy middle part of the flowers at the end of the story?* LOCATE (seeds)

■ *How did the boy help the flowers grow?* COMBINE (He pulls weeds, sows seeds, waters them, and shoos birds away.)

■ *What conclusion can you draw about why the playhouse is special?* CONNECT (It is made from sunflowers that the boy grew.)

Retell

GUIDED RETELLING Have children retell main events in the story.

■ *What happened at the beginning of the story?* (The boy planted seeds, and they grew into big sunflowers.)

■ *What happened in the middle of the story?* (The boy used the sunflowers as a playhouse. His friends all played inside it.)

■ *What happened at the end of the story?* (The sunflowers died, and the boy and his friends saved the seeds and planted them.)

Fluency: Echo-Read

MODEL Reread page 7, using different voices for the narration and for the dialogue. Then reread page 9 and have children echo-read.

Quick Check

Can children draw conclusions to help understand a story?
Can children retell a main event from a story read aloud?

Vocabulary

Position Words

Chant the following jingle:

Look out *of the window.*

Look in *the drawer.*

Look under *the desk.*

Look over *the chair.*

■ Remind children that many position words are prepositions. When a preposition is used with a naming word, it is called a prepositional phrase. For example, *in the drawer.* The word *in* is the preposition and *drawer* is the naming word. Say the above sentences one at a time and have children identify the prepositional phrase.

■ Place a box on the floor. Give each child a few small items and have him or her follow directions using position words. For example: *Put the car* in *the box. Take it* out. *Put the pencil* under *the box.*

USE PREPOSITIONAL PHRASES Have children play "I Spy," taking turns saying clues using prepositional phrases. For example: *I spy something* under *the desk; I spy something* in *the box.*

Story Words: *mammoth, castle*

Display and read pages 12–13 of *Sunflower House* and point out the sunflowers. *Is the sunflower big or little? What word does the author use to describe it?* Explain that *mammoth* means "huge or really big."

Display and read pages 16–17 of *Sunflower House. The children pretend that the sunflower house is a* castle. *Who knows what a castle is?* Explain that a *castle* is a large house for a king or other royalty. *How might you describe a huge castle?*

TIME TO MOVE!

Have children sing and march in time to the following verse of "Old MacDonald": *Old MacDonald had a farm, E-I-E-I-O; And on that farm he had some sunflowers, E-I-E-I-O; With a sunflower here and a sunflower there; Here a sunflower, there a sunflower, everywhere a sunflower; Old MacDonald had a farm, E-I-E-I-O.*

Objectives

- **Identify and use position words**
- **Use prepositional phrases**
- **Learn story words** *mammoth, castle*

Materials

- **Read-Aloud Trade Book:** *Sunflower House*
- **box**
- **small items**

Digital Learning

 LOG ON For children who need additional language support and oral vocabulary development, use the activities found at **www.macmillanmh.com**.

ELL

Reinforce Meaning Say the following as you demonstrate the actions: *First, put your hand over your head. Next, put one hand under the other. Last, put your hand in and out of the box.* Repeat with children copying your actions. Continue with two or three other sets of actions involving position words.

`Objectives

- Segment sounds in words
- Review sound-spellings /u/u, /k/k, /b/b, /l/l
- Blend the sounds in words with -ot

Materials

- Sound Box
- WorkBoard Sound Boxes; Teacher's Resource Book, p. 136
- markers
- Word-Building Cards
- pocket chart

Phonemic Awareness

Phoneme Segmentation

Model

Use the **Sound Box** and markers.

Point to each box as you say the sounds.

Repeat with *lake*.

I am going to say each sound in the word *lick*. I'll place a marker in a box as I say each sound in *lick*: /lll/ /iii/ /k/. There are three sounds in *lick*: /lll/, /iii/, and /k/. So I put a marker in each box.

Say the sounds in *lick* with me: /l/ /i/ /k/.

Guided Practice/Practice

Distribute Sound Boxes and markers.

Children say the word and its sounds. Guide practice with the first row.

I will say a word. Say each sound in the word and put a marker in a box for each sound. Then we'll say the word and its sounds together.

/d/ /o/ /t/	/m/ /o/ /p/	/t/ /i /k/
/b/ /ī/ /t/	/p/ /i/ /k/	/h/ /ō/ /p/

Phonics

Cumulative Review

u k b l

Model

Hold up **Word-Building Card** *u*.

Repeat for the letters *b, k, l, o, t*.

This is the letter *u*. The letter *u* stands for /u/ at the beginning of *umbrella*. What is the letter? What sound does it stand for?

Say the word. Write the letter *u*.

Repeat with *bat, koala, lemon, octopus, turtle*.

Listen to the sound at the beginning of the word *umbrella*: /u/. I will write the letter *u* because *u* stands for the beginning /u/ sound.

Guided Practice/Practice

Children write the letter that stands for the initial sound. Do the first word with children.

Listen as I say each word. Write the letter that stands for the beginning sound.

kit	up	boy	lock	ox
us	kind	light	bike	time

Build Fluency: Sound-Spellings

 Display the following **Word-Building Cards**: *a, b, c, d, e, f, h, i, k, l, m, n, o, p, r, s, t, u*. Have children chorally say each sound. Repeat and vary the pace.

 Blend with -ot

Model

Place Word-Building Card *l* in the pocket chart.

This letter is *l*. The letter *l* stands for the /l/ sound.

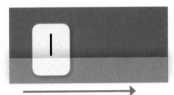

Place the letters *ot* in the pocket chart, leaving space after *l*.

These are the letters *o* and *t*. The letters *o* and *t* stand for the /o/ and /t/ sounds. Let's blend these two sounds together: /ooot/.

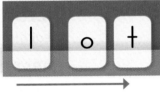

Place the letters *ot* closer to the letter *l*. Move your hand from left to right.

Repeat the routine with *hot*.

The beginning sound in the word is /l/, and the rest of the word is /ot/. Let's blend the beginning sound and the rest of the word together: /lllooot/, *lot*.

Guided Practice/Practice

Children blend the onset and rime in other words that end with -ot. Guide practice with the word *dot*, using the routine.

dot cot not

pot rot tot

What do you notice about the words *lot, hot, dot, cot, not, pot, rot,* and *tot*?

(They end with the letters *ot*; they end with the /ot/ sounds; they rhyme.)

ELL

Build Vocabulary Review the meanings of the words in the Guided Practice portion of the lesson. For example, tell children that a small circle is a *dot*. Draw a dot on the board. Have children draw and say *dot*.

Vowel Pairs
ACCELERATE

Explain Hold up the *Book* **Sound-Spelling Card.** *Two o's together can stand for the /ü/ sound in the word* book. Hold up the *Spoon* Sound-Spelling Card. *Two o's together can stand for the /ü/ sound we hear in the word* spoon. *What sounds can two o's together stand for?*

Model Place Word-Building Cards for *lock* in the pocket chart. Run a finger below the letters and say *lock*. Replace the *c* with *o*, track the print, and say *look*. Repeat for *tock/took*. Place Word-Building Cards for *rot* in the pocket chart. Track the print and say *rot*. Then add a second *o*, track the print, and say *root*. Repeat for *lot/loot*.

Guided Provide children with small Word-Building Cards. Assist them in building the following sets: *rock/rook, lock/look, tock/took*. Remind children that *oo* can make two sounds. Assist them in building the following sets: *rom/room, cop/coop, lop/loop*.

Objectives

- Read decodable words with /k/k, /u/u
- Review high-frequency words
- Respond to questions about text
- Reread for fluency

Materials

- Decodable Reader: *Pick It!*
- High-Frequency Word Cards: *is, can, a, do, I, to, the, little, here, said, was*

Decodable Text

For additional decodable passages, see pages 39–44 of the **Teacher's Resource Book**.

Decodable Reader

Read *Pick It!*

Pick It!

 REVIEW HIGH-FREQUENCY WORDS Display **High-Frequency Word Cards** for **is**, **can**, **a**, **do**, **I**, **to**, **the**, **little**, **said**, **here**, and **was**. Review the words using the **Read/Spell/Write** routine.

MODEL CONCEPTS ABOUT PRINT Guide children to follow along with their books. *I hold the book so that the cover is on the front. Then I turn each page as I read it, starting with the cover and ending with the last page.*

PREDICT *Look at the cover. What is the boy holding? What is he reaching for? What time of year is it? What might this story be about?*

FIRST READ Have children point to each word, sounding out decodable words and saying the high-frequency words quickly. Children should chorally read the story the first time through. If needed, provide corrective feedback and guide them page by page.

DEVELOP COMPREHENSION Ask the following: *Why does the boy want to pick things?* (He wants to help.) *Why does the boy ask the girl for permission to pick things?* (She knows more about gardens.)

 SECOND READ Have partners reread the book together. Circulate, listen in, and provide corrective feedback.

It is a red bud.
Do not pick it.

2

It is not red.
Can I pick it?

3

Do not pick it.
Let it sit.

4

It is a sick pod.
Can I pick it?

5

Hop to it.
Pick the sick pod.

6

Kick the rock.
I can not pick it up.

7

I can tip it up a lot.
It can pop up.

8

Decodable Reader

Writing

Interactive Writing: A Poem

REVIEW
Display and read aloud the list that children created for the Shared Writing activity.

WRITE
Today we are going to write a poem about sunflowers. Collaborate with children to write the following sentence frame four times: *Sunflowers are _____.* Read the sentence aloud with children as you track the print.

- Have children suggest a word to complete the first sentence, using the list as a resource. Ask children to help you by writing all of the letters that they know.

- Repeat with the other sentence frames. Remind children that lines of a poem can rhyme, but that they do not have to.

- Read the completed sentences together with children as you track the print.

- Save the poem to refer to in other writing activities this week.

- To extend the activity, share poems with children from the **Big Book of Explorations** or the classroom library. Then work with children to write a poem about something in the classroom or outside of the window.

Write About It
Ask children to write a poem using another type of flower and the same sentence frame used in the lesson.

Objectives
- Write a short poem
- Use letter knowledge to write letters in words

Materials
- Shared Writing lists from Day 1

5-Day Writing	
Poems	
DAY 1	Shared: A List
DAY 2	Interactive: A Poem
DAY 3	Independent: Prewrite and Draft Poems
DAY 4	Independent: Revise and Edit Poems
DAY 5	Independent: Publish and Present

ELL

Prewriting Planning
Ask children to draw and describe their favorite flowers. Tell them to look through picture books to help them find illustrations of flowers.

Transitions That Teach
While lining up, have children name the five **senses** and how they are used.

WHOLE GROUP

Oral Language
- Build Robust Vocabulary
- Oral Vocabulary Cards: "Anansi and the Melon"

✔ **Comprehension**
- Read "How Does a Garden Grow?"
- Text Feature: Photographs

✔ **High-Frequency Words**
- Review *little*, *said*, *here*, *was*

✔ **Phonemic Awareness**
- Phoneme Deletion

✔ **Phonics**
- Cumulative Review
- Blend with *-op*

Grammar
- Describing Words (Adjectives)

Writing
- Independent Writing: Prewrite and Draft Poems

SMALL GROUP

- Differentiated Instruction, pages 2038–2063

Additional Vocabulary

To provide 15–20 minutes of additional vocabulary instruction, see Oral Vocabulary Cards 5-Day Plan. The pre- and posttests can be found in the **Teacher's Resource Book**, pages 228–229.

Oral Language

Talk About It ## Build Robust Vocabulary

BUILD BACKGROUND

Introduce the story "Anansi and the Melon" using **Oral Vocabulary Card 1** and read the title aloud. *Have you tried different kinds of melons? What senses do you use when you eat a melon?* Ask children to tell what they think is happening in the picture and to make a prediction about what will happen based on the illustration.

- Read the story on the back of the cards. Pause at each oral vocabulary word and read the definition. Check children's understanding using the Identify Story Elements, Recognize Cause and Effect, and Words with Multiple Meanings prompts.

Oral Vocabulary Cards

Vocabulary Routine

Use the routine below to discuss the meaning of each word.

Define: To **arrange** means "to organize, put in order, or make happen." Say the word with me.
Example: We can arrange the crayons by color.
Ask: How should we arrange the books in our classroom library?

Define: To **tend** means "to take care of something." Say the word with me.
Example: The gardener tends to his garden by pulling out the weeds.
Ask: Who tends to the potted plants in our classroom? What does he or she do?

Define: Something that is **basic** is important and necessary. You cannot do without it. Say the word with me.
Example: For our camping trip, we packed some basic things, such as food, a tent, and sleeping bags.
Ask: What are the basic needs of a plant?

- Use the routine on Cards 2 and 3 to review the words **senses** and **garden**.

- Review last week's words: *gradually, moist, necessary, observe,* and *seed.*

Listen for Rhyme

IDENTIFY RHYME

Tell children that they will recite another rhyme about a tree. Show them the "Lovely Little Cherry Tree" rhyme on chart paper. Play the rhyme and ask children to join in.

Have children list other fruit plants that might be in a garden, such as pear or apple trees. Ask children to write the names of the fruits on self-stick notes and place them on the chart paper to change the rhyme. For example: *Lovely little apple tree*. Have them read the revised rhyme together.

Ask children to identify words in "Lovely Little Cherry Tree" that rhyme. (*tree/me, low/snow*) Have them look at the rhyming words on the chart and tell how the words that rhyme look alike. (*tree/me* end in -*e*, *low/snow* end in -*ow*)

Lovely Little Cherry Tree

Lovely little cherry tree

Holds a bird that sings for me,

Grows up high or bends down low,

Sunshine, wind, or rain, or snow.

Objectives

- Discuss the theme
- Use oral vocabulary words *arrange, basic, garden, senses,* and *tend*
- Listen and respond to a folktale
- Orally generate rhymes in response to spoken words

Materials

- Oral Vocabulary Cards: "Anansi and the Melon"
- rhyme written on chart paper

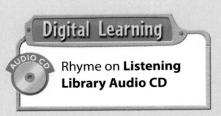

Digital Learning

Rhyme on **Listening Library Audio CD**

Objectives

- Retell important facts
- Use photographs to find information
- Identify the topic and details in expository text
- Discuss what plants need to grow
- Follow pictorial directions
- Grow seeds indoors

Material

- Big Book of Explorations, Vol. 2: "How Does a Garden Grow?" pp. 29–32
- lima bean seeds and potting soil
- foam cups

Content Vocabulary

soil dirt

blossom a flower

ripe fully grown and ready to eat

Informational Text

Genre

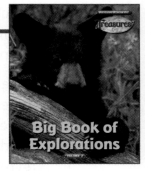

Big Book of Explorations

INFORMATIONAL TEXT: EXPOSITORY Tell children that this selection is **expository** text, a text that explains or gives information. Tell children that in this nonfiction article they will learn how gardens grow.

READ "HOW DOES A GARDEN GROW?"

- **Preview and Predict** Display the first page and read the title as you track the print. Access children's knowledge of gardens. Point to the tomato at the top of page 29. *Is it a flower or a vegetable?* Turn the pages and display the photos. *What will this selection be about? Which kind of garden will we learn about?*

- **Content Vocabulary** Introduce and discuss the vocabulary words.

- **Text Feature: Photographs** *Photographs tell the reader that the book is about real people, places, or things.* Point to the photograph in Step 3 on page 31. *I look at the photograph to see what information I can learn. I can see what a full-grown tomato plant looks like.*

CONTENT FOCUS

As you read pages 30–31, point out the numbers that accompany the photographs. Remind children that the selection will tell them how to grow tomatoes in a garden. Explain that the numbers show readers the steps to follow in the right order. *How many steps does it take to grow tomatoes? Which number shows us what to do first? What is the last thing you should do?*

Read aloud the "How Heavy?" section on page 31 as you point to the photograph. Ask why the woman is in the photo. (to show how big the cabbage is) *What helped the cabbage grow so big?* (lots of sun) Encourage children to ask and answer other questions about this section.

After reading and discussing the questions on page 32, ask children to respond to the Think Big! question.

page 29 pages 30–31 page 32

Retell and Respond

- *What is the topic, or main idea, of this selection?*

- *Why are there numbers in the selection?*

- *What do plants use to make food? What else do plants need to grow?*

- *Why are the blossoms on a tomato plant important?*

- *Use the photographs on pages 30–31 to tell how to grow tomatoes.*

Connect to Content

Science: Grow a Bean Plant

- You will need a small foam cup for each child, a packet of lima bean seeds, potting soil, and a plastic tray.

- Review the things that plants need to grow.

- Have children use the point of a pencil to poke a few small holes in the bottom of their cups. Guide them to fill their cups halfway with soil, plant one bean seed, and cover it with soil.

- Help children water their seeds. Place the cups on a tray to catch any excess water. Place the tray on a sunny windowsill and keep the soil moist. After bean plants sprout, have children continue to care for them.

Objective

- Read the high-frequency words *little, said, here, was*

Materials

- High-Frequency Word Cards: *a, He, Here, here, is, little, said, She, the, was*
- pocket chart
- Photo Cards: *farm, man, lamp, violin, book*
- index card with: period mark
- Activity Book, pp. 27–28
- Practice Book, pp. 175–176

Activity Book, pages 27–28
Practice Book, pages 175–176

High-Frequency Words

 **little, said, here, was**

| little | said |
| here | was |

SPIRAL REVIEW **REVIEW** Display **High-Frequency Word Cards** for **little**, **said**, **here**, and **was**. Review the words using the **Read/Spell/Write** routine.

APPLY Build sentences using the High-Frequency Word Cards and the **Photo Cards**. Read each sentence aloud, then have children chorally read it as you track the print with your finger. Use the sentence below and the following: *He said the book was here. She said the book was little.*

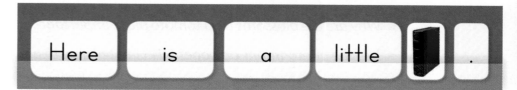

| Here | is | a | little | 📖 | . |

READ FOR FLUENCY Chorally read the Take-Home Book with children. Then have them reread the book to review high-frequency words and build fluency.

Quick Check

Can children read the words *little*, *said*, *here*, and *was*?

During **Small Group Instruction**

If No → **Approaching Level** Provide additional practice with high-frequency words, page 2048.

If Yes → **On Level** Children are ready to read the Take-Home Book.

Beyond Level Children are ready to read the Take-Home Book.

TIME TO MOVE!

Put the Photo Cards in the pocket chart. Have children look at the cards and then close their eyes. Remove a card and give it to a child. When children open their eyes, point to the empty space. Ask: *What was here?* Have the child replace it and say: *The violin was here.*

Phonemic Awareness

Phoneme Deletion

Model

Use the Puppet.

Listen as I ask Happy a question: Happy, what is *bit* without the /b/? Now listen to Happy say *bit* without the /b/: Bit *without /b/ is* it. Say the new word with Happy: *it.*

Repeat with *sat/at.*

Guided Practice/Practice

Say each sentence. Children practice phoneme deletion by deleting the onset in a word and saying the rime.

It is *bus* without the /b/. (*us*)

It is *cup* without the /k/. (*up*)

It is *can* without the /k/. (*an*)

It is *ham* without the /h/. (*am*)

It is *bed* without the /b/. (*ed*)

Guide practice with the first two sentences.

It is *fit* without the /f/. (*it*)

For Tier 2 instruction, see page 2048.

Objectives

- Review sound-spellings for /u/u, /k/k, /b/b, /l/l, /o/o, /p/p
- Blend with the -*op* phonogram

Materials

- Photo Cards: *baby, book, bowl, king, kite, kitten, ladder, leaf, lock, October, ostrich, otter, paint, penny, pot, umpire, under, upside down*
- Word-Building Cards
- pocket chart

Phonics

  Cumulative Review

Model

Display the **Photo Card** for *umpire*.

Repeat for *kitten, book, lock, otter, pot*.

This is an umpire. The sound at the beginning of *umpire* is /u/. The letter *u* stands for the /u/ sound at the beginning of *umpire*.

Guided Practice/Practice

Display and name each Photo Card. Children identify the initial sound and letter. Guide practice with the first card.

Now choose a picture. Say the name and the beginning sound. Then say the letter that stands for the beginning sound.

Build Fluency: Sound-Spellings

 Display the following **Word-Building Cards**: *a, b, c, d, e, f, h, i, k, l, m, n, o, p, r, s, t, u*. Have children chorally say each sound. Repeat and vary the pace.

For Tier 2 instruction, see page 2049.

Blend with -*op*

Model

Place **Word-Building Card** *t* in the pocket chart.

This is letter *t*. It stands for /t/. Say /t/.

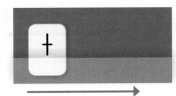

Place the letters *op* in the pocket chart, leaving space after the *t*. Point to the letters *op*.

These are the letters *o* and *p*. The letters *o* and *p* stand for /o/ and /p/. Let's blend these two sounds together: /ooop/.

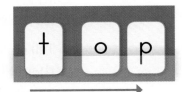

Place the letters *op* next to letter *t*. Move your hand from left to right below the letters.

The beginning sound in the word is /t/, and the sound of the rest of the word is /op/.

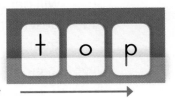

Repeat the routine with *hop*.

Let's blend the beginning sound and the rest of the word together: /tooop/, *top*.

Guided Practice/Practice

Children blend the onset and rime in other words ending with -*op*. Guide practice with *pop*, using the routine.

pop mop bop cop sop lop

What do you notice about the words *top*, *hop*, *pop*, *mop*, *bop*, *cop*, *sop*, and *lop*?

(They end with the letters *op*; they end with the sounds /op/; they rhyme.)

Read Words

Apply

Write the words and sentences. Guide practice with the first word, using the **Sound-by-Sound Blending Routine**. Read the sentences with children.

| What said bop? |
| Was it the pop top? |
| No, the cop said bop. |

Corrective Feedback

Blending: Sound Error Model the sound that children missed, then have them repeat the sound. For example, for the word *top*, say: *My turn.* Tap under the letter *o* in the word *top* and say: *Sound? What's the sound?* Then return to the beginning of the word. Say: *Let's start over.* Blend the word with children again.

Objective

- Recognize describing words (adjectives)

Materials

- Oral Vocabulary Cards: "Anansi and the Melon"
- Photo Cards: *ant, apple, ax, berries, bird, carrots, celery, cherry, corn, deer, dog, egg, feather, gate, grapes, inchworm, insect, kitten, ladder, ladybug, leaf, lemon, moth, mouse, nest, nut, owl, pea, peach, pear, pumpkin, rabbit, rake, rock, rope, rose, saw, soil, strawberry, string, tree, vegetables, vine, water, watermelon, web, zucchini*

ELL

Basic and Academic Language Display the Photo Cards from the lesson and pair English Language Learners with fluent English speakers. Have partners make up sentences that describe the pictured items. Encourage them to use more than one descriptive word. Write children's sentences, read them chorally, and ask: *What descriptive words did you use in your sentence? What are other descriptive words you can use?*

Grammar

Describing Words (Adjectives)

MODEL Use the **Oral Vocabulary Cards** for "Anansi and the Melon" to discuss describing words. Remind children that describing words help us tell what we learn from using our **senses**. Read lines 3–4 of Card 2: *He used his eyes to find the biggest melon. He used his nose to smell the sweetest one.*

- Tell children that the sentences you read include describing words that tell more about the melons. Repeat the sentences. *Which words in the sentences describe the melons?* (biggest, sweetest)

PRACTICE Tell children that they will work in groups. Each child will get a picture of something found in a garden. They will use describing words and what they know about the pictured item to tell their group more about the item.

- Show children the **Photo Card** for *rake* and name it. *I think about how rakes are used in a garden. Rakes pick up clumps of grass left after mowing the lawn. Grass grows in gardens. How can I use my senses to describe raking grass? My eyes see green grass. My nose smells cut grass when I pick up the rake. My ears hear the rake make a scratchy sound. My hands feel soft grass. I do not taste the grass. I will tell the class that I rake soft, green grass in the garden. The rake smells grassy. It makes a scratchy sound while I work. Which describing words did I use to talk about using the rake in the garden?* (soft, green, grassy, scratchy)

- Divide children into small groups. Distribute the Photo Cards and have children name them. Remind children to think about how the pictured item would appear in a garden and how they would use their senses to describe it. After each child describes the pictured item, have members of the group list the describing words used.

- If children have difficulty, help them name the card. *Why would this item be in a garden? What would it look like? What would it smell like? What sound would it make? What would it feel like? What would it taste like?*

Writing

Independent Writing: Poems

Display and read aloud the lists and poem from the Shared and Interactive Writing activities.

BRAINSTORM

WRITING TRAIT: ORGANIZATION Tell children that today they will write poems about a flower.

Think Aloud Good writers connect the ideas they write about and put them in the right order. To write a poem about a flower, I'll think about what words to use and what order to put them in.

Ask children to name flowers they like and words that can be used to describe them. List children's ideas for them to use as a reference.

PREWRITE

Write the following sentence frames on the board:

_____ are _____.

_____ are _____.

Ana

Roses

Roses are round.
Roses are red.
Roses are curved.

- Complete the first sentence by writing the words *Daffodils* and *yellow*. Note that you write from left to right, and when you finish a sentence, you start the next one on the next line. Complete the second sentence by writing *Daffodils* and *gentle*. Read the sentences aloud as you track the print. Have children chorally repeat the sentences.

- Have children select a flower and choose words to describe what their **senses** tell them about that flower.

DRAFT

- Ask children to write the sentence frames and complete them by writing the name of a flower and descriptive words from the list. Have them illustrate their poems.

- Collect and save children's work to use tomorrow.

Write About It

Ask children to draw and label a picture of a flower.

Objectives
- Write poems
- Use letter knowledge to write letters and words

Materials
- lists and poem from Day 2
- gardening books or catalogs, or nature magazines

5-Day Writing

Poems	
DAY 1	Shared: A List
DAY 2	Interactive: A Poem
DAY 3	Independent: Prewrite and Draft Poems
DAY 4	Independent: Revise and Edit Poems
DAY 5	Independent: Publish and Present

ELL

Use New Language Give children gardening catalogs, nature magazines, or gardening books to help them name and describe flowers.

Transitions That Teach

While packing up, have children describe how to **tend** to classroom plants.

WHOLE GROUP

Oral Language
- Build Robust Vocabulary

✔ **Comprehension**
- Read Aloud: "The Rabbit and the Elephant"

Vocabulary
- Position Words
- Story Words: *mammoth, castle*

✔ **Phonemic Awareness**
- Phoneme Blending

✔ **Phonics**
- Cumulative Review
- Blend with *-ick* and *-uck*
- Decodable Reader: *Pick It!*

Writing
- Independent Writing: Revise and Edit Poems

SMALL GROUP
- Differentiated Instruction, pages 2038–2063

Oral Language

 Talk About It ## Build Robust Vocabulary

GARDEN TOOLS
Show the action of hoeing the ground. *I'm working in my* **garden**. *What am I doing? I am using a tool called a hoe to break up the dirt. What other tool might I use to* **tend** *to my garden?*

CREATE A WORD WEB
Draw a word web, or use **Teaching Chart G1**. Write the title *Garden Tools* as shown and read the words as you track the print.

Think Aloud I know that a *hoe* is a garden tool. A *hoe* has a thin flat blade on a long handle. It is used to loosen the soil or to pull weeds. So I will write the word *hoe* in our word web to name one garden tool. I'll add a picture of a *hoe* next to its name.

Ask children to name other garden tools to add to the web. Guide children to take turns and speak one at a time. Have them add a simple drawing of each tool. Read the words with children as you track the print.

ELL ENGLISH LANGUAGE LEARNERS

Beginning	Intermediate	Advanced
Confirm Understanding Point to each tool on the web. *This is a shovel.* Have children repeat the word. *Show me what you do with a shovel.* Ask and confirm: *Do you dig with a shovel? Yes, you use a shovel to dig in a garden.*	**Enhance Understanding** Prompt children to use words and pictures from the web to make up riddles about tools. For example: *What garden tool is very long and has water running through it?*	**Compare and Contrast** Ask children to choose two tools from the web and tell how they are the same or different. For example: *Rakes and hoes both have long handles. A rake has a set of teeth, and a hoe has one blade. Both move dirt.*

Listen for Rhyme

IDENTIFY RHYME

Remind children that words rhyme when they have the same ending sounds. *The word clap rhymes with flap.* Tell children *clap* and *flap* end with the sounds: /aaap/, *ap*. Have children say other words that rhyme with *clap* and *flap*. Have children distinguish rhyming pairs from non-rhyming pairs: *why/dry; stay/hay; fin/flip; pet/pat; silly/frilly.*

SEED RHYME

Tell children that they will recite "I'm a Little Acorn Brown," the rhyme they learned about an oak tree seed. Play the rhyme and ask children to join in.

Ask children to name and describe plants they could find in a garden. List the plants on chart paper. Have children describe the seeds for each type of plant and add them to the list. For example, sunflower seeds are from sunflowers and pine cones are from pine trees.

Ask children to change the poem by substituting a different plant seed for acorn and changing subsequent lines to rhyme. Have them use the list of plants and seeds for ideas. For example: *I'm a sunflower seed lying under a weed.*

Tell children that seeds grow to become the plant they came from. Note any plants for which children cannot identify seeds and research how they regenerate. Explain to children that some plants, such as tulips and potatoes, do not make seeds.

I'm a Little Acorn Brown

I'm a little acorn brown

Lying on the cold, cold ground.

Everyone walks over me.

That's why I'm cracked, you see.

I'm a nut

In a rut.

I'm a nut

In a rut.

Objectives

- Discuss the theme
- Contribute to a garden tools word web
- Use oral vocabulary words *arrange, basic, garden, senses,* and *tend*
- Distinguish rhyming pairs from non-rhyming pairs of words
- Dictate information for a list

Materials

- Graphic Organizer; Teaching Chart G1

Oral Vocabulary

Have children use each word in a sentence about this week's stories.

arrange	basic
garden	senses
tend	

Review Work with children to review last week's words. *What things are* necessary *for a* seed *to grow? What kind of rain would leave the ground* moist*? What things might you* observe *in the sky? Show me how you would* gradually *eat a cookie.*

gradually	moist
necessary	observe
seed	

Digital Learning

Rhyme on **Listening Library Audio CD**

Objectives

- Listen and respond to a folktale
- Describe characters' reasons for their actions
- Recognize sensory details

Materials

- Read-Aloud Anthology: "The Rabbit and the Elephant," pp. 117–121

ELL

Reinforce Understanding
Display the picture of the rabbit and the elephant. *Would you work for this big, strong elephant? Would you rather work for a gentle, fun rabbit? He has musical hoes to use in his fields!* Discuss ways to make work fun. You may want to review the meaning of *hoe,* from the word web.

Readers Theater

BUILDING LISTENING AND SPEAKING SKILLS
Distribute copies of "A Pinch of Pepper," Read-Aloud Anthology pages 191–198. Have children practice performing the play throughout the unit. Assign parts and have children present the play or perform it as a dramatic reading at the end of the unit.

Interactive Read Aloud

Listening Comprehension

GENRE: LITERARY TEXT/FOLKTALE
A folktale is a story passed down from family to family using spoken words. The folktale you will read today includes a lesson about the importance of being kind and friendly. See the information about this folktale in the **Read-Aloud Anthology** lesson.

Read Aloud

CULTURAL PERSPECTIVES
Explain to children that "The Rabbit and the Elephant" story is from Ghana, a country in west Africa. Tell them that Africa has many large and powerful elephants.

READ "THE RABBIT AND THE ELEPHANT"

- **MODEL ASKING QUESTIONS ABOUT STORY STRUCTURE** Use the Think Alouds at point of use in the folktale.

- **MODEL FLUENT READING** Read aloud the folktale with fluent expression. Stop occasionally and have children discuss the story structure and predict what might happen next.

- **EXPAND VOCABULARY** See page 117 of the **Read-Aloud Anthology** to teach new words using the **Define/Example/Ask** routine.

Respond to Literature

TALK ABOUT IT Ask children to retell the folktale.

- *What does Elephant think about his neighbors in the beginning of the story? What does Rabbit decide to do? Why did he act the way he did? Which senses does he use?*

- *What happens in the middle and end of the story?*

- Have children write or draw in response to the folktale. Add their work to their Writing Portfolios.

Write About It

Ask children to draw part of the folktale and label their picture.

Vocabulary

Position Words

REVIEW POSITION WORDS

Draw a tall tree on a sheet of butcher paper and place the paper on the floor. Give each child several colored pieces of paper. Tell children to pretend the colored paper is fruit. Give directions, such as: *Put the fruit on the top branches of the tree. Put the fruit on the bottom branches of the tree.*

Have children take turns giving one another directions on where to place the paper fruit, using the words *top, middle,* and *bottom*.

Story Words: *mammoth, castle*

Display and read pages 12–13 of *Sunflower House* and point out the picture of the sunflowers. Remind children that *mammoth* means "huge or really big." Ask children to name things that might be described as mammoth.

Display and read pages 16–17 of *Sunflower House*. Remind children that a *castle* is a large house for a king or other royalty. *What might you do in a castle?*

Objectives

- Use position words
- Review story words
  mammoth, castle

Materials

- small pieces of colored construction paper
- large sheet of butcher paper
- Read-Aloud Trade Book: *Sunflower House*
- Activity Book, p. 26

ELL

Reinforce Meaning Have children draw three items in a column. Then share the drawings with the class. Ask children to point to the objects and identify their position as *top, middle,* or *bottom*. Review the position of each item.

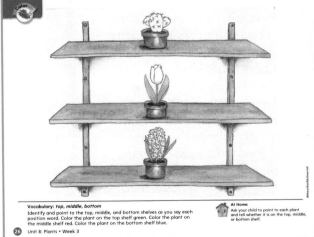

Vocabulary: *top, middle, bottom*
Identify and point to the top, middle, and bottom shelves as you say each position word. Color the plant on the top shelf green. Color the plant on the middle shelf red. Color the plant on the bottom shelf blue.

26 Unit 8: Plants • Week 3

At Home:
Ask your child to point to each plant and tell whether it is on the top, middle, or bottom shelf.

Activity Book, page 26

TIME TO MOVE!

Arrange children in a circle. Ask those with blue shoes to tap the top of their heads. Continue giving directions using position words. Have children use a complete sentence where they are tapping. For example: *I tap the middle of my back.*

Objectives

- Blend sounds to form words
- Review sound-spellings for /u/u, /k/k, /b/b, /l/l, /i/i
- Blend with -*ick* and -*uck* phonograms

Materials

- Puppet
- Word-Building Cards
- pocket chart
- Activity Book, pp. 29–30
- Practice Book, p. 177

Beyond
ACCELERATE

Display the *Book* and *Spoon* **Sound-Spelling Cards**. Remind children that two *o*'s together can stand for two sounds: the /ù/ sound and the /ü/sound.

Practice Place the *Book* and *Spoon* Sound-Spelling Cards picture-side up on **Teaching Chart G3**. Say *spoon. I hear the /ü/ sound in* spoon, *so I will write the word under the spoon. Say* book. *I hear the /ù/ sound in* book, *so I will write the word under the book.* Continue sorting with *room, foot, cook, loon, toot,* and *good.*

Phonemic Awareness

✔ Phoneme Blending

Model

Use the **Puppet** to model how to blend sounds to form *nut*.

Repeat with *luck*.

Happy is going to say the sounds in a word. Listen to Happy: /n/ /u/ /t/. Happy can blend these sounds together: /nnnuuut/, *nut*. Say the sounds with Happy: /n/ /u/ /t/. Now blend the sounds to say the word with Happy: *nut*.

Guided Practice/Practice

Children blend sounds to form words.

Guide practice with the first word, using the same routine.

Happy is going to say the sounds in a word. Listen to Happy as he says each sound. Then blend the sounds to say the word.

/g/ /u/ /l/	/p/ /i/ /k/	/h/ /u/ /g/
/u/ /p/	/b/ /u/ /s/	/s/ /i/ /k/
/b/ /u/ /k/	/j/ /u/ /g/	/t/ /u/ /k/

Phonics

✔ Review

u k b l

Model

Display **Word-Building Card** *u*. Repeat the routine for final *k*, and initial *b, l, i*.

This is the letter *u*. The letter *u* stands for the /u/ sound you hear at the beginning of *umbrella*. The word *up* begins with the same sound as *umbrella*: /u/.

Guided Practice/Practice

Children choose a Word-Building Card, name the letter, say the letter sound, and name another word that begins or ends with the same sound.

Pick a card. Say the name of the letter, say the sound the letter stands for, and name a word that begins or ends with that sound. Then have children read the following words: *bud, hum, lip*.

Build Fluency: Sound-Spellings

 SPIRAL REVIEW Display the following **Word-Building Cards**: *a, b, c, d, e, f, h, i, k, l, m, n, o, p, r, s, t, u*. Have children chorally say each sound. Repeat.

 ## Blend with *-ick* and *-uck*

Model

Place Word-Building Card *l* in the pocket chart.

This is letter *l*. It stands for /l/. Say /l/.

Place the letters *ick* in the pocket chart, leaving space after the *l*. Point to the letters *ick*.

These are the letters *ick*. They stand for /i/ and /k/. Let's blend the sounds: /iiik/.

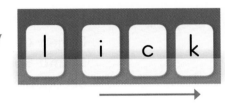

Place the letter *l* closer to *ick*. Move your hand from left to right below the letters.

The beginning sound is /l/ and and the rest of the word is /ik/. Blend the beginning sound and the rest of the word: /llliiik/, *lick*.

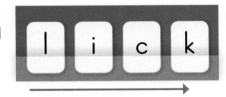

Repeat with *duck*.

Guided Practice/Practice

Children blend the onset and rime in other words that end with *-ick* and *-uck*. Guide practice with *kick*, using the routine.

kick   Rick   Nick   tick   pick

What is the same about the words? (They end with the letters *ick*; they end with the /ik/ sounds; they rhyme.)

luck   puck   tuck   buck

What is the same about the words? (They end with the letters *uck*; they end with the /uk/ sounds; they rhyme.)

Corrective Feedback

Blending: Sound Error Model the sound that children missed, then have them repeat the sound. For example, for the word *lick*, say: *My turn.* Tap under the letter *i* in the word *lick* and say: *Sound? What's the sound?* Then return to the beginning of the word. Say: *Let's start over.* Blend the word with children again.

ELL

Build Vocabulary Pair English Language Learners with more proficient partners. Have them choose two or three examples from the words they blend in the Guided Practice portion of the lesson and use those words in sentences.

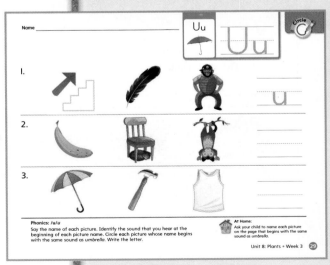

Activity Book, pages 29–30
Practice Book, page 177

Objectives

- Read decodable words with /k/ck, /k/k, /u/u
- Review high-frequency words
- Reread for fluency

Materials

- **Decodable Reader:** *Pick It!*
- **High-Frequency Word Cards:** *a, can, do, here, I, is, little, said, the, to, was*
- **Sound-Spelling Cards:** *Koala, Umbrella*

Decodable Text

For additional decodable passages, see pages 39–44 of the **Teacher's Resource Book**.

Decodable Reader

Read *Pick It!*

 REVIEW Review this week's high-frequency words and phonics skills using the word lists on the inside back cover of *Pick It!*

Pick It!

Review the high-frequency words **a**, **can**, **do**, **here**, **I**, **is**, **little**, **said**, **the**, **to**, and **was** using the **Read/Spell/Write** routine. Then have children chorally read the high-frequency word list.

Review the phonics skills /k/k and /u/u using the *Koala* and *Umbrella* **Sound-Spelling Cards**. Then have children chorally read the decodable word list. Model blending as needed and note children who struggle while reading these words. Provide additional instruction and practice during Small Group time.

MODEL CONCEPTS ABOUT PRINT Guide children to follow along. *I open the book by turning the cover. Then I turn each page as I read it, starting with the first page and ending with the last page.*

 REREAD FOR FLUENCY Have children reread the book with a partner. Circulate and listen in, providing corrective feedback as needed. Then have children reread the book independently.

It is a red bud.
Do not pick it.

2

It is not red.
Can I pick it?

3

Do not pick it.
Let it sit.

4

It is a sick pod.
Can I pick it?

5

Hop to it.
Pick the sick pod.

6

Kick the rock.
I can not pick it up.

7

I can tip it up a lot.
It can pop up.

8

Decodable Reader

Writing

Independent Writing: Poems

REVISE AND EDIT

Distribute children's poems. Have children reread them and check for the following:

- Did I write two or more sentences to make a poem?

- Did I write the name of a flower and words that describe it?

- Are my sentences in an order that makes sense to me?

Circulate and help children as they review and revise their poems. Guide children to check that their poems are grammatically correct. Have children share their poems with a partner.

> Jennifer
>
> Peonies are pink.
> Peonies are pretty.
> Peonies are gentle.
> Peonies are soft.

Write About It

Ask children to draw a picture of a fanciful flower **garden**. Have them label their drawing, describing what they would experience with their **senses**.

Objectives

- **Revise poems**
- **Edit poems**

Materials

- poems from Day 3
- Writer's Checklist; Teacher's Resource Book, p. 205

5-Day Writing

Poems	
DAY 1	Shared: A List
DAY 2	Interactive: A Poem
DAY 3	Independent: Prewrite and Draft Poems
DAY 4	Independent: Revise and Edit Poems
DAY 5	Independent: Publish and Present

ELL

Prewriting Planning Write *Sunflowers are _____.* twice on the board and read it aloud. Ask children to insert words to fill the blanks, creating a poem that tells about this flower.

Transitions That Teach

While lining up, have children describe how different areas of the classroom are **arranged**.

WHOLE GROUP

Oral Language
- Build Robust Vocabulary

✔ **Comprehension**
- Strategy: Recognize Story Structure
- Skill: Draw Conclusions

✔ **Vocabulary**
- Review High-Frequency Words
- Review Position Words

✔ **Phonemic Awareness**
- Phoneme Segmentation

✔ **Phonics**
- Build Fluency
- Read Words
- Dictation

Writing
- Independent Writing: Publish and Present

SMALL GROUP

- Differentiated Instruction, pages 2038–2063

Review and Assess
Oral Language
Build Robust Vocabulary

REVIEW WORDS

Review this week's oral vocabulary words with children. Explain that all of the words will be used to discuss plants.

Use the following questions to check children's understanding:

- What are some things you would see in a **garden**?

- How would you **arrange** a flower garden?

- How would you **tend** a vegetable garden?

- What are some of the **basic** things people need to care for plants?

- How could you use your **senses** in a vegetable garden?

REVIEW RHYMES ABOUT TREES AND SEEDS

Recite the rhyme "Lovely Little Cherry Tree" and have children join in. Have children name other trees that could grow in a garden. Tell them to use complete sentences as they tell how they might change through the year. For example, they lose leaves in the winter; grow leaves and flowers in the spring; grow fruit in the summer; and lose fruit in the fall.

Then recite the rhyme "I'm a Little Acorn Brown" with children. Ask children to name other plant seeds, such as corn kernels, coconuts, avocado pits, and beans.

Review and Assess
Comprehension

STRATEGY Recognize Story Structure

REFLECT ON THE STRATEGY Remind children that stories can be organized in different ways.

Think Aloud I think about the beginning, middle, and end of a story to understand and remember it. The structure of *Sunflower House* follows the life of the sunflowers. In the beginning they are planted, in the middle they grow, and at the end they die.

SKILL Draw Conclusions

Remind children that they have learned how to use the **plot** and story clues to figure out more things about it. Page through *Sunflower House* and "The Rabbit and the Elephant" with children. Then use the following questions to review drawing conclusions.

■ *Why does the sunflower house droop and disappear? How did you figure that out?*

■ *Why is Elephant surprised that his neighbors are working in Rabbit's garden instead of in his? How could you tell?*

Reading Across Texts

Create a chart to compare and contrast *Sunflower House*, "How Does a Garden Grow?" and "The Rabbit and the Elephant." Then have children write or draw about the similarities and differences between characters and settings in the selections. Add their work to their Writing Portfolios.

Sunflower House	How Does a Garden Grow?	The Rabbit and the Elephant
fiction	expository text	folktale
could really happen	about real plants	could not really happen
lines of the story rhyme, like a poem	no rhyming lines	the song in the story rhymes
about how to grow sunflowers	about how to grow tomatoes	about starting a farm
all illustrations	photographs and illustrations	illustrations

Objectives
- Review recognizing story structure and drawing conclusions
- Listen to and share information
- Make connections to ideas in other texts

Materials
- Read-Aloud Trade Book: *Sunflower House*
- Big Book of Explorations, Vol. 2: "How Does a Garden Grow?"
- Read-Aloud Anthology: "The Rabbit and the Elephant"
- Activity Book, p. 31

Activity Book, page 31

Objectives

- Review the high-frequency words *little, said, here, was, and, what*
- Review position words
- Build fluency

Materials

- High-Frequency Word Cards; Teacher's Resource Book, pp. 103–110
- Read-Aloud Trade Book: *Sunflower House*
- position words on index cards: *bottom, in, middle, over, out, top, under*

Fluency

Connected Text Have children reread this week's **Decodable Reader** with a partner. Circulate, listen in, and note those children who need additional instruction and practice reading this week's decodable and sight words.

Review and Assess
Vocabulary

 ## High-Frequency Words

Distribute one of the following **High-Frequency Word Cards** to each child: **little**, **said**, **here**, **was**, **and**, and **what**. *When you hear the word that is on your card, stand and hold up your card.*

- *I* said, *"This cookie is* little.*"*
- What *can we do* here?
- *We can run* and *jump here.*
- *I* was *tired from running.*

Build Fluency: Word Automaticity

Display the High-Frequency Word Cards. Point quickly to each card, at random, and have children read the word as fast as they can.

little	said
here	was
and	what

Position Words

Use position words to talk about the illustrations in *Sunflower House*. *The birds are flying* over *the boy. The roots are growing* under *the ground.* Ask children to make sentences describing the location of objects around the classroom using position words.

Rapid Naming Display the position words on index cards and have children read the words as quickly as they can.

TIME TO MOVE!

Play "Simon Says" using position words. For example: *Simon says put your hand under your foot.* Have children take turns being Simon.

Review and Assess
Phonemic Awareness

 ## Phoneme Segmentation

Guided Practice

Segment the sounds in the word *luck*.

Listen as I say each sound in the word *luck*: /l/ /u/ /k/. How many sounds are in *luck*? (3) What are the sounds? (/l/ /u/ /k/)

I'll place a marker in a box for each sound: /l/ /u/ /k/. There are three sounds in *luck*, so I'll put a marker in three boxes.

Say the sounds in *luck* with me: /l/ /u/ /k/.

Practice

Distribute **Sound Boxes** and markers.

I will say a word. Place a marker in a box for each sound you hear. Then say the word and its sounds.

Children say the word and its sounds.

duck	lot	kick	pot
peck	tuck	pick	deck
buck	tack	sock	lick

For Tier 2 instruction, see page 2058.

Objective
- Segment sounds in words

Materials
- Sound Box
- WorkBoard Sound Boxes; Teacher's Resource Book, p. 136
- markers

Objectives

- Read simple one-syllable words
- Write simple one-syllable words

Materials

- Word-Building Cards
- 8 index cards with: *Pam, said, the, little, pup, was, here,* period mark
- 9 index cards with: *What, is, the, tip, for, Bob, and, Pat,* question mark
- pocket chart
- Sound Box
- WorkBoard Sound Boxes; Teacher's Resource Book, p. 136
- markers
- Activity Book, p. 32

Phonics: /k/k, /u/u
Say the name of each picture. Then write the letter that stands for the sound you hear at the beginning of the word.

At Home:
Ask your child to name each picture and its beginning letter and sound.

978-0-02-206194-4
MHID: 0-02-206194-0

32 Unit 8: Plants • Week 3

Activity Book, page 32

Review and Assess
Phonics

Build Fluency: Sound-Spellings

Rapid Naming Display the following **Word-Building Cards**: *a, b, c, d, e, f, h, i, k, l, m, n, o, p, r, s, t, u.* Have children chorally say each sound as quickly as they can.

✔ Read Words

Apply

Distribute the first set of cards. Have children stand in sequence.	Let's read the sentence together. *Pam said the little pup was here.*
Repeat, using the other set of cards.	Let's read the sentence together. *What is the tip for Bob and Pat?*

✔ Dictation

Dictate sounds for children to spell.

Listen as I say a sound. Repeat the sound, then write the letter that stands for the sound.

/l/   /a/   /r/   /h/   /e/

/k/   /o/   /b/   /u/   /d/

Then dictate words for children to spell. Model for children how to use the **Sound Boxes** to segment the sounds in the words. Have them repeat.

Now let's write some words. I will say a word. I want you to repeat the word, then think about how many sounds are in the word. Use your Sound Boxes to count the sounds. Then write one letter for each sound you hear.

run	cut	bud	fun
pod	tap	top	dip
bib	rub	bad	pan

Write the letters and words on the board for children to self-correct.

For Tier 2 instruction, see page 2058.

Review and Assess
Writing

Independent Writing: Poems

PUBLISH
Explain to children that you will gather their illustrated poems together to make a classroom book.

- Brainstorm ideas for a title, such as "Our Poetry **Garden**."

- Have a few children work on a book cover.

- Make holes along the side of the cover and each page of the book and then have children bind the pages together with yarn.

PRESENT
Ask children to take turns reading their poems to the class.

LISTENING, SPEAKING, AND VIEWING
- Remind children to speak audibly and clearly and to be good listeners when a classmate is speaking. Praise children for their hard work.

- Display the book of poems in the library for all to appreciate. Have children add copies of their poems to their Writing Portfolios.

- Ask children to write and draw about how they have progressed as writers.

Write About It
Ask children to draw and label a picture of themselves picking flowers.

Objectives
- Publish and present poems
- Speak audibly and clearly

Materials
- poems from Day 4

5-Day Writing

Poems	
DAY 1	Shared: A List
DAY 2	Interactive: A Poem
DAY 3	Independent: Prewrite and Draft Poems
DAY 4	Independent: Revise and Edit Poems
DAY 5	Independent: Publish and Present

Transitions That Teach
While children are lining up, have them name **basic** things they need to paint a picture or to make a sand castle.

My Garden

Have children draw a picture of a garden they would like to have. Ask them to label their picture *My Garden*.

ELL

Partners When pairing children to make up sentences, pair English Language Learners with children who are more proficient. Write their sentences, read them together, and point out the high-frequency words.

Approaching Level

Oral Language

Objective	Preteach oral vocabulary
Materials	• none

THEME WORDS: *senses, garden*

- Tell children the meanings for **senses** and **garden**. *You have five senses. You have eyes to see, ears to hear, a nose to smell, fingers to touch, and a mouth to taste. A garden is a plot of land where plants, such as flowers, trees, and vegetables, grow.*

- Discuss the words with children. *What senses do you use when you are in a kitchen? If you had a garden, what would you grow in it?*

- Have children use the following sentence frames to generate complete oral sentences using the words: *When I go to a concert, I use my senses to _____. If I had a vegetable garden, I would grow _____.*

High-Frequency Words

Objective	Review high-frequency words
Materials	• **High-Frequency Word Cards:** *little, said, here, was*

REVIEW WORDS: *little, said, here, was*

- Display the **High-Frequency Word Card** for **here**.
- **Read** Point to and say the word *here*. *This is the word* here. *It means "this place." My flower garden is here.*
- **Spell** *The word* here *is spelled* h-e-r-e. Have children read and spell *here*.
- **Write** Finally, have children write the word *here*. Repeat the routine with **little**, **said**, and **was**.

- Have children work with a partner to make up sentences using the words *here, was, said,* and *little*. Ask them to talk about something little that was in the classroom.

HIGH-FREQUENCY WORDS REVIEW

Display the High-Frequency Word Cards for words previously taught, one card at a time, and have children chorally read and spell the words. Mix and repeat. Note words children need to review.

Tier 2

Approaching Level

Phonemic Awareness

Objective   Identify initial /k/ and /u/ sounds
Materials   • **Photo Cards:** *kangaroo, key, king, kitten, koala, umpire, undershirt, up*

✔ PHONEME ISOLATION

Model

■ Display the **Photo Card** for *king. This is a king. Listen for the beginning sound in* king: */k/. King begins with /k/. Now you say /k/: /k/. What sound do you hear at the beginning of* king? Repeat with the remaining Photo Cards.

Guided Practice/Practice

■ Display the Photo Cards. Have children take turns selecting a picture, naming it, and saying the initial sound as they complete these sentences: *This is a(n)* _____. _____ *begins with* _____. Guide practice with the first card.

■ Have children note their mouth and tongue position as they say /k/ and /u/. *Is your mouth open or closed when you say the sound?*

Phonics

Objective   Recognize words that begin with /u/u, /k/k, and /l/l
Materials   • **Photo Cards:** *kangaroo, key, king, koala, ladder, ladybug, lamp, lemon, lion, umbrella, umpire, undershirt, under, up*
        • **Word-Building Cards**

✔ PRETEACH: RECOGNIZE /u/u, /k/k, /l/l

Model

■ Display **Word-Building Card** *u* and the Photo Card for *umbrella. This letter is* u. U *stands for the /u/ sound that you hear at the beginning of* umbrella. *I will place a* u *card on the picture of the umbrella because* umbrella *begins with /u/.* Repeat with *k* and *l.*

Guided Practice/Practice

■ Display the Photo Cards on a table. *This is an umpire. What sound do you hear at the beginning of* umpire? *What letter stands for /u/? Let's place the* u *card on the umpire because* umpire *begins with /u/.* Repeat with remaining Photo Cards for /u/u, /k/k, and /l/l.

■ Guide children to trace the letters *u, k,* and *l* on their small Word-Building Cards.

SOUND-SPELLINGS REVIEW

Tier 2

Display Word-Building Cards *m, a, s, p, t, i, n, c, o, f, h, d, r, e, b, l, k,* and *u,* one at a time. Have children chorally say the sound. Repeat and vary the pace.

Corrective Feedback

Mnemonic Error Display the *Koala* and *Umbrella* **Sound-Spelling Cards**. *These are the letters* k *and* u. *K stands for the /k/ sound. Let's say it together: /k/. U stands for the /u/ sound. Let's say it together: /uuu/. What words can help us remember the* k *and* u *sounds? What are the sounds? What are the letters?*

ON YOUR OWN

Letter Garden

Provide paper for children to draw flowers for a letter garden. On each flower have them write the letter *l, u,* or *k*.

ELL

Extra Practice Provide additional practice in recognizing and naming letters for children whose native languages do not use the symbols of the Latin alphabet.

On Level

High-Frequency Words

Objective Review high-frequency words *little, said, here, was, and, what*

Materials • **High-Frequency Word Cards:** *little, said, here, was, and, what*

REVIEW

- Display the **High-Frequency Word Card** for **little**.

- **Read** Point to and say the word *little*. *This is the word* little. *It is a word we use when we talk about the size of something. The little doll fit in my pocket.*

- **Spell** *The word* little *is spelled* l-i-t-t-l-e. Have children read and spell *little*.

- **Write** Finally, have children write the word *little*.

- Repeat with **here**, **was**, **said**, **and**, and **what**. Then have partners make up questions and answers using the words *little, and,* and *what*. Ask them to talk about what things are little.

Phonemic Awareness/Phonics

Objective Segment words into sounds and review recognizing /u/u, /k/k, and /l/l

Materials • **Word-Building Cards** • pocket chart
• **Sound-Spelling WorkBoards**

PHONEME SEGMENTATION

Model

- *I will say the sounds in* rock. *Listen:* /r/ /o/ /k/, rock. *There are three sounds in* rock: /r/ /o/ /k/. *Say the word with me:* rock. *Now say the three sounds:* /r/ /o/ /k/.

Practice

- Have children practice segmenting words into sounds. *I will say a word. Break the word into its sounds and tap them out.* Use the following words: *sock, Rick, lock, pack, tuck, neck, deck, Jack.*

REVIEW: /u/u, /k/k, /l/l

- Display **Word-Building Card** u. *The name of this letter is* u. *This letter stands for the /u/ sound we hear at the beginning of* umbrella. *What is the sound? I'll hold up the* u *card because* umbrella *begins with /u/.* Repeat with *k* and *kit*, and *l* and *lap*.

- Distribute small Word-Building Cards to children. Say: *up, kick, pack, led, king, umpire, unzip, back, luck, Ken, lemon.* Children hold up their small Word-Building Cards and say the initial sound of the word you name. Guide practice with the first two words.

ELL

Sound-Letter Relationships Provide additional practice in pronouncing and blending the /u/, /k/, /l/ sounds and naming the corresponding letters as children point to them.

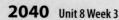

Beyond Level

High-Frequency Words/Vocabulary

Objective Review high-frequency words
Materials • none

ACCELERATE

■ Write *plant* and *wait* on the board. Point to and say the word *plant*. *Trees, bushes, grass, and flowers are plants. The word* plant *is spelled* p-l-a-n-t. Have children read and spell *plant*. Finally, have children write the word *plant*. Repeat the routine with *wait*.

■ Have children work with a partner to make up oral sentences with *plant* and *wait*. Ask them to talk about plants that they would grow in a window box garden. Have them describe what they would do while they wait for the plants to grow.

EXPAND ORAL VOCABULARY

■ **Synonyms** Review the meaning of the oral vocabulary word *basic* with children. Then explain that a *synonym* is a word that means the same thing as another word.

■ Say: *A synonym for the word* basic *is* essential. *Bread is a basic ingredient in a sandwich. You can't make a sandwich without it.*

■ Have children take turns using the new word *basic* in a complete sentence. Then tell children they will work with a partner to name ingredients that are basic to a variety of meals.

Phonics

Objectives Read words with /k/*k*, /k/*ck*, /u/*u*; blend and build words with long /ā/*a*
Materials • **Sound-Spelling Cards:** *Koala, Umbrella* • **Word-Building Cards**

ENRICH

■ Say the /k/ /ā/ /k/ sounds. Ask children to blend the sounds to say the word *cake*.

■ Display the *Koala* **Sound-Spelling Card**. Remind children that the /k/ sound is spelled with the letter *k* or the letters *ck*. *Kit begins with the /k/ sound. Pick ends with the /k/ sound. What other words begin or end with /k/?* Repeat with *u*.

■ Have children apply their skills to more complex words. Write words for children to read. Model blending each word: *stuck, blunt, flush, kiss, spunk, crush, king, buck, must*.

■ Display **Word-Building Cards** *b, c, e, h, i, k, l, m, p, r, s, t,* and *u*. Have partners make as many words as they can and list them.

ELL ENGLISH LANGUAGE LEARNERS

Oral Language Warm-Up

Content Objective Learn theme vocabulary
Language Objective Repeat and act out a rhyme to demonstrate understanding
Materials • **Listening Library Audio CD** • **Photo Cards**

BUILD BACKGROUND KNOWLEDGE

All Language Levels

- Continue developing vocabulary around the unit theme "Plants" using the rhyme "Lovely Little Cherry Tree." Display a picture of a cherry using the **Photo Card**. Teach the word *cherry* as you point to the cherry in the picture. Explain that many gardens have cherry trees. Say: *Cherries are sweet. They grow on trees.* Have children repeat the word *cherry* three times.

- Play "Lovely Little Cherry Tree" on the **Audio CD**. Act out each line as you chant the rhyme. For example: hold out your hand, palm up, as if presenting the cherry tree; use actions or gestures for "holds" and "grows up high or bends down low."

- Then teach children the motions. Emphasize key words such as *tree, grows, bends, sunshine, wind,* and *rain*.

- Ask children to tell what they know about fruit trees. Build on their responses to model speaking in complete sentences. For example: *Fruit grows on trees. I have a cherry tree in my yard.*

Academic Language

Language Objective Use academic language in classroom conversations

All Language Levels

- This week's academic words are **boldfaced** throughout the lesson. Define the word in context and provide a clear example from the selection. Then ask children to generate an example or a word with a similar meaning.

Academic Language Used in Whole Group Instruction

Oral Vocabulary Words	Vocabulary and Grammar Concepts	Strategy and Skill Words
arrange basic garden senses tend	position words describing words	structure/organization story order conclusion retell describing words

Cognates

Help children identify similarities and differences in pronunciation and spelling between English words and Spanish cognates:

Cognates

Cognates	
basic	*básico*

ELL ENGLISH LANGUAGE LEARNERS

Vocabulary

Language Objective Demonstrate understanding and use of key words by discussing gardens

Materials • **Visual Vocabulary Resources**

PRETEACH KEY VOCABULARY

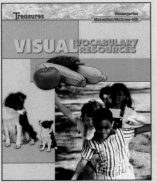

Visual Vocabulary Resources

All Language Levels

Use the **Visual Vocabulary Resources** to preteach the weekly oral vocabulary words *arrange, basic, garden, senses,* and *tend*. Focus on one or two words per day. Use the following routine that appears in detail on the cards.

- Define the word in English and provide the example given.

- Define the word in Spanish, if appropriate, and indicate if the word is a cognate.

- Display the picture and explain how it illustrates or demonstrates the word.

- Then engage children in structured partner-talk about the image, using the key word.

- Ask children to chorally say the word three times.

- Point out any known sound-spellings or focus on a key aspect of phonemic awareness related to the word.

PRETEACH FUNCTION WORDS AND PHRASES

All Language Levels

Use the Visual Vocabulary Resources to preteach the function phrases *in a line* and *round and round*. Focus on one phrase per day. Use the detailed routine on the cards.

- Define the phrase in English and, if appropriate, in Spanish. Point out if the phrase is a cognate.

- Refer to the picture and engage children in talk about the phrase. For example, children will partner-talk using sentence frames, or they will listen to sentences and replace a word or phrase with the new function phrase.

- Ask children to chorally repeat the phrase three times.

TEACH BASIC WORDS

Beginning/Intermediate

Use the Visual Vocabulary Resources to teach the basic words *house, roof, walls, floor, ceiling* and *door*. Teach these "house words" using the routine provided on the card.

Approaching Level

Oral Language

Objective Reinforce oral vocabulary
Materials • none

THEME WORDS: *senses, garden*

- *We've talked about our five **senses**. Our sense of smell is one of them. We've also talked about different types of **gardens**. Rose gardens smell wonderful.*

- *Which sense do you use when you pet a kitten? Which sense do you use when you watch a movie?*

- *What kind of garden do you prefer to look at: a vegetable garden or a flower garden? Why?*

- *A blind person is missing his sense of sight. How can he use his other senses to get around? How can this person enjoy a flower garden?* Tell children to respond in complete sentences.

High-Frequency Words

Objective Reteach high-frequency words
Materials • **High-Frequency Word Card:** *little, said, here, was, and, what*
• **Sound-Spelling WorkBoards**

RETEACH WORDS: *little, said, here, was, and, what*

Tier 2

- Distribute a **WorkBoard** to each child. Then display the **High-Frequency Word Card** for **little**.

- Use the **Read/Spell/Write** routine to reteach the word. Point to and say the word. *This is the word* little. *It is a word that describes the size of something. It means the same as* small. Little *is spelled* l-i-t-t-l-e. Have children read and spell *little*. Then have them write the word on their WorkBoards. Repeat the routine with **said**, **here**, **was**, **and**, and **what**.

- Have children work with a partner to make up sentences using the words *little* and *and*. Ask them to talk about small things found in a garden. Tell them to speak in complete sentences.

CUMULATIVE REVIEW

Display the High-Frequency Word Cards for words previously taught and have children chorally read and spell each word. Mix and repeat. Note words children need to review.

ELL

Partners When pairing children to make up sentences, pair English Language Learners with children who are more proficient. Write their sentences, read them together, and point out the high-frequency words.

Approaching Level

Phonemic Awareness

Objective Segment sounds in words with medial /o/o and /i/i
Materials • **Puppet**

Tier 2

PHONEME SEGMENTATION

Model
- *Happy will say the sounds in* top. *Listen:* /t/ /o/ /p/, top. *There are three sounds in* top: /t/ /o/ /p/. *Say the word with me:* top. *Now say the three sounds:* /t/ /o/ /p/. *Repeat with* pit.

Practice
- Continue practicing with the **Puppet.** *Happy will say a word. Say each sound in the word. Then say the word again:* sock, /s/ /o/ /k/. *Repeat with* kick, Bob, hop, lip, dock, pick, *and* rock.

Phonics

Objective Reinforce letter-sound correspondence for /u/u, /k/k, /b/b, /l/l
Materials • **Sound-Spelling Cards:** *Umbrella, Koala, Bat, Lemon*
• **Sound-Spelling WorkBoards** • **Word-Building Cards**
• **Decodable Reader:** *Pick It!*

RECOGNIZE /b/b, /k/k, /l/l, /u/u

Model
- Display the *Umbrella* **Sound-Spelling Card.** *The letter* u *stands for the /u/ sound as in* umbrella. *What is this letter? What sound does it stand for?* Repeat with *k, b,* and *l.*

- Trace *u, k, b,* and *l* on small **Word-Building Cards.** *I will say a sentence. We will trace* u *on the cards when we hear /u/ at the beginning of words. My uncle is under the umbrella.* Repeat for the letters *k, b,* and *l* using the following sentences: *King Karl has a kite; Ben is busy with big bugs; Lucy likes little lollipops.*

Guided Practice/Practice
- Distribute a **WorkBoard** to each child. Say: *up, bat, koala, kit, lion, karate, umpire, bear, bean, love, uncle.* Children write *u, k, b,* or *l* on their WorkBoards when they hear a word that begins with /u/, /b/, /k/, or /l/. Guide them with the first two words.

- **Read the Decodable Reader** Read *Pick It!* with children. Have them echo-read each page. Chorally reread the story.

CUMULATIVE REVIEW

Display Word-Building Cards *a, i, n, o, r, e, b, l, k,* and *u.* Point to the letters randomly. Have children chorally say the sound.

Puppet

Decodable Reader

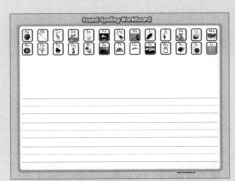

Sound-Spelling WorkBoard

Corrective Feedback

Sound Error Say: *My turn. When I say the word* kit, *I hear the /k/ /i/ /t/ sounds. I do not hear /u/, so I will not write* u. *Listen again: /k/ /i/ /t/,* kit. *Do you hear the /u/ sound?* Continue with the other words and then repeat *kit.*

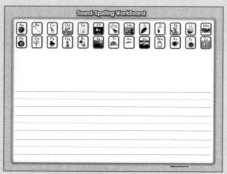

Sound-Spelling WorkBoard

On Level

Phonics

Objective Review recognizing and blending initial /k/k, /b/b, /l/l, and /u/u

Materials
- **Word-Building Cards**   • pocket chart
- **Sound-Spelling WorkBoards**

REVIEW /b/b, /k/k, /l/l, /u/u

- Display **Word-Building Card** b. *This letter is* b. B *stands for the /b/ sound we hear at the beginning of* balloon. *What is the sound?* Repeat with *k* and *kangaroo, u* and *up,* and *l* and *lion.*

- Distribute Word-Building Cards to children. Say: *umpire, lemon, lime, koala, umbrella, bat, banana, kit.* Children hold up their cards and say whether the word begins with the /u/, /k/, /b/, or /l/ sound. Guide practice with the first two words.

- **Blend Words** Place Word-Building Cards *b, u, c,* and *k* in the pocket chart. Point to each letter for children to identify the letter name and sound. Move your hand from left to right below the letters as you blend the word. Remind children that *ck* at the end of a word has the /k/ sound. *Listen as I blend the three sounds together: /buuuk/,* buck. *What's the word?* Repeat with *luck.*

- Have children write *buck* several times on their **WorkBoards** as they say /b/ /u/ /k/. Repeat with *luck.*

Beyond Level

Phonics

Objective Blend and build words with long /a/a

Materials
- **Word-Building Cards**   • pocket chart

ACCELERATE

- Display the Word-Building Cards for *made* in a pocket chart. Point to the letters as you say each sound. *The word* made *has three sounds: /m/ /ā/ /d/. Let's say the sounds together: /m/ /ā/ /d/. Listen as I blend the sounds: /mmmāāād/. The final e is silent, and it makes the a say its name: /ā/.*

- Help children read words with long *a*. Write words on the board and model blending as needed. Use the following: *shade, lake, plane, blade, grade, stake, cake, crate, spade, flake, shake, trade.*

ELL ENGLISH LANGUAGE LEARNERS

Access to Core Content

Content Objective Develop listening comprehension
Language Objective Discuss text using key words and sentence frames
Materials • **ELL Resource Book**, pp. 222–229

✔ PRETEACH TRADE BOOK

All Language Levels

Use the Interactive Question-Response Guide on **ELL Resource Book** pages 222–229 to introduce children to *Sunflower House*. Preteach half of the selection on Day 1 and half on Day 2.

■ Use the prompts provided in the guide to develop meaning and vocabulary. Use the partner-talk and whole-class responses to engage children and increase student talk.

■ When completed, revisit the selection and prompt children to talk about the illustrations. Provide sentence starters as needed and build on children's responses to develop language.

ELL Resource Book

Trade Book

Beginning	**Intermediate**	**Advanced**
Use Visuals During the Interactive Reading, select several pictures. Describe them and have children summarize what you said.	**Summarize** During the Interactive Reading, select a few lines of text. After you read them and explain them, have children summarize the text.	**Expand** During the Interactive Reading, select a larger portion of text. After you read it and explain it, have children summarize the text.

Approaching Level

High-Frequency Words

Objective Recognize high-frequency words *little, said, here, was*

Materials
- **High-Frequency Word Cards:** *little, said, here, was*
- **Word-Building Cards**

REVIEW WORDS: *little, said, here, was*

- Display the **High-Frequency Word Card** for **little**. Say the word and have children repeat it. Point to each letter and have children name it.

- Distribute small **Word-Building Cards** *l, i, t, t, l,* and *e*. Model putting the letters together to form the word *little*. Then have children form *little*.

- Repeat the above routines with the words **said**, **here**, and **was**.

- Ask a question with the word *little*: *What little thing can you find in a garden?* Have children use *little* to answer the question in a complete sentence. Continue with the other words.

CUMULATIVE REVIEW

Display High-Frequency Word Cards for words previously taught, one card at a time, and have children chorally read and spell the words. Mix and repeat. Note words children need to review.

Phonemic Awareness

Objective Delete sounds to form new words

Materials • Puppet

PHONEME DELETION

Tier 2

Model
- Hold up the **Puppet**. *Listen as Happy says the sounds for* bus: */b/ /u/ /s/. Now Happy will say* bus *without the /b/: /uuusss/, us. What's left is the word* us: bus, us. *Now I'll do another word.* Repeat with *kit* and *win*.

Guided Practice/Practice
- Have the Puppet provide the following clues:

  Say cup *without /k/. What do you have?* (up)

  Say bin *without /b/. What do you have?* (in)

  Say mat *without /m/. What do you have?* (at)

  Say bit *without /b/. What do you have?* (it)

  Say pan *without /p/. What do you have?* (an)

- Guide practice as needed.

ELL

Extra Practice During the Cumulative Review, pair children at different levels of proficiency and have partners take turns reading and spelling the high-frequency words to each other.

Puppet

Approaching Level

Phonics

Objective	Blend letter sounds to form words with *op* and build fluency
Materials	• **Word-Building Cards** • pocket chart

Tier 2

REVIEW SKILLS

Model

- Place **Word-Building Card** *t* in the pocket chart. *This letter is* t. *Letter* t *stands for the /t/ sound. Say /t/. What is the letter? What is the sound?*

- Place *o* next to *t*. Repeat the routine for *o*.

- Place *p* next to *o*. Repeat the routine for *p*.

- Move your hand from left to right below the letters. *Listen as I blend the three sounds together: /tooop/, top. What's the word? Let's blend the word together: /t/ /o/ /p/, /tooop/, top.*

Guided Practice/Practice

- Give *m, o, p* cards to three children and line them up to spell *mop*. Have each child say the sound for the letter on his or her card. Have children blend the sounds to say the word *mop*. Repeat with *hop* and *pop*.

Build Fluency

- Have children blend *top, mop, hop,* and *pop* quickly.

Decodable Reader

Objective	Reread Decodable Reader *Pick It!*
Materials	• **Decodable Reader:** *Pick It!*

REREAD *Pick It!*

- Have children identify the front cover of the book and read the title. Open to the title page and point out the title. *Let's read the title together.* Have children sound out each word as you run your finger under it. *Look at the picture. What is the boy doing? What do you think we will read about in this book?*

- Page through the book. Ask children what they see in each picture. Ask children to find the words *can* and *the.*

- Read the book chorally with children. Have children point to each word as they read it. Provide corrective feedback as needed.

- Ask children to use *can* and *the* to talk about the pictures. *Can they pick the red bud?*

- After reading, ask children to recall what they read.

Corrective Feedback

Association Error If children have difficulty identifying initial and medial /o/, say: *My turn: /tooop/,* top. *I hear the /o/ sound at the middle of* top: */tooop/. What is the sound? What is the letter? Let's start over.* Repeat the word *top* for children to identify the position of /o/.

Decodable Reader

ON YOUR OWN

Write Captions

Have children draw a picture of something in a garden that is ready to be picked. Have them write a caption.

ON YOUR OWN

Draw the Garden

Have children draw a picture of the garden from *Pick It!* and label the plants that grow there. Have children share their drawings with the group.

Decodable Reader

On Level

Decodable Reader

Objective   Reread *Pick It!* to develop fluency
Materials   • **Decodable Reader:** *Pick It!*

REREAD FOR FLUENCY

- Ask children to review the illustrations in *Pick It!* Have them use their own words to identify and describe the characters and to retell what the book was about.

- Have children reread a page or two of *Pick It!* Work with them to read with accuracy and expression. Model reading a page. Point out how you used your voice to read the question: *When I read page 3, I see a question mark. I read the question by raising my voice at the end:* Can I pick it? *That's how a question sounds when people speak.*

- Provide time to listen as children read their page(s). Comment on their accuracy and expression, and provide corrective feedback by modeling proper fluency.

Beyond Level

Decodable Reader

Objective   Reread *Pick It!* to reinforce fluency
Materials   • **Decodable Reader:** *Pick It!*

REREAD FOR FLUENCY

- Have partners reread *Pick It!*

- Provide time to listen as children read. Comment on their accuracy and expression, and provide corrective feedback by modeling proper fluency.

INNOVATE

- Have children create a new title by replacing the word *Pick* with another word that ends with *ck*. For example, *Pluck It!* or *Trick It!* Ask children to draw a new cover illustration for the story and tell a partner how the story with the new title would change.

ELL ENGLISH LANGUAGE LEARNERS

Access to Core Content

Content Objective Develop listening comprehension
Language Objective Discuss text using key words and sentence frames
Materials • **ELL Resource Book,** pp. 230–231

PRETEACH BIG BOOK OF EXPLORATIONS

All Language Levels

Use the Interactive Question-Response Guide on **ELL Resource Book** pages 230–231 to introduce children to *How Does a Garden Grow?* Preteach half of the selection on Day 3 and half on Day 4.

Grammar

Content Objective Identify describing words
Language Objective Speak in complete sentences, using sentence frames
Materials • **Trade Book:** *Sunflower House* • **Photo Cards**

DESCRIBING WORDS

All Language Levels

- Review describing words. Remind children that describing words tell more about something. Say this sentence: *The big red flower is for you.* Point out that this sentence has two describing words that tell more about the flower: *big, red.*

- Remind children of the **Trade Book** *Sunflower House.* Say this sentence from the story: *They're much too big and wide and tall.*

- Point out that the sentence is about Mom and Dad. Ask: *What three words describe Mom and Dad?* (*big, wide, tall*) Big, wide, *and* tall *tell how Mom and Dad look to the child in the story.*

PEER DISCUSSION STARTERS

All Language Levels

- Distribute **Photo Cards** of food items, such as *carrots, sandwich, pizza, peach, watermelon,* and *juice.*

- Pair children and have them complete sentence frames such as *The _____ are _____.* Ask them to expand on their sentences by providing as many describing words as they can. For example: *The carrots are orange and delicious.* Circulate, listen in, and take note of each child's language use and proficiency.

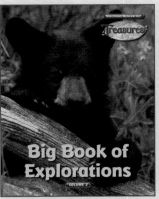

Big Book of Explorations

Transfer Skills

In Spanish, adjective forms reflect number and gender. For example, children may say *the bigs flowers* instead of *the big flowers.* Point to the describing word and say it aloud, then point to the noun, emphasizing the difference in endings.

Puppet

Corrective Feedback

Sound Error If children miss making the letter-sound correspondence, say: *My turn: pick, /piiik/. I hear /i/ in the middle of pick, /piiik/. I'll hold up my i card because I hear /i/ in the middle of /piiik/. What is the sound? What letter stands for that sound? Let's start again.*

ELL

Extra Practice Provide additional practice in recognizing and naming letters for children whose native languages do not use the symbols of the Latin alphabet.

Approaching Level

Phonemic Awareness

Objective Blend sounds to form words
Materials • **Puppet**

PHONEME BLENDING

Tier 2

Model

■ Hold up the **Puppet**. *Happy is going to say the sounds in a word: /k /u/ /t/. Happy will blend these sounds together: /kuuut/. Now you say the sounds in the word: /k/ /u/ /t/. Say the word with Happy:* cut. Repeat with *luck*.

Guided Practice/Practice

■ Have the Puppet say the following sounds: /d/ /u/ /k/ (*duck*), /f/ /u/ /n/ (*fun*), /t/ /u/ /k/ (*tuck*), /n/ /u/ /t/ (*nut*), /b/ /u/ /d/ (*bud*), /r/ /u/ /n/ (*run*). Guide children to blend the sounds together to say the words.

Phonics

Objective Blend letter sounds to form words with -ick
Materials • **Word-Building Cards** • pocket chart

BLEND SOUNDS IN CVC WORDS

Tier 2

Model

■ Place **Word-Building Cards** k, i, c, k in the pocket chart. *This letter is* k. *The letter* k *stands for the /k/ sound. Say /k/.*

■ *This letter is* i. *The letter* i *stands for the /i/ sound. Say /i/.*

■ *These letters are* c *and* k. *The letters* ck *together stand for the /k/ sound at the end of words. Say /k/.*

■ *Point under the word and say the sound each letter stands for: /k/ /i/ /k/. Now I blend the three sounds together: /kiiik/,* kick.

Guided Practice/Practice

■ Keep the Word-Building Cards in the pocket chart. Have children take turns pointing under the cards, saying the letter sounds, and blending the word: /k/ /i/ /k/, /kiiik/, *kick*.

■ Repeat with *pick, sick,* and *tick*. Guide practice as necessary.

Approaching Level

Leveled Reader Lesson 1

Objective Read *It Was Here!* to apply skills and strategies
Materials • **Leveled Reader:** *It Was Here!*

BEFORE READING

- **Preview and Predict** Read the title and author's name. *Who do you see on the cover? What do you think the book is about?* Turn to the title page and point out that it also has the title and author.

- **Review High-Frequency Words** Write **little**, **said**, **here**, **was**, **and**, and **what** and read the words aloud. Guide children as they name the letters in each word. Have children find each word in the book and point to the word as they read it.

- **Page Through the Book** Name unfamiliar terms and clarify any details that are confusing to children.

- **Model Concepts About Print** Demonstrate book handling for children. Guide them as they follow along with their books. *I hold the book so that the cover faces me. I open the book by turning the cover. Then I turn each page as I read it, starting with the first page and ending with the last page.*

- **Set a Purpose for Reading** *Let's find out what Gus's problem is.*

DURING READING

- Remind children to use the illustrations to gain information and to look for the high-frequency words *little, said, here, was, and,* and *what.* Show children how to monitor and adjust comprehension if a word doesn't sound right or doesn't make sense in the sentence. *On page 5, I read the sentence very quickly. I thought the sentence was "It was there!" That makes sense, but then I look again at the sentence. The word is* here, *not* there. Here *and* there *look a lot alike, and that's why I got confused. I will read the sentence again using the correct word: "It was here!"*

- Monitor children's reading and encourage children to reread a portion of the story to help with their comprehension.

AFTER READING

- Ask children to point out words that they had trouble reading and to share strategies they used to figure them out. Reinforce good behaviors. Say: *Jared, I noticed that you used picture clues to help you figure out the name of each food missing from the garden.*

- Ask children to retell important events from the story and to share responses. *How did Gus know that foods were missing from his garden? What kinds of animals take food from a garden?*

Leveled Reader

Digital Learning

Use the **Leveled Reader Audio CD** for fluency building *after* children read the book with your support during Small Group time.

ON YOUR OWN

Food for Gus

Have children think of the kinds of foods Gus might like to eat, based on what has been taken from his garden. Have them write a sentence and draw a picture to tell about one of these foods.

Leveled Reader

ELL

Retell Use the Interactive Question-Response Guide Technique to help English Language Learners understand *I Like This Flower*. As you read, make meaning clear by pointing to pictures, demonstrating word meaning, paraphrasing text, and asking children questions.

Favorite Flowers

Have children describe the flower that Honey Bee, Little Ant, and Butterfly liked. Then have them draw their favorite flower and write a caption, such as *I like this flower.*

I like this flower.

On Level

Leveled Reader Lesson 1

Objective Read *I Like This Flower* to apply skills and strategies

Materials • **Leveled Reader:** *I Like This Flower*

BEFORE READING

- **Preview and Predict** Read the title and the name of the author. *What do you see on the cover? Is the flower inside or outside? What are the insects doing? What do you think the book will be about?* Open and page through the book. Name unfamiliar items.

- **Model Concepts About Print** Demonstrate book handling. *I hold the book so that the cover is facing me and the words are not upside down. I open the book by turning the cover. Then I turn each page as I read it.*

- **Review High-Frequency Words** Write **little**, **said**, **here**, **was**, **I**, **like**, and **and** on chart paper. Have children find each word in the book and point to the word as they read it.

- **Set a Purpose for Reading** *Let's read to find out what animal friends like.*

DURING READING

- Have children turn to page 2 and begin by whisper-reading the first two pages.

- Remind children to look for the new high-frequency word and to use the illustrations.

- Tell children to monitor and adjust their comprehension as they read. Suggest that they use sensory images or reread a section. Stop during the reading and ask open-ended questions to facilitate discussion, such as: *Why is the kangaroo taking a photograph? How does he feel about the insects?* Build on children's responses to develop deeper understanding.

AFTER READING

- Ask children to point out words they had trouble reading and to share strategies they used. Reinforce good behaviors. For example: *Jemiah, I noticed that you sounded out the sounds in each word in* Honey Bee *and* Butterfly.

- **Retell** Ask children to ask each other questions *Do you like flowers? What is your favorite kind of flower?* Tell children to respond in complete sentences.

Beyond Level

Leveled Reader Lesson 1

Objective   Read *Kim's Garden* to apply skills and strategies
Materials   • **Leveled Reader:** *Kim's Garden*

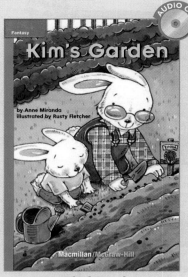

Leveled Reader

BEFORE READING

- **Preview and Predict** Read the title and the name of the author. *Who do you see on the cover? Where are they? What are they doing? What time of year is it?* Turn to the title page and point out that it also has the title and the name of the author. Page through the book with children and name unfamiliar items.

- **Introduce Story Words** Point to the flower names *petunia, marigold,* and *zinnia* on page 7. Point out each flower in the illustration so children will know what Kim is planting.

- **Set a Purpose for Reading** *Let's read to find out what changes when seeds begin to sprout and grow into flowers.*

DURING READING

- Remind children that when they come to an unfamiliar word, they can look for familiar chunks in the word, break the word into syllables and sound out each part, or think about what the word might mean. If the word does not sound right or make sense in the sentence, children can self-correct.

- Monitor children's reading and provide help as needed.

AFTER READING

- Have children point out words they had trouble reading and share the strategies they used.

- Ask pairs of children to ask each other questions and share their personal responses. *What did you learn about planting a garden that you did not know before? How was the way that they planted seeds in the book different from your experiences? What tools did they use in the story?*

- **Synthesize** *Gram taught Kim how to plant a garden. What might Kim teach Gram to do?*

- Have children work in pairs to list activities that Kim might teach Gram, such as using a computer or playing a board game. Encourage children to come up with at least two ideas.

- **Model** Tell children to write a short story about Kim teaching Gram how to do an activity from the list. Write on the board: *How will the story begin? Will Gram have to be patient? What questions will Gram ask Kim? How will the story end?*

Extend the Book

Ask children to draw and write about an activity they do with a grandparent or an older family member.

Grandpa and I make a birdhouse.

Leveled Reader

Vocabulary

Preteach Vocabulary Use the routine in the **Visual Vocabulary Resources**, pages 347–348, to preteach the ELL Vocabulary listed on the inside front cover of the Leveled Reader.

ELL ENGLISH LANGUAGE LEARNERS

Leveled Reader

Content Objective Read to apply skills and strategies

Language Objective Retell information using complete sentences

Materials • **Leveled Reader:** *I Will Sit Here*

BEFORE READING

All Language Levels

- **Preview** Read the title *I Will Sit Here*. Ask: *What's the title? Say it again.* Repeat with the author's name. Point to the cover illustration and say: *Look at the insects on this flower.* Point to the insects and flower as you name them. *The ant is an insect. The butterfly is an insect. Now turn to a partner and tell about this picture.*

- **Page Through the Book** Use simple language to tell about the illustration on each page. Immediately follow up with questions, such as: *Is this a butterfly or an ant? Where is it sitting?*

- **Review Skills** Use the inside front cover to review the phonics skill and high-frequency words.

- **Set a Purpose** Say: *Let's read to find out where the insects sit.*

DURING READING

All Language Levels

- Have children whisper-read each page, or use the differentiated suggestions below. Circulate, listen in, and provide corrective feedback, such as modeling how to use the illustrations for clues to figure out a word.

- **Retell** Stop after every two pages and ask children to state what they have learned so far. Reinforce language by restating children's comments when they have difficulty using story-specific words. Provide differentiated sentence frames to support children's responses and engage children in partner-talk.

Beginning	Intermediate	Advanced
Echo-Read Have children echo-read after you.	**Choral-Read** Have children choral-read with you.	**Choral-Read** Have children choral-read.
Check Comprehension Point to pictures and ask questions such as: *Do you see the ant? Point to the ant.*	**Check Comprehension** Ask questions/prompts such as: *Describe what you see in this picture. Who sits on the flower?*	**Check Comprehension** Ask: *Where does Kangaroo sit? Read the sentence that tells where Kangaroo sits.*

ELL ENGLISH LANGUAGE LEARNERS

AFTER READING

All Language Levels

Book Talk Children will work with peers of varying language abilities to discuss their books for this week. Display the four Leveled Readers read this week: *Kim's Garden* (Beyond Level), *I Like This Flower* (On Level), *It Was Here!* (Approaching Level), and *I Will Sit Here* (English Language Learners).

Ask the questions and provide the prompts below. Call on children who read each book to answer the questions or respond to the prompt. If appropriate, ask children to find the pages in the book that illustrate their answers.

- **What color flowers did your book show?**
- **Where are the flowers?**
- **Describe the garden in your book.**
- **Who else is in the book?**
- **Which flower do you like best?**

Develop Listening and Speaking Skills Tell children to remember the following:

- Share information in cooperative learning interactions. Remind children to work with their partners to retell the story and complete any activities. Ask: *What happened next in the story?*

- Employ self-corrective techniques and monitor their own and other children's language production. Children should ask themselves: *What parts of this passage were confusing to me? Can my classmates help me clarify a word or sentence that I don't understand?*

- Use high-frequency English words to describe people, places, and objects.

- Narrate, describe, and explain with specificity and detail. Ask: *Where did the story take place? Can you describe the setting? What else did you notice?*

- Express opinions, ideas, and feelings on a variety of social and academic topics. Ask: *What do you think about the characters in the story?*

Approaching Level

Phonemic Awareness

Objective Segment words into sounds
Materials • **Sound Boxes** • markers
• **WorkBoard Sound Boxes; Teacher's Resource Book**, p. 136

 PHONEME SEGMENTATION

Tier 2

Model
- Use the **Sound Boxes**. *I will say the sounds in the word* luck. *Listen: /l/ /u/ /k/,* luck. *How many sounds are in* luck? *I will place a marker in a box as I say each sound in* luck. *There are three sounds in* luck, */l/ /u/ /k/, so I will put a marker in three boxes. Say the sounds in* luck *with me: /l/ /u/ /k/.* Repeat with *pick.*

Guided Practice/Practice
- Distribute Sound Boxes and markers. *I will say a word. Say each sound in the word as you place a marker in a box. Then tell me the sounds.* Say the following words:

duck	lot	kick
pot	peck	tuck
Rick	deck	kick

Phonics

Objective Reinforce medial /i/i, /o/o, and /u/u and build fluency
Materials • **Photo Cards:** *bus, lock, mix, mop, nut, sock, six, sun* • pocket chart
• **Word-Building Cards** • **Sound-Spelling WorkBoards**

 BUILD FLUENCY: LETTER-SOUND CORRESPONDENCE

Tier 2

Model
- Place **Word-Building Cards** *i, o,* and *u* in the top row of the pocket chart. Place the **Photo Cards** facedown in a stack. Pick the first card, name the picture, and identify the medial sound. Then place it in the pocket chart under the corresponding letter.

Guided Practice/Practice
- Have each child choose a Photo Card, say the name of the picture, identify its medial sound, and place it in the pocket chart under *i, o,* or *u*. Guide practice with the first Photo Card.

Build Fluency
- Display the Word-Building Cards. Have children name each letter as quickly as they can. Then ask them to write the letters *i, o,* and *u* on their **WorkBoards** several times as they say /i/, /o/, and /u/.

Approaching Level

Leveled Reader Lesson 2

Objective Reread *It Was Here!* to reinforce fluency and drawing conclusions
Materials • **Leveled Reader:** *It Was Here!*

Leveled Reader

FOCUS ON FLUENCY

- Tell children that you will read one page of the book and they should read that page right after you. They should follow along in their books and try to read at the same speed and with the same expression that you use.

SKILL DRAW CONCLUSIONS

- *Look at pages 2 and 3. What do you think the rabbit is doing? Why does Gus look confused as he looks for his vegetables? How did looking at the illustrations and following the **plot** help you learn more about the story? How did you use your experiences to figure out what happens in the story?*

REREAD BOOKS

- Distribute copies of the past six **Leveled Readers**. Tell children that rereading the books will help them develop their skills.

- Circulate and listen in as children read. Stop them periodically and ask them how they are figuring out words or checking their understanding. Suggest that children reread a portion aloud to help them adjust their comprehension. Tell children to read other previously read Leveled Readers during independent reading time.

High-Frequency Words

Objective Review high-frequency words *little, said, here, was, and, what*
Materials • **High-Frequency Word Cards**

BUILD WORD AUTOMATICITY: *little, said, here, was, and, what*

- Distribute copies of the word **little**. Say the word and have children repeat it. Ask children to name the letters in the word. Repeat with the words **said**, **here**, **was**, **and**, and **what**.

- **Build Fluency** Use the High-Frequency Word Cards to review previously taught words. Display the words and have children read them aloud. Repeat, guiding children to read more rapidly.

Meet Grade-Level Expectations

As an alternative to this day's lesson, guide children through a reading of the On Level Leveled Reader. See page 2054. Because both books contain the same vocabulary, phonics, and comprehension skills, the scaffolding you provided will help most children gain access to this more challenging text.

Extend *It Was Here!*

Children can extend the story by drawing pictures that show Gus catching the rabbit who is stealing his vegetables. Have them use speech bubbles showing what the characters would say.

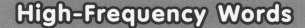

Leveled Reader

Write Facts

Ask children to recall the animals in the story and choose one to write a fact about. Have them draw a picture of the animal and write a fact about a real honeybee, butterfly, ant, or kangaroo.

On Level

Leveled Reader Lesson 2

Objective Reread to apply skills and strategies to retell a story
Materials • **Leveled Reader:** *I Like This Flower*

BEFORE READING

- Ask children to look through *I Like This Flower* and recall what the book is about. Reinforce vocabulary by repeating children's sentences using more sophisticated language. For example: *Yes, the animal friends like the flower. Red Kangaroo likes it so much, he takes a picture of it.*

DURING READING

- Have children join you in a choral-reading of the story. Model reading with expression. *I read* Click! Click! Click! *on page 8 so that it sounds like a camera taking a picture.* Ask children to use the same kind of expression when they read.

- Assign each child a page. Have children practice by whisper-reading. *Follow along as other children read, and be ready to come in when it is your turn. Remember, use lots of expression.*

AFTER READING

- Have children retell the selection in their own words. *What happened at the beginning of the story? What happened in the middle of the story? What happened at the end of the story?*

- *Look at page 4. Why do you think Little Ant, Butterfly, and Honey Bee all like flowers? Do you think they like one another, too? How can you tell? Why do you think Red Kangaroo said he could not sit by the flower?*

Beyond Level

Leveled Reader Lesson 2

Objective Reread to apply skills and strategies to retell a story

Materials • **Leveled Reader:** *Kim's Garden*

BEFORE READING

■ Ask children to page through *Kim's Garden* and recall what the book is about. Have them retell important events in the story. *Why did Kim not want to use seeds in the garden? Why did she change her mind?*

DURING READING

■ Assign each child a page of the book to read aloud. Have children practice by whisper-reading. *Follow along as each child reads, and be ready to come in when it is your turn. Remember, use lots of expression.*

AFTER READING

■ Remind children that all stories have a beginning, a middle, and an end. Discuss what happened at the beginning of *Kim's Garden*. Guide children to continue looking through the book to find out what problem occurs in the middle and how the problem is solved in the end.

Expand Vocabulary

Objective Brainstorm words for flowers

Materials • **Leveled Reader:** *Kim's Garden*

ENRICH: *words for flowers*

■ Reread the sentence *"I'm planting roses," said Gram,* on page 2.

■ Tell children that the word *rose* names a kind of flower. Ask children to point to the picture of the roses on page 2.

■ Reread the sentences *"Here is a pack of petunias. Here is a pack of marigolds. Here is a pack of zinnias," said Gram,* on page 6. Work with children to identify the words that name types of flowers. (*petunias, marigolds, zinnias*) Point out the flowers in the illustration on page 6.

■ Draw a word web and write *Flowers* in the center circle and the words *rose, petunia, marigold,* and *zinnia* around the center circle. Ask children to think of other words they know that name flowers and add them to the word web.

Leveled Reader

ON YOUR OWN

Create a Story Map

Provide each child with a story map labeled *Beginning, Middle,* and *End.* Have children draw pictures to show what happens in each part of *Kim's Garden.*

ELL

Partners When children add to the word web, pair English Language Learners with children who are more proficient.

ELL ENGLISH LANGUAGE LEARNERS

Fluency

Content Objectives Reread the Decodable Reader to develop fluency; develop speaking skills

Language Objective Tell a partner what a selection is about

Materials • **Decodable Reader:** *Pick It!*

REREAD FOR FLUENCY

Beginning

■ Review the high-frequency words **little**, **said**, **here**, and **was** using the **Read/Spell/Write** routine.

Intermediate/Advanced

■ Use each word in a sentence that illustrates its use, such as: *Here is a little table.* Point to the table. *What else is little?* Gesture around the class.

■ Then provide sentence starters for children to complete. Where appropriate, act out children's responses. For example: *Here is a little cup.*

All Language Levels

■ Guide children through a choral-reading of *Pick It!* Point to the exclamation mark in the title. Tell children that the exclamation mark tells us we should read the title with excitement: *Pick It!* Model reading the title in a normal way and with excitement and have children chorally repeat.

DEVELOP SPEAKING/LISTENING SKILLS

All Language Levels

■ Have children reread *Pick It!* to a partner. Remind them to listen carefully and follow along in their book as their partner is reading. Work with children to read with accuracy and appropriate expression.

■ Ask children to tell their partner about the pictures on each page. Then have the other partner describe the pictures. Circulate, listen in, and provide additional language as needed.

Beginning	Intermediate	Advanced
Confirm Understanding Point to the pictures for partners to identify. Ask: *What do you see?* Restate the correct answer in a complete sentence.	**Express Opinions** Ask partners to tell you which is their favorite picture in the book. Prompt them to explain why it is their favorite picture.	**Compare and Contrast** Have partners compare two different pictures and describe them. Prompt them to explain how they are alike and different.

ELL

ENGLISH LANGUAGE LEARNERS

High-Frequency Words

Content Objective Spell high-frequency words correctly
Language Objective Write in complete sentences, using sentence frames
Materials • Sound-Spelling WorkBoards • Sound-Spelling Cards • Photo Cards

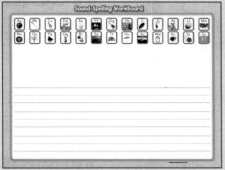

Sound-Spelling WorkBoard

Beginning/Intermediate

- Write the high-frequency words **little**, **said**, **here**, and **was** on the board. Have children copy the words on their **WorkBoards**. Then help them say, then write, a sentence for each word. Provide the following sentence starters: *Look at the little _____. I said, "_____." Here is a _____. The flower was _____.*

Advanced

- Children should first orally state each sentence. Correct as needed. Then they can draw a picture to complete the sentence. For children who are ready, help them spell words using their growing knowledge of English sound-spelling relationships. Model how to segment the word children are trying to spell and attach a spelling to each sound. Use the **Sound-Spelling Cards** to reinforce the spellings for each English sound.

Writing

All Language Levels

- Dictate the following words and ask children to write them: *pick, up, kid.* Use the words in sentences and explain the meaning as needed. Have children write each word five times as they say them. Demonstrate correct letter formation, as needed.

- Then display a set of **Photo Cards**. Select at least five cards whose picture names begin with /k/*k* (koala, key, kitten, kite, king) and /u/ (umpire, under, undershirt, up, upside down), and two that end with /k/*ck* (sock, lock).

- Say the name of each card, stretching or reiterating the initial sound to emphasize it. You may also need to model correct mouth formation when forming the sound. Use the articulation pictures and prompts on the back of the small Sound-Spelling Cards for support. Tell children to write the first letter in each picture name that begins with /k/ or /u/ on their WorkBoards. If the word ends with /k/, they should write *ck.*

Phonemic Awareness/ Phonics

For English Language Learners who need more practice with this week's phonemic awareness and phonics skills, see the Approaching Level lessons. Focus on minimal contrasts, articulation, and those sounds that do not transfer from the child's first language to English. For a complete listing of transfer sounds, see pages T10–T31.

Weekly Assessment

Use your Quick Check observations and the assessment opportunities identified below to evaluate children's progress in key skill areas.

Skills		Quick Check Observations	Pencil and Paper Assessment
PHONEMIC AWARENESS/ PHONICS /k/k, /u/u, /l/l	u k	1997	Activity Book, pp. 24, 29–30, 32 Practice Book, pp. 173, 177
HIGH-FREQUENCY WORDS *little, said, here, was*	little	2018	Activity Book, pp. 27–28 Practice Book, pp. 175–176
COMPREHENSION Draw Conclusions		2008	Activity Book, pp. 25–26, 31 Practice Book, p. 174

Quick Check Rubric

Skills	1	2	3
PHONEMIC AWARENESS/ PHONICS	Does not connect the /k/, /u/ sounds with the letters *Kk, Uu* and has difficulty blending the words *deck, kick, lick, rock, dock, tack, rub, cut, cup, fun, dud, Pam, mop, map, tip, bit.*	Usually connects the /k/, /u/ sounds with the letters *Kk, Uu* and blends the words *deck, kick, lick, rock, dock, tack, rub, cut, cup, fun, dud, Pam, mop, map, tip, bit* with only occasional support.	Consistently connects the /k/, /u/ sounds with the letters *Kk, Uu* and blends the words *deck, kick, lick, rock, dock, tack, rub, cut, cup, fun, dud, Pam, mop, map, tip, bit.*
HIGH-FREQUENCY WORDS	Does not identify the high-frequency words.	Usually recognizes the high-frequency words with accuracy, but not speed.	Consistently recognizes the high-frequency words with speed and accuracy.
COMPREHENSION	Does not draw conclusions using the pictures and text.	Usually draws conclusions using the pictures and text.	Consistently draws conclusions using the pictures and text.

DIBELS LINK

PROGRESS MONITORING

Use your DIBELS results to inform instruction.

IF...

Initial Sound Fluency (**ISF**)   0–34

THEN...

Evaluate for Intervention

TPRI LINK

PROGRESS MONITORING

Use your TPRI scores to inform instruction.

IF...

Phonemic Awareness	Still Developing
Graphophonemic Knowledge	Still Developing
Listening Comprehension	Still Developing

THEN...

Evaluate for Intervention

End-of-Week Assessment

Diagnose		Prescribe
Review the assessment answers with children. Have them correct their errors. Then provide additional instruction as needed.		
PHONEMIC AWARENESS/ PHONICS /k/k, /u/u, /l/l	**IF...** **Quick Check Rubric:** Children consistently score 1 or **Pencil and Paper Assessment:** Children get 0–2 items correct	**THEN...** Reteach Phonemic Awareness and Phonics Skills using the **Phonemic Awareness** and **Phonics Intervention Teacher's Editions**. *SPIRAL REVIEW* Use the Build Fluency lesson in upcoming weeks to provide children practice reading words with /k/k, /u/u, and /l/l.
HIGH-FREQUENCY WORDS *little, said, here, was*	**Quick Check Rubric:** Children consistently score 1 or **Pencil and Paper Assessment:** Children get 0–2 items correct	Reteach High-Frequency Words using the **Phonics Intervention Teacher's Edition**. *SPIRAL REVIEW* Use the High-Frequency Words lesson in upcoming weeks to provide children practice reading the words *little, said, here,* and *was*.
COMPREHENSION Skill: Draw Conclusions	**Quick Check Rubric:** Children consistently score 1 or **Pencil and Paper Assessment:** Children get 0–2 items correct	Reteach Comprehension Skill using the **Comprehension Intervention Teacher's Edition**.

Response to Intervention

To place children in Tier 2 or Tier 3 Intervention use the *Diagnostic Assessment*.

- Phonemic Awareness
- Phonics
- Vocabulary
- Comprehension
- Fluency

Use this page to record lessons that work well or need to be adapted for future reference.

Lessons that work well

Lessons that need adjustments

Use this page to record lessons that work well or need to be adapted for future reference.

Lessons that work well

Lessons that need adjustments

Unit 8 Computer Literacy

Objectives

- Use the paintbrush tool to make a picture
- Use a digital camera

Materials

- www.macmillanmh.com
- paint program at www.macmillanmh.com
- digital camera

Vocabulary

graphics pictures that are created, stored, or printed on a computer

paintbrush tool a tool in a paint program used to draw graphics

icon a picture that represents a file or command on a computer display

color palette a set of available colors

digital camera a camera that takes digital images that can be loaded and manipulated on a computer

display screen a screen on a digital camera that shows the picture

Computer Literacy
Focus on Keyboard and Internet Skills and Media Literacy
www.macmillanmh.com

Remind children never to bring drinks around electronic equipment.

Drawing on the Computer
Using a Paint Program

ACCESS PRIOR KNOWLEDGE

Discuss with children:

- *In art, what do you make with a paintbrush?*

- *How do you think you can use a paintbrush on the computer?*

EXPLAIN

- *When working with a **graphic** on the computer, we use the mouse as our paintbrush.*

- *We can use the **paintbrush tool** to draw shapes by clicking on a shape **icon** or by using the free draw tool icon.*

MODEL

- Connect to **www.macmillanmh.com**. Go to the Computer Literacy lessons and open the paint program.

- Demonstrate how to use the paintbrush tool to free draw.

- Show children how to use the mouse to click on a shape icon. Model how to drag the shape to the size you want.

- Model how to select a color from the **color palette** and fill in a shape. Have children draw a shape and fill it in with a color.

Technology Makes a Difference

Explain that

▶ **digital cameras** are used to take pictures of people, places, and events;

▶ digital cameras have a viewfinder and **display screen** you can use to preview images when taking pictures;

▶ after you press the button, the picture you took appears on the display screen;

▶ you can then hook the camera's memory card to the computer to transfer the pictures to the computer.

Media Literacy

Media in Motion

ACCESS PRIOR KNOWLEDGE

Discuss with children:

- *What are some ways that you can move?* (walk, run, skip, hop, jump, dance, march, spin)

- *What are the differences between television and radio?* (Television involves pictures and sound while radio only involves sound; there is more variety on television; radio is more portable.)

EXPLAIN

Introduce the lesson vocabulary by discussing each word and its definition with children.

- **Movement** is the changing of position of an object or person. When we walk, skip, jump, and dance, we are moving. The makers of media use movement to make information more interesting for their **audience**.

- Media that uses **images** often involves movement. Television and movies use images that move to tell a story.

- Web sites sometimes also use movement. Moving pictures or video can be part of a **Web site**.

MODEL

- Teach children the song "My Bonnie Lies Over The Ocean." Have children begin in a seated position. The first time the word "Bonnie" is sung, children should stand up. The second time it is sung they should sit down, continuing in this manner until the end of the song. Sing the song a second time, having children sit and stand each time a word beginning with the letter "B" is sung.

- Play children an age-appropriate television clip. Have children sit with their backs to the television set so they can hear what is happening on screen, but they cannot see it. Ask children to describe what happened in the clip. Then, play the clip a second time. This time, have children face the television and watch the movement on screen. Ask children which way was easier to understand and which way they preferred.

- Play the clip a third time. If possible, have children mimic the movements portrayed on screen.

Objectives

- Identify movement techniques used in media
- Examine how movement makes information more interesting

Materials

- television clips containing examples of movement

Media Literacy Activities
Lessons that help children explore and identify the use of motion in different forms of media

Theme: Plants

Theme Project Wrap-Up
Research/Organizing and Presenting Ideas

After children complete their projects, they can have a Garden Day to present what they have learned.

Step 3 **Review and Evaluate**

How do I share what I have learned?

The following checklists and Scoring Rubric will help you and children assess their projects.

seed   root   stem

Teacher's Checklist

Assess the Research Project

Plan the Project

✔ Used descriptive words to describe how various plants grow.

✔ Identified sources or people to answer research questions.

✔ Gathered information from provided text sources.

Do the Project

✔ Used pictures and words to record information.

✔ Sorted information with guidance.

✔ Identified purpose of research.

Assess the Presentation

Speaking

✔ Spoke audibly, clearly, and to the point.

✔ Shared information and ideas.

✔ Used appropriate vocabulary to describe experiences.

Representing

✔ Described project with appropriate visuals.

✔ Visuals added details and interest to the presentation.

✔ Communicated message clearly.

Assess the Listener

Listening

✔ Listened critically to presentations and asked clarifying questions.

✔ Connected own experiences with that of the speaker.

✔ Applied comprehension strategies while listening.

Children's Checklist

Research Process

✔ Which resource was difficult to use?

✔ Did you choose sources that could answer your research questions?

Presenting

Speaking

✔ Did you explain your project's purpose?

✔ Did you use details to make your report interesting?

✔ Did you speak audibly? Did you use complete, coherent sentences?

Representing

✔ Did you use writing with your visuals?

✔ What other visuals could you have used?

✔ Did you think about the audience as you planned your project?

SCORING RUBRIC FOR THEME PROJECT

4 Excellent	**3** Good	**2** Fair	**1** Unsatisfactory
The child	The child	The child	The child
• presents the main idea with supporting details; • may make sophisticated observations; • presents accurate, well-produced visuals that enhance the topic.	• clearly fulfills all the steps of the project; • provides adequate details; • makes several relevant observations.	• attempts to present some of the required steps; • demonstrates some difficulty with research; • may make somewhat unclear observations.	• does not appear to grasp the task in its entirety; • has great difficulty with organizational skills; • presents unnecessary or inaccurate information.

 Home-School Connection

Garden Day provides an excellent opportunity for home and community involvement.

■ Invite family and community members to come to school to view children's presentations and projects. Children may enjoy planting a small garden with their family and community members on the school grounds.

Big Question Wrap-Up

Review the Big Question for this unit with children. Discuss what they learned about plants.

Help children respond to the following questions: *What kinds of plants grow where you live? What do plants need to survive?* Remind children to take turns when speaking.

Administer the Test

Unit and Benchmark Assessment

Unit 8 TEST

TESTED SKILLS AND STRATEGIES

COMPREHENSION STRATEGIES AND SKILLS

- Strategies: Recognize text and story structure
- Skills: Identify sequence of events, draw conclusions, retell

HIGH-FREQUENCY WORDS

- *little, said, here, was*

PHONEMIC AWARENESS

- Phoneme isolation
- Phoneme blending
- Phoneme segmentation

PHONICS

- *k, ck, u*
- Review *-ot, -op, -ick* phonograms

CONCEPT WORDS

- Position words

Use Multiple Assessments for Instructional Planning

To create instructional profiles for your children, look for patterns in the results from any of the following assessments.

Running Records

Use the instructional reading level determined by the Running Record calculations for regrouping decisions.

Running Records
LEVELS: REBUS–80

Benchmark Assessments

Administer tests three times a year as an additional measure of both children's progress and the effectiveness of the instructional program.

Unit and Benchmark Assessment

Analyze the Data

Use information from a variety of informal and formal assessments, as well as your own judgment, to assist in your instructional planning. Children who consistently score at the lowest end of each range should be evaluated for Intervention. Use the **Diagnostic Assessment** for guidelines in the **Intervention Teacher's Editions**.

Diagnose		Prescribe
ASSESSMENTS	**IF...**	**THEN...**
UNIT TEST	0–15 Correct	Reteach skills using the **Intervention Teacher's Editions**.
RUNNING RECORDS	Rebus–Level 2	Reteach skills using the **Intervention Teacher's Editions**.

For users of DIBELS

Use the results from the DIBELS Progress Monitoring tests to confirm instructional decisions.

DIBELS LINK

PROGRESS MONITORING

Use your DIBELS results to inform instruction.

IF...
Initial Sound Fluency (ISF)   0–7
Phoneme Segmentation Fluency (PSF)   Start midyear

THEN...
Evaluate for Intervention

For users of TPRI

Use the scores from the TPRI as a progress monitoring tool to confirm instructional decisions.

TPRI LINK

PROGRESS MONITORING

Use your TPRI scores to inform instruction.

IF...
Phonemic Awareness   Still Developing
Graphophonemic Knowledge   Still Developing
Listening Comprehension   Still Developing

THEN...
Evaluate for Intervention

Response to Intervention

To place children in Tier 2 or Tier 3 Intervention use the *Diagnostic Assessment*.

- Phonemic Awareness
- Phonics
- Vocabulary
- Comprehension
- Fluency

Additional Resources

Contents

Instructional Routines

Professional Development

- Read the routine prior to using *Treasures*. Use the Routine QuickNotes as a reminder of key routine steps throughout Unit 1, or as needed.

- View the online classroom video clip through **TeacherWorks Plus**. Watch master teachers use these routines.

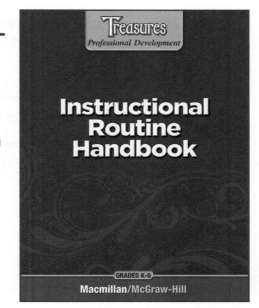

1. **Phonological Awareness/ Phonemic Awareness**
   Rhyme
   Oddity Tasks
   Sound Categorization
   Oral Blending
   Oral Segmentation
   Manipulation

2. **Phonics**
   Blending
   Introducing Sound-Spelling Cards
   Letter Recognition
   Building Words
   Building Fluency
   Reading Decodables
   Multisyllabic Words Routine

3. **Fluency**
   Strategies

4. **Vocabulary**
   Define/Example/Ask Routine
   Strategies

5. **High-Frequency Words**
   Read/Spell/Write Routine
   Reading Pre-decodables

6. **Spelling**
   Dictation

7. **Comprehension**
   Strategies
   Skills
   Reading Big Books
   Reading Student Book

8. **Writing**
   Conferences
   Revision Assignments
   Writing Process
   Using Rubrics
   Using Anchor Papers
   Writers' Express Sequence

9. **Research Process**
   Big Question Board

10. **Classroom Management**
    Workstation Flip Charts
    Contracts
    Centers
    Small Groups

11. **Listening/Speaking/Viewing**

12. **Assessment**

Theme Bibliography

By the Authors and Illustrators

For additional information on authors, illustrators, and selection content, go to **www.macmillanmh.com**.

Mitchell, Melanie. *Snakes (Life Cycles).* **Lerner, 2002.** In this series on life cycles, the author introduces young children to snakes with captivating photos and simple text.

Related to the Theme

Use these and other classroom or library resources to provide additional read alouds to build academic language.

Cook, Trish. *The Grandad Tree.* **Candlewick Press, 2000.** A brother and sister remember their grandfather and how they played under the apple tree that continues to grow and change in their garden.

Ehlert, Lois. *A Pie in the Sky.* **Harcourt, 2004.** A father and child watch cherries, on the tree in their yard, ripen until they are ready to be used in a pie.

Ehlert, Lois. *Red Leaf, Yellow Leaf.* **Harcourt, 1991.** The life of a sugar maple tree is examined through the eyes of a young child.

Oppenheim, Joanne. *Have You Seen Trees?* **Scholastic, 1995.** Trees are celebrated in all their beauty in different seasons and climates.

Pearson, Debora. *Leo's Tree.* **Annick Press, 2004.** Through a cycle of seasons, a baby boy and a tree each grow and change; told in simple rhyming text.

Udry, Janice May. *A Tree Is Nice.* **HarperTrophy, 1987.** Here is a celebration of all the pleasure a tree brings to the many people and creatures who come in contact with it.

WEEK 2	WEEK 3
Leonard, Tom. *One Small Place by the Sea.* **HarperCollins, 2004.** Stop and observe! Tom Leonard's illustrations take you underwater to a secret world with his detailed depictions of mussels, seaweed, and algae. A feast for the eyes!	**Bunting, Eve.** *A Day's Work.* **Clarion, 1997.** Children will be able to get a glimpse into immigration and day labor as they follow Abuelo and his grandfather while they look for work.
Carle, Eric. *The Tiny Seed.* **Aladdin, 1991.** A tiny seed travels great distances amid many obstacles to survive and grow into a beautiful flower.	**Coy, John.** *Two Old Potatoes.* **Alfred A. Knopf, 2003.** A little girl and her father plant two old potatoes in their garden and tend to them month by month, until in September they have a garden full of potatoes.
Doyle, Malachy. *Jody's Beans.* **Candlewick Press, 1999.** Jodi and her grandfather plant some runner beans in the garden and watch them grow through each season, until the beans finally end up on the dinner table.	**Ehlert, Lois.** *Planting a Rainbow.* **Voyager Books, 1992.** A variety of colorful flowers are planted, and the cycle of planting, growing, and picking flowers is celebrated.
Greenstein, Elaine *One Little Seed.* **Viking, 2004.** Just a few words on each page convey the process a seed goes through before it blossoms.	**Fleming, Candace.** *Muncha! Muncha! Muncha!* **Atheneum, 2002.** Mr. McGreely finally has the garden he has always wanted. His only problem is keeping the bunnies from eating his vegetables.
Jordan, Helene J. *How a Seed Grows.* **HarperTrophy, 1992.** Children see the botanical process from sowing seeds, to the sprouting of roots, to transplanting young plants.	**Ford, Miela.** *Sunflower.* **Greenwillow, 1995.** Here is a happy spring story on the basics of planting a garden, with bright, glowing illustrations.
Krauss, Ruth. *The Carrot Seed.* **HarperCollins, 1945.** A small boy patiently waits for his carrot seed to sprout, despite all the people around him who say it will not grow.	**Heap, Sue.** *Four Friends in a Garden.* **Candlewick, 2004.** Four friends—a bear, a rabbit, a sheep, and a little girl named Mary—welcome a butterfly to the garden and enjoy the outdoor experience.
Wallace, Nancy Elizabeth. *Seeds! Seeds! Seeds!* **Marshall Cavendish, 2004.** Buddy Bear discovers a surprise in each of the bags his grandfather sends to him.	**Roberts, Bethany.** *The Wind's Garden.* **Henry Holt, 2001.** There are two kinds of gardens being described in this appealing picture book; one that a young girl has cared for, and the other that the wind has planted.

Theme Bibliography

Selection Honors, Prizes, and Awards

 Sunflower House

by *Eve Bunting*

Illustrated by *Kathryn Hewitt*

Author: *Eve Bunting*, winner of ALA Notable Children's Book (1990), IRA-CBC Children's Choice, and School Library Journal Best Book (1989) for *The Wednesday Surprise*; Missouri Mark Twain Award, Florida Sunshine State Young Reader's Award (1989) for *Sixth Grade Sleepover*; ALA Notable Children's Book (1992) for *Fly Away Home*; Edgar Allen Poe Juvenile Award (1993) for *Coffin on a Case*; ALA Notable Children's Book, Caldecott Medal (1995) for *Smoky Night*; Booklist Editors' Choice (1995), Pennsylvania Young Reader's Choice Award (1998) for *Spying on Miss Müller*; Parents' Choice Gold Award (1996) for *Red Fox Running*; ALA Notable Children's Book, Booklist Editors' Choice (1997) for *Train to Somewhere*; Young Reader's Choice Award (1997) for *Nasty Stinky Sneakers*; Parents' Choice Gold Award (1997) for *A Day's Work*; National Council for Social Studies Notable Children's Book Award (1998) for *Moonstick, I Am the Mummy Heb-Nefert*, and *On Call Back Mountain*; Parents' Choice Recommended Award (2003) for *Whales Passing*

Illustrator: *Kathryn Hewitt*, winner of Association of Booksellers for Children, Children's Choice Award (1998) for *Lives of the Athletes: Thrills, Spills (and What the Neighbors Thought)*; Boston Globe-Horn Honor Award (1993) and ALA Notable Children's Book (1994) for *Lives of the Musicians: Good Times, Bad Times (and What the Neighbors Thought)*

Resources

Audio Bookshelf
44 Ocean View Drive
Middletown, RI 02842
800-234-1713
www.audiobookshelf.com

Discovery Communications
4540 Preslyn Drive
Raleigh, NC 27616
888-892-3484

Dorling Kindersley
375 Hudson Street
New York, NY 10014
Tel: 800-631-8571
Fax: 201-256-0000
http://us.dk.com

**Great Plains National
Instructional Television
Library**
GPN Educational Media
1407 Fleet Street
Baltimore, MD 21231
800-228-4630
http://shopgpn.com

Innovative Educators
P.O. Box 520
Montezuma, GA 31063
888-252-KIDS
Fax: 888-536-8553
www.innovative-educators.com

Library Video Co.
P.O. Box 580
Wynnewood, PA 19096
800-843-3620
www.libraryvideo.com

Listening Library
400 Hahn Road
Westminster, MD 21157
800-243-4504

Live Oak Media
P.O. Box 652
Pine Plains, NY 12567
800-788-1121
www.liveoakmedia.com

Macmillan/McGraw-Hill
220 East Danieldale Road
DeSoto, TX 75115-9960
Tel: 800-442-9685
Fax: 972-228-1982
www.macmillanmh.com

MCA Video
MCA Records/Universal Studios
100 Universal City Plaza
Universal City, CA 91608
818-777-1000

Microsoft Corp.
One Microsoft Way
Redmond, WA 98052
800-426-9000
www.microsoft.com

**National Geographic
Society**
1145 17th Street N.W.
Washington, DC 20036
800-647-5463
www.nationalgeographic.com

Recorded Books
270 Skipjack Road
Prince Frederick, MD 20678
800-636-3399
www.recordedbooks.com

Sunburst Communications
Sunburst Technology
1550 Executive Drive
Elgin, IL 60123
888-492-8817
www.sunburst.com

SVE & Churchill Media
6465 North Avondale Avenue
Chicago, IL 60631
800-253-2788

Tom Snyder Productions
100 Talcott Avenue
Watertown, MA 02472
800-342-0236
www.tomsnyder.com

Weston Woods
143 Main Street
Norwalk, CT 06851
800-243-5020
www.teacher.scholastic.com/products/
westonwoods/

Web Sites

Go to www.macmillanmh.com.
Use the zip code finder to locate other resources in your area.

The Academy of Natural Sciences
http://www.ansp.org/

Acadia National Park
http://www.nps.gov/acad

Agriculture in the Classroom
http://www.agclassroom.org/

Arches National Park
http://www.nps.gov/arch

Asian American History Resources Online - CET
http://www.cetel.org/res.html

Association of Zoos and Aquariums
http://www.aza.org/

Bronx Zoo
http://www.bronxzoo.com/

Cincinnati Zoo
http://www.cincinnatizoo.org/

Colonial Williamsburg
http://www.history.org/

Denali National Park and Preserve
http://www.nps.gov/dena

Ellis Island
http://www.ellisisland.org/

Glacier National Park
http://www.nps.gov/glac

Grand Canyon National Park
http://www.nps.gov/grca

Grand Teton National Park
http://www.nps.gov/grte

High Museum of Art, Atlanta
http://www.high.org/

International Civil Rights Center and Museum
http://www.sitinmovement.org/

Japanese American National Museum
http://www.janm.org/

K12Station – Library of K–12 Education Links
http://www.k12station.com/k12link_library.html

Kids.gov
http://www.kids.gov/

KidsHealth in the Classroom
http://classroom.kidshealth.org/

Meteorology
http://www.wxdude.com/

The Metropolitan Museum of Art, New York
http://www.metmuseum.org/

Minneapolis Institute of Arts
http://www.artsmia.org/

Minnesota Zoo
http://www.mnzoo.com/

MoMA | The Museum of Modern Art
http://www.moma.org/

Monterey Bay Aquarium
www.montereybayaquarium.org

Mount Rushmore National Memorial
http://www.nps.gov/moru

Museum of Fine Arts, Boston
http://www.mfa.org/

Museum of Science, Boston
http://www.mos.org/

Museum of Science and Industry, Chicago
http://www.msichicago.org/

NASA
http://www.nasa.gov/

NASA Kids' Club
http://www.nasa.gov/audience/forkids/kidsclub/flash/index.html

National Air and Space Museum
http://www.nasm.si.edu/

National Civil Rights Museum
http://www.civilrightsmuseum.org/home.htm

National Museum of African American History and Culture
http://nmaahc.si.edu/

National Museum of American History
http://americanhistory.si.edu/

National Museum of the American Indian
http://www.nmai.si.edu/

National Museum of Women in the Arts
http://www.nmwa.org/

National Music Museum
http://www.usd.edu/smm/

National Park Service
http://www.nps.gov/

National Weather Service Education Resources
http://www.nws.noaa.gov/om/edures.shtml

National Women's History Museum
http://www.nwhm.org/

National Zoo
http://nationalzoo.si.edu/

Native American Facts for Kids: Resources on American Indians for Children and Teachers
http://www.native-languages.org/kids.htm

New England Aquarium
http://www.neaq.org/index.php

New York Aquarium
http://www.nyaquarium.com/

Newseum
http://www.newseum.org/

Omaha's Henry Doorly Zoo
http://www.omahazoo.com/

Philadelphia Museum of Art
http://www.philamuseum.org/

Philadelphia Zoo
http://www2.philadelphiazoo.org/

Plimoth Plantation
http://www.plimoth.org/

Redwood National and State Parks
http://www.nps.gov/redw

Rocky Mountain National Park
http://www.nps.gov/romo

Saint Louis Art Museum
http://www.slam.org/

San Diego Zoo
http://www.sandiegozoo.com/

San Francisco Museum of Modern Art
http://www.sfmoma.org/

Shedd Aquarium
http://www.sheddaquarium.org/

Smithsonian Education
http://www.smithsonianeducation.org/

Smithsonian: Science and Technology
http://www.si.edu/Encyclopedia_SI/science_and_technology/

Space Center Houston
http://www.spacecenter.org/

Tennessee Aquarium
http://www.tennis.org/

United States Holocaust Memorial Museum
http://www.ushmm.org/

University of California Museum of Paleontology
http://www.ucmp.berkeley.edu/

The White House Historical Association
http://www.whitehousehistory.org/

Yellowstone National Park
http://www.nps.gov/yell

Yosemite National Park
http://www.nps.gov/yose

Zion National Park
http://www.nps.gov/zion

High-Frequency Words	UNIT/WEEK
I	Start Smart Week 1
can	Start Smart Week 2
we	Unit 1 Week 1
the	Unit 1 Week 2
like	Unit 2 Week 1
a	Unit 2 Week 2
see	Unit 3 Week 1
go	Unit 3 Week 2
to	Unit 4 Week 1
have	Unit 4 Week 2
is	Unit 5 Week 1
play	Unit 5 Week 2
are	Unit 6 Week 1
for	Unit 6 Week 2
you	Unit 6 Week 2
this	Unit 7 Week 1
do	Unit 7 Week 1
and	Unit 7 Week 2
what	Unit 7 Week 2
little	Unit 8 Week 1
said	Unit 8 Week 1
here	Unit 8 Week 2
was	Unit 8 Week 2
she	Unit 9 Week 1
he	Unit 9 Week 1
has	Unit 9 Week 2
look	Unit 9 Week 2
with	Unit 10 Week 1
my	Unit 10 Week 1
me	Unit 10 Week 2
where	Unit 10 Week 2

Oral Vocabulary

Week		Theme Words	Oral Vocabulary Card Words	
1	**Oak Trees**	grow plant	conceited equal charming	plant grow
2	**Seed Secrets**	observe seed	necessary moist gradually	seed observe
3	**Sunflower House**	senses garden	arrange tend basic	senses garden

Language Transfers:

The Interaction Between English and Students' Primary Languages

Dr. Jana Echevarria
California State University, Long Beach

Dr. Donald Bear
University of Nevada, Reno

It is important for teachers to understand why English Language Learners (ELLs) use alternative pronunciations for some English words. Many English sounds do not exist or transfer to other languages, so English Language Learners may lack the auditory acuity to "hear" these English sounds and have difficulty pronouncing them. These students are not accustomed to positioning their mouth in a way the sound requires. The charts that appear on the following pages show that there is variation among languages, with some languages having more sounds in common and thus greater transfer to English than others.

For example, an English speaker may be able to pronounce the /r/ in the Spanish word *pero* ("but"), but not the /rr/ trill in *perro* ("dog"). The English speaker may also lack the auditory acuity to detect and the ability to replicate the tonal sounds of some Chinese words. Similarly, a Vietnamese speaker may have difficulty pronouncing /th/ in words such as *thin* or *thanks*.

Further, English Language Learners make grammatical errors due to interference from their native languages. In Spanish, the adjective follows the noun, so often English Language Learners say "the girl pretty" instead of "the pretty girl." While English changes the verb form with a change of subject (*I walk. She walks.*), some Asian languages keep the verb form constant across subjects. Adding /s/ to the third person may be difficult for some English Language Learners. Students may know the grammatical rule, but applying it consistently may be difficult, especially in spoken English.

When working with English Language Learners, you should also be aware of sociocultural factors that affect pronunciation. Students may retain an accent because it marks their social identity. Speakers of other languages may feel at a social distance from members of the dominant English-speaking culture.

English Language Learners improve their pronunciation in a nonthreatening atmosphere in which participation is encouraged. Opportunities to interact with native English speakers provide easy access to language models and give English Language Learners practice using English. However, students should not be forced to participate. Pressure to perform—or to perform in a certain way—can inhibit participation. In any classroom, teacher sensitivity to pronunciation differences contributes to a more productive learning environment.

Phonics, word recognition, and spelling are influenced by what students know about the sounds, word structure, and spelling in their primary languages. For example, beginning readers who speak Spanish and are familiar with its spelling will often spell short *o* with an *a*, a letter that in Spanish makes the short *o* sound. Similarly, English Language Learners who are unaccustomed to English consonant digraphs and blends (e.g., /ch/ and *s*-blends) spell /ch/ as *sh* because /sh/ is the sound they know that is closest to /ch/. Students learn about the way pronunciation influences their reading and spelling, beginning with large contrasts among sounds, then they study the finer discriminations. As vocabulary advances, the meaning of words leads students to the sound contrasts. For example, *shoe* and *chew* may sound alike initially, but meaning indicates otherwise. Students' reading and discussions of what they read advances their word knowledge as well as their knowledge in all language and literacy systems, including phonics, pronunciation, grammar, and vocabulary.

Phonics Transfers:
Sound Transfers

This chart indicates areas where a positive transfer of sounds and symbols occurs for English Language Learners from their native languages into English. This symbol (✔) identifies a positive transfer. "Approximate" indicates that the sound is similar.

Sound Transfers	Spanish	Cantonese	Vietnamese	Hmong	Korean	Khmer
Consonants						
/b/ as in bat	✔	approximate	approximate	approximate	approximate	✔
/k/ as in cake, kitten, peck	✔	✔	✔	✔	✔	✔
/d/ as in dog	✔	approximate	approximate	✔	approximate	✔
/f/ as in farm	✔	✔	✔	✔		
/g/ as in girl	✔	approximate	✔	approximate	approximate	
/h/ as in ham	✔	✔	✔	✔	✔	approximate
/j/ as in jet, page, ledge		approximate	approximate		approximate	
/l/ as in lion	✔	✔	✔	✔	✔	
/m/ as in mat	✔	✔	✔	✔	✔	✔
/n/ as in night	✔	✔	✔	✔	✔	✔
/p/ as in pen	✔	✔	✔	approximate	✔	✔
/kw/ as in queen	✔	approximate	✔		✔	✔
/r/ as in rope	approximate					✔
/s/ as in sink, city	✔	✔	✔	✔	✔	approximate
/t/ as in ton	✔	✔	approximate	approximate	✔	✔
/v/ as in vine	✔		✔	✔		
/w/ as in wind	✔	✔			✔	✔
/ks/ as in six	✔				✔	✔
/y/ as in yak	✔	✔		✔	✔	✔
/z/ as in zebra			✔			
Digraphs						
/ch/ as in cheek, patch	✔	approximate		✔	✔	✔
/sh/ as in shadow			✔	✔	✔	
/hw/ as in whistle					✔	✔
/th/ as in path	approximate		approximate			
/TH/ as in that	approximate					
/ng/ as in sting	✔	✔	✔	✔	✔	approximate

Sound Transfers	Spanish	Cantonese	Vietnamese	Hmong	Korean	Khmer
Short Vowels						
/a/ as in cat	approximate		approximate	✔	✔	
/e/ as in net	✔	approximate	approximate		✔	
/i/ as in kid	approximate	approximate			✔	
/o/ as in spot	approximate	approximate	approximate	approximate	approximate	✔
/u/ as in cup	approximate	approximate	✔		✔	✔
Long Vowels						
/ā/ as in lake, nail, bay	✔	approximate	approximate	approximate	✔	✔
/ē/ as in bee, meat, cranky	✔	approximate	✔	✔	✔	✔
/ī/ as in kite, tie, light, dry	✔	approximate	✔	✔	✔	✔
/ō/ as in home, road, row	✔	approximate	approximate		✔	
/ū/ as in dune, fruit, blue	✔	approximate	✔	✔	✔	✔
/yū/ as in mule, cue	✔	approximate			✔	
r-Controlled Vowels						
/är/ as in far	approximate	approximate				
/ôr/ as in corn	approximate	approximate				
/ûr/ as in stern, bird, suburb	approximate	approximate				
/âr/ as in air, bear						
/îr/ as in deer, ear						
Variant Vowels						
/oi/ as in boil, toy	✔	approximate	approximate		✔	✔
/ou/ as in loud, down	✔	approximate	✔	approximate	✔	✔
/ô/ as in law	approximate	✔	✔	approximate	approximate	✔
/ô/ as in laundry	approximate	approximate	✔	approximate	approximate	✔
/ôl/ as in salt, call	approximate	approximate			approximate	✔
/ü/ as in moon, drew	✔	approximate	approximate	✔	✔	✔
/u̇/ as in look		approximate	approximate		approximate	✔
/ə/ as in askew			approximate		✔	

Phonics Transfers:
Sound-Symbol Match

Sound-Symbol Match	Spanish	Cantonese	Vietnamese	Hmong	Korean	Khmer
Consonants						
/b/ as in bat	✔		✔			
/k/ as in cake	✔		✔			
/k/ as in kitten	✔		✔	✔		
/k/ as in peck						
/d/ as in dog	✔		✔	✔		
/f/ as in farm	✔			✔		
/g/ as in girl	✔		✔			
/h/ as in ham			✔	✔		
/j/ as in jet, page, ledge						
/l/ as in lion	✔		✔	✔		
/m/ as in mat	✔		✔	✔		
/n/ as in night	✔		✔	✔		
/p/ as in pen	✔		✔	✔		
/kw/ as in queen			✔			
/r/ as in rope	approximate					
/s/ as in sink, city	✔		✔			
/t/ as in ton	✔		✔	✔		
/v/ as in vine	✔		✔	✔		
/w/ as in wind	✔					
/ks/ as in six	✔					
/y/ as in yak	✔			✔		
/z/ as in zebra						
Digraphs						
/ch/ as in cheek, patch	✔					
/sh/ as in shadow						
/hw/ as in whistle						
/th/ as in path			✔			
/TH/ as in that						
/ng/ as in sting	✔		✔			
Short Vowels						
/a/ as in cat			✔	✔		
/e/ as in net	✔		✔			
/i/ as in kid						
/o/ as in spot			✔	✔		
/u/ as in cup						

T14

Sound-Symbol Match	Spanish	Cantonese	Vietnamese	Hmong	Korean	Khmer
Long Vowels						
/ā/ as in lake						
/ā/ as in nail						
/ā/ as in bay						
/ē/ as in bee						
/ē/ as in meat						
/ē/ as in cranky						
/ī/ as in kite, tie, light, dry						
/ō/ as in home, road, row						
/ū/ as in dune			✔	✔		
/ū/ as in fruit, blue						
/yü/ as in mule, cue						
_r_-Controlled Vowels						
/är/ as in far	✔					
/ôr/ as in corn	✔					
/ûr/ as in stern	✔					
/ûr/ as in bird, suburb						
/âr/ as in air, bear						
/îr/ as in deer, ear						
Variant Vowels						
/oi/ as in boil	✔		✔			
/oi/ as in toy	✔					
/ou/ as in loud						
/ou/ as in down						
/ô/ as in law						
/ô/ as in laundry						
/ôl/ as in salt	✔					
/ôl/ as in call						
/ü/ as in moon, drew						
/ů/ as in look						
/ə/ as in askew						

How to Use the Phonics Transfer Charts

To read and speak fluently in English, English Language Learners need to master a wide range of phonemic awareness, phonics, and word study skills. The Phonics Transfer Charts are designed to help you anticipate and understand possible student errors in pronouncing or perceiving English sounds.

1. **Highlight Transferrable Skills** If the phonics skill transfers from the student's primary language to English, state that during the lesson. In most lessons an English Language Learner feature will indicate which sounds do and do not transfer in specific languages.

2. **Preteach Non-Transferrable Skills** Prior to teaching a phonics lesson, check the chart to determine if the sound and/or spelling transfers from the student's primary language into English. If it does not, preteach the sound and spelling during Small Group time. Focus on articulation, using the backs of the small **Sound-Spelling Cards**, and the minimal contrast activities provided.

3. **Provide Additional Practice and Time** If the skill does NOT transfer from the student's primary language into English, the student will require more time and practice mastering the sound and spellings. Continue to review the phonics skill during Small Group time in upcoming weeks until the student has mastered it. Use the additional resources, such as the extra decodable stories in the **Teacher's Resource Book**, to provide oral and silent reading practice.

Teaching Supports for Students Transitioning from Spanish to English

The **Sound-Spelling Cards** have been created to assist you in working with English Language Learners. For example:

1. The dotted border on many of the cards indicates that the sound transfers from Spanish to English. On these cards, the same image is used in both English and Spanish (e.g., *camel/camello*). Therefore, students learning the sound in Spanish can easily transfer that knowledge to English.

2. Students whose primary language is not English will need additional articulation support to pronounce and perceive non-transferrable English sounds. Use the articulation photos on the backs of the Sound-Spelling Cards and the student-friendly descriptions of how to form these sounds during phonics lessons.

Sound-Spelling Cards

Transfer Skill Support

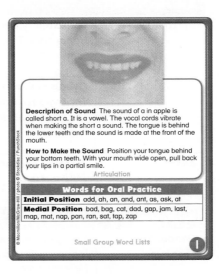

Articulation Support

Grammar Transfers:
Grammatical Form

This chart can be used to address common mistakes that some English Language Learners make when they transfer grammatical forms from their native languages into English.

Grammatical Form	Transfer Mistakes in English	Native Language	Cause of Difficulty
Nouns			
Plural Marker -s	**Forgets plural marker -s** *I have 3 sister.*	Cantonese, Haitian Creole, Hmong, Korean, Vietnamese, Khmer	Native language does not use a plural marker.
Countable and Uncountable Nouns	**Confuses countable and uncountable nouns** *the homeworks* or *the informations*	Haitian Creole, Spanish	Countable and uncountable nouns are different in English and native language.
Possessives	**Uses prepositions to describe possessives** *the book of my brother* as opposed to *my brother's book*	Haitian Creole, Hmong, Spanish, Vietnamese	Possession is often described using a prepositional phrase.
	Avoids using 's *dog my father* as opposed to *my father's dog*	Haitian Creole, Vietnamese, Khmer	A noun follows the object in the native language.
Articles			
	Consistently omits articles *He has book. They want dog not cat.*	Cantonese, Haitian Creole, Hmong, Korean, Vietnamese, Khmer	There is no article in the native language or no difference between *the* and *a*.
	Overuses articles *The English is difficult. The soccer is popular in the Europe.*	Haitian Creole, Hmong, Spanish	Some languages use articles that are omitted in English.
a/an	**Mistakes *one* for *a/an*** *She is one nurse.*	Haitian Creole, Hmong, Vietnamese	The native language either does not use articles or uses articles differently.
Pronouns			
Gender-Specific Pronouns	**Uses pronouns with the inappropriate gender** *He is my sister.*	Cantonese, Haitian Creole, Hmong, Korean, Spanish, Khmer	The third person pronoun in the native language is gender free, or the personal pronoun is omitted.
	Uses inappropriate gender, particularly with neutral nouns *The day is sunny. She is beautiful.*	Spanish	Nouns have feminine or masculine gender in the native language, and the gender may be carried over into English.

Grammatical Form	Transfer Mistakes in English	Native Language	Cause of Difficulty
Pronouns			
Object Pronouns	**Confuses subject and object pronouns** *Her talks to me.*	Cantonese, Hmong, Khmer	The same pronoun form is used for subject and object in the native language.
	Omits object pronouns *That girl is very rude, so nobody likes.*	Korean, Vietnamese	The native language does not use direct objects.
Pronoun and Number Agreement	**Uses the wrong number for pronouns** *I saw many red birds. It was pretty.*	Cantonese, Korean	The native language does not require number agreement.
Subject Pronouns	**Omits subject pronouns** *Mom isn't home. Is at work.*	Korean, Spanish	Subject pronouns may be dropped because in the native language the verb ending gives information about the number and/or gender.
Pronouns in Clauses	**Omits pronouns in clauses** *If don't do homework, they will not learn.*	Cantonese, Vietnamese	The native language does not need a subject in the subordinate clause.
Pronouns and Nouns	**Overuses pronouns with nouns** *This school, it very good.*	Hmong, Vietnamese	This is popular in speech in some languages. The speaker mentions a topic, then makes a comment about it.
	Avoids pronouns and repeats nouns *Carla visits her sister every Sunday, and Carla makes a meal.*	Korean, Vietnamese	In the native language, the speaker repeats nouns and does not use pronouns.
Pronoun *one*	**Omits the pronoun *one*** *I saw two dogs, and I like the small.*	Spanish	Adjectives can stand alone in the native language, but English requires a noun or *one*.
Possessive Forms	**Confuses possessive forms** *The book is my.*	Cantonese, Hmong, Vietnamese	Cantonese and Hmong speakers tend to omit the final *n* sound, which may create confusion between *my* and *mine*.

Grammar Transfers:
Grammatical Form

Grammatical Form	Transfer Mistakes in English	Native Language	Cause of Difficulty
Verbs			
Present Tense	**Omits -s in present tense, third person agreement** He *like* pizza.	Cantonese, Haitian Creole, Hmong, Korean, Vietnamese, Khmer	Subject-verb agreement is not used in the native language.
Irregular Verbs	**Has problems with irregular subject-verb agreement** Tom and Sue *has* a new car.	Cantonese, Hmong, Korean, Khmer	Verbs' forms do not change to show the number of the subject in the native language.
Inflectional Endings	**Omits tense markers** I *study* English yesterday.	Cantonese, Haitian Creole, Hmong, Korean, Vietnamese, Khmer	The native language does not use inflectional endings to change verb tense.
Present and Future Tenses	**Incorrectly uses the present tense for the future tense** I *go* next week.	Cantonese, Korean	The native language may use the present tense to imply the future tense.
Negative Statements	**Omits helping verbs in negative statements** Sue *no coming* to school.	Cantonese, Korean, Spanish	The native language does not use helping verbs in negative statements.
Present-Perfect Tense	**Avoids the present-perfect tense** Marcos *live* here for three months.	Haitian Creole, Vietnamese	The native language does not use the present-perfect verb form.
Past-Continuous Tense	**Uses the past-continuous tense for recurring action in the past** When I was young, I *was talking* a lot.	Korean, Spanish	In the native language, the past-continuous tense is used but in English the expression *used to* or the simple past tense is used.
Main Verb	**Omits the main verb** *Talk in class not good.*	Cantonese	Cantonese does not require an infinitive marker when using a verb as a noun. Speakers may confuse the infinitive for the main verb.
Main Verbs in Clauses	**Uses two or more main verbs in one clause without any connectors** I *took* a book *went studied* at the library.	Hmong	In Hmong, verbs can be used consecutively without conjunctions or punctuation.
Linking Verbs	**Omits the linking verb** He *hungry.*	Cantonese, Haitian Creole, Hmong, Vietnamese, Khmer	In some languages, *be* is implied in the adjective form. In other languages, the concept is expressed with a verb.
Helping Verb in Passive Voice	**Omits the helping verb in the passive voice** The homework *done.*	Cantonese, Vietnamese	In Cantonese and Vietnamese, the passive voice does not require a helping verb.

Grammatical Form	Transfer Mistakes in English	Native Language	Cause of Difficulty
Verbs			
Passive Voice	**Avoids the passive voice** *They speak English here.* *One speaks English here.* *English is spoken here.*	Haitian Creole	The passive voice does not exist in the native language.
Transitive Verbs	**Confuses transitive and intransitive verbs** *The child broke.* *The child broke <u>the</u> <u>plate</u>.*	Cantonese, Korean, Spanish	Verbs that require a direct object differ between English and the native language.
Phrasal Verbs	**Confuses related phrasal verbs** *I ate at the apple.* *I ate up the apple.*	Korean, Spanish	Phrasal verbs are not used in the native language, and there is often confusion over their meaning.
Have* and *be	**Uses *have* instead of *be*** *I have thirst.* *He has right.*	Spanish	Spanish and English have different uses for *have* and *be*.
Adjectives			
Word Order	**Places adjectives after nouns** *I saw a car red.*	Haitian Creole, Hmong, Spanish, Vietnamese, Khmer	Nouns often precede adjectives in the native language.
	Consistently places adjectives after nouns *This is a lesson new.*	Cantonese, Korean	Adjectives always follow nouns in the native language.
***-er* and *-est* Endings**	**Avoids *-er* and *-est* endings** *I am more old than you.*	Hmong, Korean, Spanish, Khmer	The native language shows comparative and superlative forms with separate words.
***-ing* and *-ed* Endings**	**Confuses *-ing* and *-ed* forms** *Math is bored.*	Cantonese, Korean, Spanish, Khmer	Adjectives in the native language do not have active and passive meanings.
Adverbs			
Adjectives and Adverbs	**Uses an adjective where an adverb is needed** *Talk quiet.*	Haitian Creole, Hmong, Khmer	Adjectives and adverb forms are interchangeable in the native language.
Word Order	**Places adverbs before verbs** *He quickly ran.* *He ran quickly.*	Cantonese, Korean	Adverbs usually come before verbs in the native language, and this tendency is carried over into English.
Prepositions			
	Omits prepositions *I like come school.*	Cantonese	Cantonese does not use prepositions the way that English does.

How to Use the Grammar Transfer Charts

The grammar of many languages differs widely from English. For example, a student's primary language may use a different word order than English, may not use parts of speech in the same way, or may use different verb tenses. The Grammar Transfer Charts are designed to help you anticipate and understand possible student errors in speaking and writing standard English. With all grammar exercises, the emphasis is on oral communication, both as a speaker and listener.

1. Highlight Transferrable Skills If the grammar skill transfers from the student's primary language to English, state that during the lesson. In many lessons an English Language Learner feature will indicate which skills do and do not transfer.

2. Preteach Non-Transferrable Skills Prior to teaching a grammar lesson, check the chart to determine if the skill transfers from the student's primary language into English. If it does not, preteach the skill during Small Group time. Provide sentence frames and ample structured opportunities to use the skill in spoken English. Students need to talk, talk, and talk some more to master these skills.

3. Provide Additional Practice and Time If the skill does NOT transfer from the student's primary language into English, the student will require more time and practice mastering it. Continue to review the skill during Small Group time. Use the additional resources, such as the grammar lessons in the **Intervention Kit** (K–3) or review lessons, in upcoming weeks.

4. Use Contrastive Analysis Tell students when a skill does not transfer and include contrastive analysis work to make the student aware of how to correct their speaking and writing for standard English. For example, when a student uses an incorrect grammatical form, write the student sentence on a **WorkBoard**. Then write the correct English form underneath. Explain the difference between the student's primary language and English. Have the student correct several other sentences using this skill, such as sentences in their Writer's Notebooks.

5. Increase Writing and Speaking Opportunities Increase the amount of structured writing and speaking opportunities for students needing work on specific grammatical forms. Sentence starters and paragraph frames, such as those found in the lessons, are ideal for both written and oral exercises.

6. Focus on Meaning Always focus on the meanings of sentences in all exercises. As they improve and fine-tune their English speaking and writing skills, work with students on basic comprehension of spoken and written English.

To help students move to the next level of language acquisition and master English grammatical forms, recast their responses during classroom discussions or provide additional language for them to use as they respond further. Provide leveled-language sentence frames orally or in writing for students to use as they respond to questions and prompts. Below are samples.

English Language Learner Response Chart

Beginning (will respond by pointing or saying one word answers)	**Sample Frames** (simple, short sentences) *I see a _____.* *This is a _____.* *I like the _____.*
Early Intermediate (will respond with phrases or simple sentences)	**Sample Frames** (simple sentences with adjectives and adverbs added, and compound subjects or predicates) *I see a _____ _____.* *The _____ animal is _____.* *There are _____ and _____.*
Intermediate (will respond with simple sentences and limited academic language)	**Sample Frames** (harder sentences with simple phrases in consistent patterns; some academic language included) *The animal's prey is _____ because _____.* *The main idea is _____ because _____.* *He roamed the park so that _____.*
Early Advanced (will begin to use more sophisticated sentences and some academic language)	**Sample Frames** (complex sentences with increased academic language, beginning phrases and clauses, and multiple-meaning words) *When the violent storm hit, _____.* *As a result of the revolution, the army_____.* *Since most endangered animals are _____, they _____.*
Advanced (will have mastered some more complex sentence structures and is increasing the amount of academic language used)	Use the questions and prompts provided in the lessons for the whole group. Provide additional support learning and using academic language. These words are boldfaced throughout the lessons and sentence starters are often provided.

Cognates

Cognates are words in two languages that look alike and have the same or similar meaning (e.g., *school/escuela*, *telephone/teléfono*) and can be helpful resources for English Language Learners. This list identifies some Spanish cognates for the academic language used during the lessons.

Students must also be aware of false cognates—words that look similar in two languages, but have different meanings, such as *soap* in English and *sopa* (meaning *soup*) in Spanish.

accent	*acento*	**context**	*contexto*
action	*acción*	**contrast**	*contrastar*
action verb	*verbo de acción*	**definition**	*definición*
adjective	*adjetivo*	**demonstrative**	*demostrativo*
adverb	*adverbio*	**denotation**	*denotación*
alphabetical order	*orden alfabético*	**description**	*descripción*
analogy	*analogía*	**dialogue**	*diálogo*
analyze	*analizar*	**dictionary**	*diccionario*
antecedent	*antecedente*	**direct**	*directo*
antonym	*antónimo*	**effect**	*efecto*
apostrophe	*apóstrofe*	**evaluate**	*evaluar*
article	*artículo*	**event**	*evento*
author	*autor*	**example**	*ejemplo*
cause	*causa*	**exclamation**	*exclamación*
classify	*clasificar*	**family**	*familia*
combine	*combinar*	**fantasy**	*fantasía*
compare	*comparar*	**figurative**	*figurativo*
complex	*complejo*	**fragment**	*fragmento*
comprehension	*comprensión*	**future**	*futuro*
conclusion	*conclusión*	**generalization**	*generalización*
confirm	*confirmar*	**generalize**	*generalizar*
conjunction	*conjunción*	**glossary**	*glosario*
connotation	*connotación*	**Greek**	*Griego*
consonant	*consonante*	**homophone**	*homófono*

idea	*idea*	**prefix**	*prefijo*
identify	*identificar*	**preposition**	*preposición*
illustration	*ilustración*	**prepositional**	*preposicional*
indirect	*indirecto*	**present**	*presente*
introduction	*introducción*	**problem**	*problema*
irregular	*irregular*	**pronunciation**	*pronunciación*
language	*lenguaje*	**punctuation**	*puntuación*
Latin	*Latín*	**reality**	*realidad*
myth	*mito*	**relationship**	*relación*
negative	*negativo*	**sequence**	*secuencia*
object	*objeto*	**singular**	*singular*
opinion	*opinión*	**solution**	*solución*
order	*orden*	**structure**	*estructura*
origin	*orígen*	**subject**	*sujeto*
paragraph	*párrafo*	**suffix**	*sufijo*
part	*parte*	**syllable**	*sílaba*
perspective	*perspectiva*	**synonym**	*sinónimo*
persuasion	*persuación*	**technique**	*técnica*
phrase	*frase*	**text**	*texto*
plural	*plural*	**theme**	*tema*
possessive adjective	*adjetivo posesivo*	**verb**	*verbo*
predicate	*predicado*	**visualize**	*visualizar*
prediction	*predicción*	**vowel**	*vocal*

ELL ENGLISH LANGUAGE LEARNERS

The **English Language Learners** in your classroom have a variety of backgrounds. An increasing proportion of English Language Learners are born in the United States. Some of these students are just starting school in the primary grades; others are long-term English Language Learners, with underdeveloped academic skills. Some students come from their native countries with a strong educational foundation. The academic skills of these newly arrived students are well developed and parallel the skills of their native English-speaking peers. Other English Learners immigrate to the United States with little academic experience.

These English Learners are not "blank slates." Their oral language proficiency and literacy in their first languages can be used to facilitate literacy development in English. Systematic, explicit, and appropriately scaffolded instruction and sufficient time help English Learners attain English proficiency and meet high standards in core academic subjects.

Beginning

This level of language proficiency is often referred to as the "silent" stage, in which students' receptive skills are engaged. It is important that teachers and peers respect a language learner's initial silence or allow the student to respond in his or her native language. It is often difficult for teachers to identify the level of cognitive development at this stage, due to the limited proficiency in the second language. It is important to realize that these beginning students have a wide range of abilities in their first language. They are able to transfer knowledge and skills from their first language as they develop English and learn grade-level content. Beginning students include those with limited formal schooling: young students just starting school, as well as older students. Other beginning students have had schooling in their native language and are academically parallel to nativeEnglish-speaking peers.

The Beginning Student...

- recognizes English phonemes that correspond to phonemes produced in primary language;

- is able to apply transferable grammar concepts and skills from the primary language;

- initially demonstrates more receptive than productive English skills;

- produces English vocabulary to communicate basic needs in social and academic settings;

- responds by pointing to, nodding, gesturing, acting out, and manipulating objects/pictures;

- speaks in one-or two-word responses as language develops;

- draws pictures and writes letters and sounds being learned.

Early Intermediate

At this level, students are considered more advanced beginning English Learners. They are developing early production skills, but their receptive skills are much more advanced than their speaking ability. At this stage it is critical that the students continue to listen to model speakers.

The Early Intermediate Student...

- recognizes English phonemes that correspond to phonemes produced in primary language;
- is able to apply transferable grammar concepts and skills from the primary language;
- understands more spoken English than the beginning student;
- speaks in one- or two-word utterances;
- may respond with phrases or sentences;
- produces English vocabulary words and phrases to communicate basic needs in social and academic settings;
- begins to ask questions, role-play, and retell;
- begins to use routine expressions;
- demonstrates an internalization of English grammar and usage by recognizing and correcting some errors when speaking and reading aloud;
- increases correct usage of written and oral language conventions.

Intermediate

Students at this level begin to tailor their English language skills to meet communication and learning demands with increasing accuracy. They possess vocabulary and knowledge of grammatical structures that allow them to more fully participate in classroom activities and discussions. They are generally more comfortable producing both spoken and written language.

The Intermediate Student...

- pronounces most English phonemes correctly while reading aloud;
- can identify more details of information that has been presented orally or in writing;
- uses more complex vocabulary and sentences to communicate needs and express ideas;
- uses specific vocabulary learned, including academic language;
- participates more fully in discussions with peers and adults;
- reads and comprehends a wider range of reading materials;
- writes brief narratives and expository texts;
- demonstrates an internalization of English grammar and usage by recognizing and correcting errors when speaking and reading aloud.

Early Advanced

Students at this language proficiency level possess vocabulary and grammar structures that approach those of an English-proficient speaker. These students demonstrate consistent general comprehension of grade-level content that is presented.

The Early Advanced Student...

- applies knowledge of common English morphemes in oral and silent reading;
- understands increasingly more nonliteral social and academic language;
- responds using extensive vocabulary;
- participates in and initiates more extended social conversations with peers and adults;
- communicates orally and in writing with fewer grammatical errors;
- reads with good comprehension a wide range of narrative and expository texts;
- writes using more standard forms of English on various content-area topics;
- becomes more creative and analytical when writing.

Advanced

The student at this language proficiency level communicates effectively with peers and adults in both social and academic situations. Students can understand grade-level text but still need some English language development support, such as preteaching concepts and skills. While the English language proficiency of these students is advanced, some linguistic support for accessing content is still necessary.

The Advanced Student...

- understands increasingly more nonliteral social and academic language;
- responds using extensive vocabulary;
- communicates orally and in writing with infrequent errors;
- creates more complex narratives and expository writing in all content areas.

English Language Learner Profiles
Facilitating Language Growth

Beginning

Student's Behaviors	Teacher's Behaviors	Questioning Techniques
■ Points to or provides other nonverbal responses ■ Actively listens ■ Responds to commands ■ Understands more than he or she can produce	■ Gestures ■ Focuses on conveying meanings and vocabulary development ■ Does not force students to speak ■ Shows visuals and real objects ■ Writes words for students to see ■ Pairs students with more proficient learners ■ Provides speaking and writing frames and models	■ Point to the _____. ■ Find the _____. ■ Put the _____ next to the _____. ■ Do you have the _____? ■ Is this the _____? ■ Who wants the _____?

Early Intermediate

Student's Behaviors	Teacher's Behaviors	Questioning Techniques
■ Speaks in one- or two-word utterances ■ Uses short phrases and simple sentences ■ Listens with greater understanding	■ Asks questions that can be answered by yes/no ■ Asks either/or questions ■ Asks higher-order questions with one-word answers ■ Models correct responses ■ Ensures supportive, low-anxiety environment ■ Does not overtly call attention to grammar errors ■ Asks short "wh" questions	■ Yes/no (Did you like the story?) ■ Either/or (Is this a pencil or a crayon?) ■ One-word responses (Why did the dog hide?) ■ General questions that encourage lists of words (What did you see in the book bag?) ■ Two-word responses (Where did I put the pen?)

Intermediate

Student's Behaviors	Teacher's Behaviors	Questioning Techniques
■ Demonstrates comprehension in a variety of ways ■ Speaks in short phrases or sentences ■ Begins to use language more freely	■ Provides frequent comprehension checks ■ Asks open-ended questions that stimulate language production	■ Why? ■ How? ■ How is this like that? ■ Tell me about _____. ■ Talk about _____. ■ Describe _____. ■ What is in your book bag?

Early Advanced

Student's Behaviors	Teacher's Behaviors	Questioning Techniques
■ Participates in reading and writing activities to acquire information ■ Demonstrates increased levels of accuracy and correctness and is able to express thoughts and feelings ■ Produces language with varied grammatical structures and academic language ■ May experience difficulties in abstract, cognitively demanding subjects	■ Fosters conceptual development and expanded literacy through content ■ Continues to make lessons comprehensible and interactive ■ Teaches thinking and study skills ■ Continues to be alert to individual differences in language and culture	■ What would you recommend/why? ■ How do you think this story will end? ■ What is this story about? ■ What is your favorite part of the story? ■ Describe/compare _____. How are these similar/different? ■ What would happen if _____? ■ Why do you think that? Yes, tell me more about _____.

English Language Learners

Fostering Classroom Discussions

Strategies for English Language Learners

One of the most effective ways in which to increase the oral language proficiency of your English Language Learners is to give students many opportunities to do a lot of talking in the classroom. Providing the opportunities and welcoming all levels of participation will motivate students to take part in the class discussions. You can employ a few basic teaching strategies that will encourage the participation of all language proficiency levels of English Language Learners in whole class and small group discussions.

☑ WAIT/DIFFERENT RESPONSES

- Be sure to give students enough time to answer the question.

- Let students know that they can respond in different ways depending on their levels of proficiency. Students can
  - answer in their native language;
  - ask a more proficient ELL speaker to repeat the answer in English;
  - answer with nonverbal cues (pointing to related objects, drawing, or acting out).

> **Teacher:** Where is Charlotte?
>
> **ELL Response:** (Student points to the web in the corner of the barn.)
>
> **Teacher:** Yes. Charlotte is sitting in her web. Let's all point to Charlotte.

☑ REPEAT

- Give positive confirmation to the answers that each English Language Learner offers. If the response is correct, repeat what the student has said in a clear, loud voice and at a slower pace. This validation will motivate other ELLs to participate.

> **Teacher:** How would you describe the faces of the bobcats?
>
> **ELL Response:** They look scared.
>
> **Teacher:** That's right, Silvia. They are scared. Everyone show me your scared face.

☑ REVISE FOR FORM

- Repeating an answer allows you to model the proper form for a response. You can model how to answer in full sentences and use academic language.

- When you repeat the answer, correct any grammar or pronunciation errors.

> **Teacher:** Who are the main characters in the story *Zathura*?
>
> **ELL Response:** Danny and Walter is.
>
> **Teacher:** Yes. Danny and Walter <u>are</u> the main characters. Remember to use the verb <u>are</u> when you are telling about more than one person. Let's repeat the sentence.
>
> **All:** Danny and Walter <u>are</u> the main characters.

✓ REVISE FOR MEANING

- Repeating an answer offers an opportunity to clarify the meaning of a response.

> **Teacher:** Where did the golden feather come from?
>
> **ELL Response:** The bird.
>
> **Teacher:** That's right. The golden feather came from the Firebird.

✓ ELABORATE

- If students give a one-word answer or a nonverbal cue, elaborate on the answer to model fluent speaking and grammatical patterns.

- Provide more examples or repeat the answer using proper academic language.

> **Teacher:** Why is the girls' mother standing with her hands on her hips?
>
> **ELL Response:** She is mad.
>
> **Teacher:** Can you tell me more? Why is she mad?
>
> **ELL Response:** Because the girls are late.
>
> **Teacher:** Ok. What do you think the girls will do?
>
> **ELL Response:** They will promise not to be late again.
>
> **Teacher:** Anyone else have an idea?

✓ ELICIT

- Prompt students to give a more comprehensive response by asking additional questions or guiding them to get to an answer.

> **Teacher:** Listen as I read the caption under the photograph. What information does the caption tell us?
>
> **ELL Response:** It tells about the butterfly.
>
> **Teacher:** What did you find out about the butterfly?
>
> **ELL Response:** It drinks nectar.
>
> **Teacher:** Yes. The butterfly drinks nectar from the flower.

Making the Most of Classroom Conversations

Use all the speaking and listening opportunities in your classroom to observe students' oral language proficiency.

- Response to oral presentations
- Responding to text aloud
- Following directions
- Group projects
- Small Group work
- Informal, social peer discussions
- One-on-one conferences

The **English Language Learner Resource Book** provides Speaking and Listening Checklists to help you monitor students' oral language proficiency growth.

Support for Students with Dyslexia

Characteristics of Dyslexia

A student with dyslexia is a student who continually struggles with reading and spelling but displays an ability to learn when there are no print materials involved. Even though the student receives the same classroom instruction as most other students, he continues to have difficulties with reading and spelling.

Students identified with dyslexia often have difficulties in the following areas

- reading words in isolation
- decoding nonsense words accurately
- oral reading (slow and inaccurate)
- learning to spell

The difficulties in these areas are usually the result of student's struggles with:

- phonological awareness: segmenting, blending, and manipulating words
- naming letters and pronouncing their sounds.
- phonological memory
- rapid naming of the letters of the alphabet or familiar objects

Effective Instruction

To address the needs of a student with dyslexia, instruction should be delivered in small groups. The instruction should be explicit, intensive, employ multisensory methods, as needed, and be individualized. It should include instruction on:

- phonemic awareness that has students detect, segment, blend and manipulate sounds
- phonics, emphasizing the sound/symbol relationships for decoding and encoding words
- morphology, semantics and syntax
- fluency with patterns of language
- strategies for decoding, encoding, word recognition, fluency and comprehension

Resources:
The International Dyslexia Association Website: www.interdys.org
The Dyslexia Handbook: Procedures Concerning Dyslexia and Related Disorders (Revised 2007) Texas Education Agency, Austin, TX, Publication Number: GE8721001

 Reading and Language Arts Program

Treasures is a scientifically-based core program that offers sequential, explicit, and effective instruction in phonological awareness, phonics, morphology, fluency, vocabulary, and reading comprehension. Students are given many opportunities to practice and review these skills to help prevent reading difficulties before they begin.

Tier 2 INTERVENTION

Weekly Small Group Lessons
Intervention Teacher's Editions

Tier 2 Instruction is provided in weekly small group lessons in the *Treasures* **Teacher's Editions**. These lessons provide targeted instruction in priority skills taught in the week. *Tier 2 Intervention Teacher's Editions* provide additional instruction for struggling students in the areas of phonemic awareness, phonics, vocabulary, fluency, and comprehension, grammar and writing.

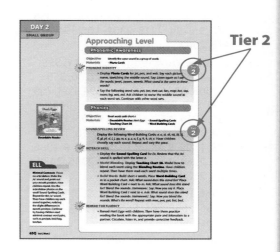

Tier 3 INTERVENTION

Reading Triumphs
Intervention Program

Reading Triumphs provides intensive instruction. Explicit, sequential lessons delivered through clear instructional routines for all the key components of reading are embedded in the program. The "no assumption instruction" allows for both teacher and student success.

A

B

Key 1 = Unit 1

D

E

F

Genre

H

I

J

Key 1 = Unit 1

L

M

Main idea and details, identifying. *See* **Comprehension strategies: main idea and details, identifying.**

Math, 8:1977

Media Literacy, 1:257, **2:**509, **3:**769, **4:**1029, **5:**1289, **6:**1549, **7:**1809, **9:**2329, **10:**2589

Mental images, creating. *See* **Comprehension skills: mental images, creating.**

Monitor Comprehension: reread. *See* **Comprehension skills: monitor comprehension: reread.**

Music, 1:S63, S81, S87

See also **Songs, rhymes, chants.**

N

National tests correlation charts. *See* **Assessment: unit assessment.**

O

On Level Options

comprehension, **1:**74, 80, 158, 164, 242, 248, **2:**326, 332, 410, 416, 494, 500, **3:**586, 592, 670, 676, 754, 760, **4:**846, 930, 1014, **5:**1106, 1190, 1274, **6:**1366, 1450, 1534, **7:**1626, 1710, 1794, **8:**1886, 1970, 2054, **9:**2146, 2230, 2314, **10:**2406, 2490, 2574

Decodable Reader, rereading the, **1:**74, 80, 158, 164, 242, 248, **2:**326, 332, 410, 416, 494, 500, **3:**586, 592, 670, 676, 754, 760, **4:**842, 926, 1010, **5:**1102, 1186, 1270, **6:**1362, 1446, 1530, **7:**1622, 1706, 1790, **8:**1966, 2050, **9:**2142, 2226, 2310, **10:**2402, 2486, 2570

high-frequency words, **1:**60, 74, 144, 158, 228, 242, **2:**312, 326, 396, 410, 480, 494, **3:**572, 586, 656, 670, 740, 754, **4:**832, 846, 916, 930, 1000, 1014, **5:**1092, 1106, 1176, 1190, 1260, 1274,

6:1352, 1366, 1436, 1450, 1520, 1534, **7:**1612, 1626, 1696, 1710, 1780, 1794, **8:**1872, 1886, 1956, 1970, 2040, 2054, **9:**2132, 2146, 2216, 2230, 2300, 2314, **10:**2392, 2406, 2476, 2490, 2560, 2574

Leveled Reader Lessons, **1:**74, 80, 158, 164, 242, 248, **2:**326, 332, 410, 416, 494, 500, **3:**586, 592, 670, 676, 754, 760, **4:**846, 852, 930, 936, 1014, 1020, **5:**1106, 1112, 1190, 1196, 1274, 1280, **6:**1366, 1372, 1450, 1456, 1534, 1540, **7:**1626, 1632, 1710, 1716, 1794, 1800, **8:**1886, 1892, 1970, 1976, 2054, 2060, **9:**2146, 2152, 2230, 2236, 2314, 2320, **10:**2406, 2412, 2490, 2496, 2574, 2580

phonemic awareness and phonics, **1:**60, 144, 228, **2:**312, 396, 480, **3:**572, 656, 740, **4:**832, 916, 1000, **5:**1092, 1176, 1260, **6:**1352, 1436, 1520, **7:**1612, 1696, 1780, **8:**1872, 1956, 2040, **9:**2132, 2216, 2300, **10:**2392, 2476, 2560

Pre-decodable Reader, rereading the, **1:**66, 150, 234, **2:**318, 402, 486, **3:**578, 662, 746

Online instruction. *See* **Digital learning.**

Oral grammar. *See* **Grammar.**

Oral language, 1:S7, S11, S21, S25, S31, S35, S39, S49, S53, S59, S63, S67, S77, S81, S87, 14, 22, 34, 44, 52, 58, 62, 98, 106, 118, 128, 136, 142, 146, 182, 190, 202, 212, 220, 226, 230, **2:**266, 274, 286, 296, 304, 310, 314, 350, 358, 370, 380, 388, 394, 398, 434, 442, 454, 464, 472, 478, 482, **3:**526, 534, 546, 556, 564, 570, 574, 610, 618, 630, 640, 648, 654, 658, 694, 702, 714, 724, 732, 738, 742, **4:**786, 794, 806, 816, 824, 830, 834, 836, 870, 878, 890, 900, 908, 914, 918, 920, 954, 962, 974, 984, 992, 998, 1002, 1004, **5:**1046, 1054, 1066, 1076, 1084, 1090, 1094, 1096, 1130, 1138, 1150, 1160, 1168, 1174, 1178, 1180, 1214, 1222, 1234, 1244, 1252, 1258, 1262, 1264, **6:**1306, 1314, 1336, 1344, 1350, 1354, 1356, 1390, 1398, 1420, 1428, 1434, 1438, 1440, 1474, 1482, 1504, 1512, 1518, 1522, 1524, **7:**1566, 1574, 1596, 1604, 1610, 1614, 1616, 1650, 1658, 1680, 1688, 1694, 1698, 1700, 1734, 1742, 1764, 1772, 1778, 1782, 1784, **8:**1826, 1834,

1864, 1870, 1874, 1876, 1910, 1918, 1930, 1940, 1948, 1954, 1958, 1960, 1994, 2002, 2014, 2024, 2032, 2038, 2042, 2044, **9:**2086, 2094, 2124, 2130, 2134, 2136, 2170, 2178, 2208, 2214, 2218, 2220, 2254, 2262, 2274, 2284, 2292, 2298, 2302, 2304, **10:**2346, 2354, 2376, 2384, 2390, 2394, 2396, 2430, 2438, 2450, 2460, 2468, 2474, 2478, 2480, 2522, 2544, 2552, 2558, 2562, 2564

See also **Vocabulary development: oral vocabulary.**

Oral Vocabulary. *See* **Vocabulary development: oral vocabulary.**

Oral Vocabulary Cards, 1:34, 118, 202, **2:**286, 370, 454, **3:**546, 630, 714, **4:**806, 890, 898, 974, 982, **5:**1066, 1150, 1234, 1242, **7:**1594, 1762, **8:**1854, 1930, 1938, 2014, **9:**2274, 2282, **10:**2450, 2458, 2542

P

Paired selections. *See* **Big Book of Explorations.**

Peer discussion starters. *See* **English Language Learners: grammar.**

Penmanship, 1:19, 103, 187, **2:**271, 355, 439, **3:**531, 615, 699, **4:**791, 875, 959, **5:**1051, 1135, 1219, **6:**1311, 1395, 1417, 1479, **7:**1571, 1655, 1677, 1739, **8:**1831, 1915, 1999, **9:**2091, 2113, 2175, 2197, 2259, **10:**2351, 2373, 2435, 2457

directionality (left-to-right, top-to-bottom), **1:**19, 103, 187, **2:**271, 355, 439, **3:**531, 615, 699, **4:**791, 875, 959, **5:**1051, 1135, 1219, **6:**1311, 1395, 1417, 1479, **7:**1571, 1655, 1677, 1739, **8:**1831, 1915, 1999, **9:**2091, 2113, 2175, 2197, 2259, **10:**2351, 2373, 2435, 2457

uppercase and lowercase letters, **1:**19, 103, 187, **2:**271, 355, 439, **3:**531, 615, 699, **4:**791, 875, 959, **5:**1051, 1135, 1219, **6:**1311, 1395, 1417, 1479, **7:**1571, 1655, 1677, 1739, **8:**1831, 1915, 1999, **9:**2091, 2113, 2175, 2197, 2259, **10:**2351, 2373, 2435, 2457

Personal response. *See* **Literary response; Talk/Sing About It.**

W

Use this page to record lessons that work well or need to be adapted for future reference.

Lessons that work well.

Lessons that need adjustments.

Use this page to record lessons that work well or need to be adapted for future reference.

Lessons that work well.

Lessons that need adjustments.

Use this page to record lessons that work well or need to be adapted for future reference.

Lessons that work well.

Lessons that need adjustments.